FREELY
I SERVED

FREELY
I SERVED

THE MEMOIR OF THE COMMANDER-
1ST POLISH INDEPENDENT PARACHUTE BRIGADE
1941 - 1944

MAJOR GENERAL
STANISLAW SOSABOWSKI

Pen & Sword
MILITARY

First published in Great Britain in 1982 by
William Kimber and Co. Ltd.

Reprinted in this format in 2013 by
PEN & SWORD MILITARY
An imprint of
Pen & Sword Books Ltd
47 Church Street
Barnsley, South Yorkshire
S70 2AS

ISBN 978 1 78346 261 2

A CIP catalogue record for this book is
available from the British Library

Printed and bound in England
By CPI Group (UK) Ltd, Croydon, CR0 4YY

Pen & Sword Books Ltd incorporates the Imprints of Aviation, Atlas,
Family History, Fiction, Maritime, Military, Discovery, Politics, History,
Archaeology, Select, Wharncliffe Local History, Wharncliffe True Crime,
Military Classics, Wharncliffe Transport, Leo Cooper, The Praetorian Press,
Remember When, Seaforth Publishing and Frontline Publishing

For a complete list of Pen & Sword titles please contact
PEN & SWORD BOOKS LIMITED
47 Church Street, Barnsley, South Yorkshire, S70 2AS, England
E-mail: enquiries@pen-and-sword.co.uk
Website: www.pen-and-sword.co.uk

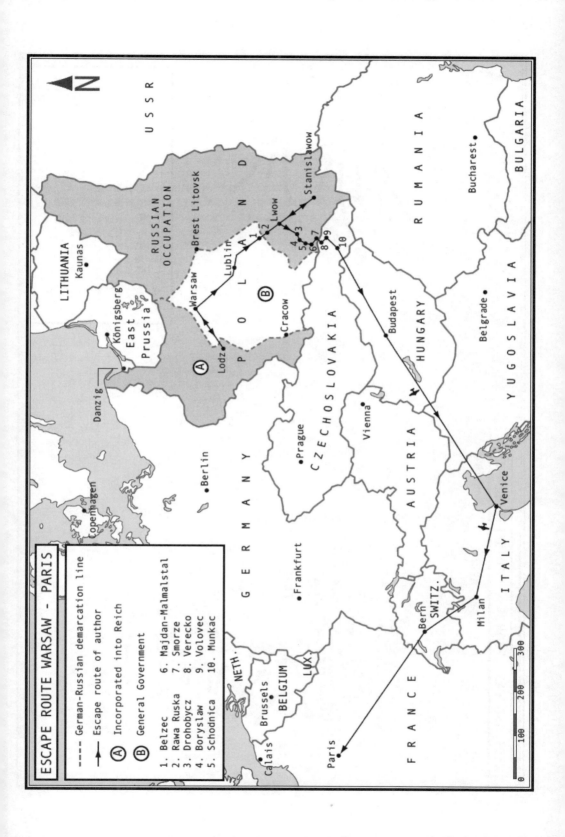

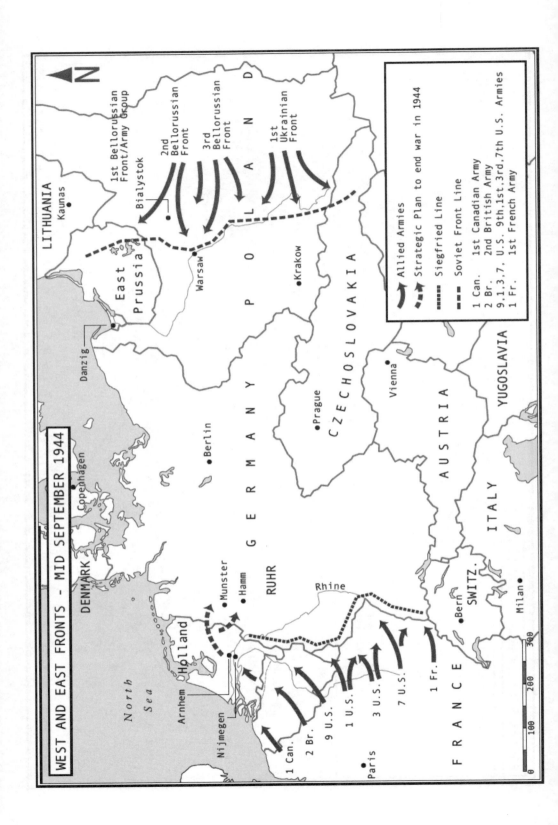

WEST AND EAST FRONTS - MID SEPTEMBER 1944

Allied Armies
Strategic Plan to end war in 1944
Siegfried Line
Soviet Front Line

1 Can. 1st Canadian Army
2 Br.   2nd British Army
9,1,3,7. U.S. 9th,1st,3rd,7th U.S. Armies
1 Fr.   1st French Army

1st Bellorussian Front/Army Group
2nd Bellorussian Front
3rd Bellorussian Front
1st Ukrainian Front

LITHUANIA
Kaunas

East Prussia

Danzig

Bialystok

Warsaw

Krakow

P O L A N D

Copenhagen

DENMARK

Berlin

G E R M A N Y

Prague

C Z E C H O S L O V A K I A

Vienna

A U S T R I A

YUGOSLAVIA

Munster
Hamm

RUHR

Rhine

Holland

Arnhem

Nijmegen

North Sea

ITALY

SWITZ.

Bern

Milan

F R A N C E

Paris

1 Can.
2 Br.
9 U.S.
1 U.S.
3 U.S.
7 U.S.
1 Fr.

0   100   200   300

FOREWORD

By General Sir Richard Gale,
G.C.B., K.B.E., D.S.O., M.C.

THIS is a stirring story of a gallant Polish officer.
Major-General Sosabowski was in command of a famous Warsaw Regiment in 1939. He writes of his early childhood in Poland, and, briefly, of his activities up to the Blitzkrieg in 1939.

Vividly he recounts his experiences during the fighting in Poland and of the gallant defence of Warsaw up to the surrender of the city. He then describes how he entered the Polish Underground Army and his experiences there. His account includes a stirring narrative of his hazardous journey to Hungary, of his mission there, and of his burning desire to get back to Warsaw.

He was ordered to go to Paris, and there to report to General Sikorski. Much to his disappointment, instead of returning to Poland he was ordered to command Polish forces in France. He gives a vivid account of things in that country as they appeared to him.

Later he was moved to the United Kingdom, where he raised and trained the Polish Parachute Brigade. In all this he still had one objective, one burning desire: this was to lead his men in the attack for the relief of Warsaw.

Nothing can be more sad than the story of the frustration of this aim. Events, far stronger than he could control, dictated otherwise. This caused an attitude of mind which many of my countrymen found it difficult to understand. Had they read this book, they might have appreciated his point of view more clearly.

He had very definite differences of opinion with those under whose command he was placed, and this led to misunderstanding and lack of confidence. In this book he hides nothing, but just contents himself with giving his own account of events as he saw them.

His description of the fighting at Arnhem as he saw it is written in a soldierly and clear manner.

When one finally closes the book one does so with a feeling of sadness. We went to war for Poland, and we ended up with Poland occupied and divided.

5

FOREWORD

In these days of alliances it is of vital importance that we British should understand our allies. They have points of view, often at variance with ours. Though their aims are the same as ours, their approach to problems will often differ.

The greatness of Marlborough as a leader lay in his ability to see this point and to make an alliance work.

ACKNOWLEDGEMENT

I would like to acknowledge the valuable help and assistance in writing this book which I received from two English friends, who prefer to remain anonymous.

CONTENTS

ILLUSTRATIONS

Major-General Stanislaw Sosabowski.

Arnhem – A Dakota, damaged while dropping supplies, after a crash landing.

The Polish Parachute Brigade and their Colours from Warsaw.

Field-Marshal Montgomery addressing the Polish troops before the Battle of Arnhem.

General 'Boy' Browning and the author.

The final preparations before Arnhem.

Paratroopers dashing for cover after grabbing arms from the containers.

Colonel Stevens; General Sosabowski and General Thomas.

The leading vehicle of the Household Cavalry troop just after it had reached the Polish position at Driel.

Members of the Dutch Underground bringing in German prisoners.

A German position near Arnhem.

A Polish Paratrooper checking a wrecked German car.

Members of the Dutch Underground with a female collaborator.

General Sosabowski, General Urquhart and Brigadier Hackett.

The return from Arnhem – the Polish Paratroopers embarking at Ostend.

MAPS

CHAPTER I

EARLY YEARS

BURIED in the garden of a small villa in the Warsaw suburb of Zoliborz there lies a rusting sabre. Perhaps it is still possible to read on the pitted blade the inscription *For honour and glory*. It was presented to me in 1912 by my men of the Underground Movement. I buried the sabre reluctantly in October 1939 after receiving orders to quit Warsaw and go to Roumania to bring back a million pounds to finance the Polish Underground Army, then battling against the Germans.

It was the same sabre that I had clutched as I stood to attention before the Commandant of the Polish War Academy in 1936, saying goodbye after six years as one of his professors.

General "Ted" Kutrzeba looked me firmly in the eye.

"Well, it is time for you to leave us, Sosabowski," he said, "I appreciate very much the good work you have done. You have turned out some first-class staff officers. But before we say goodbye I'd like to give you a bit of friendly advice. You are an independent fellow; you are outspoken and you are critical. These are good points, but I would remind you that few senior officers like to have the opinion of juniors thrust at them, and many will resent it. So watch your step."

He smiled and held out a firm hand.

"Thank you, sir," I said. "I will look out."

I saluted, turned on my heel and marched from the room.

In 1930, before joining the Academy as a Professor, I had been serving as second-in-command of the 3rd Highland Brigade. My posting came through and the Deputy Divisional Commander —later General Malinowski—sent for me.

"Now, Sosabowski," he said, "be careful at the War Academy: they won't like it if you are too outspoken. I understand you, but not many senior officers will appreciate adverse comment, no matter how right it may be."

I thanked him and went on my way. Yet, strange to say, in my six years at the Academy I can recall no unhappy incidents of this nature.

Throughout my military life people have warned me to guard my tongue and opinions. As recently as 1957 my old Commander-in-Chief, General Sosnkowski, wrote in a foreword to my book *The Shortest Way*:

General Sosabowski is a fighting soldier and a commander of determination and knowledge. He is not a man who passively says "Yes sir". He has his own viewpoint and is not afraid to express it, sometimes a little bluntly. He believes this kind of behaviour can only help a senior commander. But when a decision is taken and orders given, he is a loyal and conscientious officer.

I suppose it is true that I have a reputation for being difficult, not only with my own people but also with the British in the last war. But I was merely living up to my standards and being myself.

There are many reasons for my character, and in this book I should like to explain how I became what I am; how I learned about soldiering, and about life, the hard way; how I fought the Germans in my beloved homeland; how I escaped with vital information first to France and then to the sanctuary of Britain; why, and how, and where, the Polish Parachute Brigade was formed; and how, finally, I took my brave soldiers into the chaos and havoc of Arnhem.

My story will also tell of the determination and courage of my men. It will tell of the good times and the hard times. It will show, I hope, the light and shade of my career, and tell of some of the generals I met—Montgomery; Richard Gale; "Boy" Browning; Brian Horrocks; Roy Urquhart; and many others, with whom I worked and fought.

*　　*　　*　　*　　*

I never knew the carefree days of youth. While my friends laughed and played, through force of circumstances I worked and slaved.

In 1905, when I was twelve years old, in the second grade of the Stanislawow Secondary School, my father died, leaving my mother a small government pension and three hungry young children to rear.

In those days Stanislawow was in south-eastern Poland, now part of the Soviet Ukraine.

For about a year after my father's death my mother managed to struggle along on the pension, gradually going through her savings and then selling her scanty possessions. First to go were her few precious bits of jewellery; soon after, the carpets and covers and the less essential pieces of furniture. We moved from one apartment to another, the standard of comfort getting lower and lower, until eventually I realised that we were cold in winter and hungry all the time. Hope was almost dead. My mother was at the end of her resources.

Andrew, my brother, was eight years old; my sister Julia only five; and my mother had to stay at home to look after them. Something had to be done and I was obviously the one to do it. But what could I, a boy of thirteen, do to support a family? I was fairly bright at school, so I decided to become a tutor and coach my less learned schoolfellows. You can imagine my teacher's surprise when I told him my plan and the reasons for it. But he liked me and, recognizing my determination, gave me one of his students to coach in French.

My fees were very small, only a few pennies a lesson, but as time went on I gained a reputation and broadened my field to include mathematics as well as languages. The few shillings I earned meant the difference between life and death for my family and, with the pension, we eked out an existence. In consequence, my mother left the major decisions more and more to me. We moved from the centre of Stanislawow to the suburbs, into the cheapest rooms I could find, and there we lived on top of each other, cheek by jowl, but we did eat and we were warm indoors.

I could spare no money for text-books; so while my companions played and fought during school breaks, I pored over their books in an effort to learn the next lesson. To make up for my lack of reading material, I asked the teachers frequent questions and kept asking and asking, until I was quite sure of the subject. Then I passed on my knowledge to my young pupils.

Vividly I remember how cold those winters were, and how hot the summers. At the Gymnasium we all wore navy blue uniforms and looked very smart in our pillbox hats and silver buttons. But few people knew that my shoes often had holes in them, which I had learnt to repair with cardboard. I had no overcoat, so in winter I ran whenever I went out of doors. Most evenings I arrived home after eleven o'clock. The muddy streets would be deserted and dark, nearly all the oil lamps in the windows extinguished, and the inhabitants fast asleep in warm beds. I had to be up at seven to get to school by eight and, having had no time for homework, I would read a borrowed book as I walked along.

Frequently I was so tired I would fall asleep as I sat. Then I would force myself to my feet and pace the room. If I dozed as I walked, I would bite fiercely at my numb fingers and the pain would clear the mist of tiredness from my brain.

When I began to get results with my pupils, the teachers recommended me to parents as a suitable coach for backward boys. I was very hard on my pupils and kept them at their books until they solved the problems. This additional work was extremely useful, because during the summer holidays the boys disappeared and so did my income. I put aside this extra money and, during vacations, doled it out to my mother in small monthly lots.

Stanislawow is a country town of 70,000 inhabitants, situated in rolling country about thirty miles from the Carpathian mountains. These mountains are green and beautiful, with swift crystal streams and rocky outcrops, and in my youth they seemed a challenge; they beckoned me to their peaks and into their dark forests and, what was more, I needed no money there—only energy. I remember giving in to this urgent challenge; I set off, with a friend and borrowed tents and haversacks, for a holiday. It was such a change from the dull dreary town streets. How good it was to breathe in the country odours and to forget for a while the drains, sewers and slaughterhouses of the town! I learnt to love nature and understand animals. Living rough in the open held no fears for me. I learnt to keep warm and dry and I also became an expert skiier.

So it was that hard necessity built my character.

Each day I had to take decisions. I had to say: "This is what must be done and this is how to do it." I had to plan ahead not just for a week, but for months, for summer and winter. What I said in the family circle was accepted without question. Without realising it, I took my first steps in leadership.

That was just one side of my life, the practical everyday life. But I was also a Pole. Born in me, part of my very nature, was a strong ideology.

Before the outbreak of the First World War Poland was divided between the Russians, Austrians and Germans. Stanislawow was under the yoke of the Austrian Empire. They ruled with kid gloves rather than jackboots; they were not hard masters and left us much to ourselves. But it was occupation and oppression, and we Poles could not stand being mastered and ruled by anyone. For over a thousand years we had been a shield against the barbarians from the East for the whole of Christendom. How could we live in slavery? We had risen against oppression in Napoleonic times; in 1830, 1848 and 1863 our grandfathers and fathers had known the thrill of revolution. The spirit of freedom was born into us.

As a lad of fourteen I joined the first Polish Underground Movement and became leader of the school group. Although this was limited to talks and discussions, we received news from all over Poland. In 1908 the first armed units were formed, called Polish Rifle Units. In 1911, after passing a very stiff examination, I was one of eighty men given commissions in the Underground and was appointed Commander of its branch in Stanislawow.

How busy I was, but what a full life I led! I had no time to despair. That is one of the privileges of the truly poor—there is never time for despair. But I never knew the true joys of childhood. In my country there is a saying: "He was ripe while still young." I was a man before my time; yet, because of it, I had aims and ambitions which I have maintained throughout the years.

My life has been a life of battle and active service. I can tell you of battles I fought against the Russians, the Austrians and Germans. Battles I fought, won and lost, all over Europe, from Warsaw to Arnhem.

I first saw active service in 1914, when the Austrians conscripted all fit Poles, put us into Austrian uniforms and marched us off to fight against other young Poles in Russian uniforms. Circumstances prevented me from joining the Polish Legion, which fought under Marshal Pilsudski on the Austrian side against the Russians. God, how we marched! In the first year I marched over a thousand miles. We marched everywhere—for a short while into the attack, but mostly that autumn and winter we marched in retreat.

My introduction to the horror of battle was brutal and stark and created a vivid impression which I shall carry to my grave.

It was October 1914. I was a twenty-one-year-old corporal. Russian infantry several times our number had encircled us near the Austrian town of Przemysl.

The last leaves of autumn were still clinging to the branches— the countryside was slowly taking on the brownish greyish colour of winter. Daylight with a watery sun brought a little warmth, but the nights were frosty.

We made several abortive attempts to break out without success; the Russians closed the ring, determined to annihilate us. Methodically and deliberately their guns raked the area, cratering, scorching and blasting; their mortars probed every curve of the hills, every trench and every valley; machine guns and rifles covered every entry and exit.

Within hours of being trapped, death was our constant and

familiar companion. Here I first saw men, horribly mutilated, doomed to die slowly without help, calling to death as to a lover to give them oblivion. Death came in many ways and from all directions; death struck regardless of rank. I heard deeply religious men turn against God and curse Him for giving them birth.

Sometimes I slept with a comrade for warmth and three times I awoke with a corpse in my arms.

It was impossible to bury the dead and the midday thaw brought the indescribable and unforgettable stench of rotting human flesh. The night frosts freshened up the corpses and the rats crept and crawled in and around the bodies.

Few of us got away from that circle of death. Many gave up and offered themselves as a sacrifice to the Russian guns because their minds could stand no more.

We joined the files of ragged soldiers retreating westwards along the dusty roads. Panic crept into the high command and into the civil administration.

Justice became casual and honesty rare.

Men got lost from their units and, unable to identify themselves, were hanged on street lamps as suspected spies. I saw a Hungarian strung up like this simply because nobody spoke his language. In one small town almost every lamp-post had a broken-necked, open-mouthed doll hanging from its cross-bar, and I am sure most of them were innocent. My old school padre was being dragged away one day and, if I had not chanced to see him, he would have been hanged.

Military trials were suspended. One morning my regiment was paraded and a soldier shot in front of us. His crime I cannot remember, but he was never given a court martial or a chance to defend himself.

For the first time I realised the power of a military commander, the power over life and death. I also realised the obligations of a commander towards his men and to himself. How much more important are the obligations than the power!

The Austrian Army supply system was full of graft and corruption. The Commissariat was interested only in fat bank balances, regardless of the lives of soldiers or the fate of their country. Field kitchens, upon which we depended for life-giving soup, frequently failed to turn up and we marched on empty stomachs. Those who left the column to search for food were cut down by marauding Cossacks.

I learnt at an early age to recognize a louse. I saw men die from lack of food. I watched them freeze to death, because the general staff forgot to send winter greatcoats. I know all about dysentery, because I had it as a soldier. I remember roadsides dotted with bloody patches where rotten bowels had ejected the poison. I know the tension of having to stop to drop your trousers and sit in agony while the troops march past and then the rush to catch them up. I know what a man looks like when he is dying of typhus—and it is not pretty.

Slowly I was promoted to sergeant, and then company-sergeant-major. I learnt responsibility and how to give orders; how to assess a situation; how to look after men; and how to gain their respect. I know the hopelessness that comes over a soldier when he is tired, hungry, cold and frightened. I also know that an intelligent commander can offer himself as an example to his troops. If he is trusted and respected they will pull themselves together and follow him.

At the end of the first year of war, after many costly battles, my company of two hundred and fifty men—mostly Poles and Ukrainians—had only three original members left. All the others had been killed, wounded or taken prisoner.

New men were sent to replace them but they were raw civilians without any experience of soldiering or battle. Sometimes I even had to tell officers what to do. I taught officers and men all the tricks of saving life in battle; how to fall flat if a grenade landed and, after it exploded, how to roll into the crater it had made. I showed them how to crawl like snakes along the ground without lifting themselves clear of it. I taught them how to fight and how to live. I learnt very early how to judge men. I knew and recognized officers who were good on the parade ground, but I also knew those who would retire when the Russians appeared, leaving me to command their troops.

I have known all the stages of war except one: I have never held up my hands in surrender.

Eventually, in 1916, the Austrians, needing battle-experienced officers, promoted me to second-lieutenant, even though I had been wounded in the leg and was in hospital hobbling around on sticks. Little did I think then that I would recover and become a parachutist. I ended the war as a lieutenant. But I never forgot the lessons learnt in the vicious, pointless holocaust of war. The most important is that an officer should never ask of his men anything he would not do himself. Example is the best lesson to subordinates.

Orders are meant to be obeyed, yet I believe one should have the right to query their correctness. Bad commanders, unaware of the true position, often given impossible instructions. A bad officer will concur and fail to carry them out. A good officer will point out the true position and the order can then be reconsidered.

And so the Great World War ended with its vast toll of death and destruction. I helped to disarm the Austrians who had commanded me and to reorganize the Polish Army for war against the Bolsheviks.

In 1939 I was commanding a famous infantry brigade. It was then that this story really started, because it was then, on September 1st, that I stood a few miles from Warsaw and watched helplessly as Nazi planes opened their bomb doors and let loose their loads of explosive death on to my beloved capital and its inoffensive people.

This was the birth of the Blitzkrieg, the lightning war which paralysed and terrorised the whole of Europe, and part of Asia, before it was finally overcome.

So once again our struggle for freedom began, a struggle that did not end with the partition of Poland by Hitler and Stalin; a struggle that did not end in 1945; a struggle that has never stopped and never will. The spirit of freedom is too strong in my country to be stamped out and suppressed for ever by any political creed or dictator. Freedom will come again to Poland.

CHAPTER II

BLITZKRIEG

ON 3RD MAY 1939 I sat in dress uniform astride my horse leading the Infantry Garrison of Warsaw in a huge ceremonial march down the Aleja Ujazdowski, past the embassies and the vast public buildings. The Aleja Ujazdowski in Warsaw is the equivalent of the Mall in London, or the Champs Elysées in Paris.

Thousands of the city's inhabitants and people from the surrounding country cheered us as we marched in the bright spring sunshine, with bands playing and colours flying, past Marshal Smigly-Rydz. The white and red flags of free Poland fluttered from hundreds of mast heads, while children shouted and waved paper banners.

Overhead, our military aircraft flew in winged salute. Long lines of cavalry trotted by with immaculate precision. Our few tanks trundled past dipping their guns, and horses, trailing field artillery, stepped high, foaming at the bits. It was an impressive show and did not reveal the terrible weaknesses of our Army. With never enough money for the National Budget, our defence forces had not been built up to the required strength.

However on that day I did not realize that it was to be my last parade on the soil of my country.

Perhaps the only people there who gave it a thought were a quiet group dressed in field grey in the stand reserved for foreign Military Attachés—the German Attaché and his staff. But this was May 1939 and nothing was allowed to mar the optimism in the West that Hitler could be mollified and would keep his promises.

It was a proud day for me to be at the head of that column of marching troops. I had come a long way and travelled a hard road since I fought as a soldier in the Austrian Army and then as a leader in the Polish Underground Movement. In my right hand, at the salute, I held the sabre presented to me in 1912, which I was so proud to bear.

The leading unit was my own, the 21st Infantry "Children of Warsaw" Brigade. In the two hundred years since it was formed, it had seldom been out of action. In all the risings against foreign domination, soldiers of the Children of Warsaw had been foremost among the fighters. In 1794, 1807, 1815 and 1830 they had written Polish history with their blood. Our Colonel-in-Chief was, by tradition, the Lord Mayor of Warsaw; in 1939 Stephan Starzynski held office and he, too, stood on the saluting base. The people of Warsaw had presented us with colours and regarded us as their own regiment.

Following the 21st was another Warsaw unit, the 36th Brigade known as the "Legion of Academicians" because some troops were students from the city's universities.

Seven months later, powerful columns of jack-booted Germans goose-stepped down this same avenue past a vainglorious and victorious Hitler.

In May, however, the Germans were only preparing for war. Poland was particularly liable to suffer under Hitler's greedy expansion plans, but although weak and unprepared we were ready to fight.

We appealed to the Western nations for money and military aid. All we ever received was fifty million pounds and such a small amount was virtually useless. Hemming us in on our northern and western frontiers were division upon division of Panzer units, armed with the mightiest war weapons man had ever invented. As early as 1933, Marshal Pilsudski, our beloved elder statesman, proposed to Britain and France that we should fight a preventive war against Germany. But the future spirit of Munich was too strong—the suggestion was not even considered.

In these circumstances Poland had no choice but to prepare as well as she could for what we at last recognised as inevitable. Two months before the outbreak of war, my infantrymen started digging trenches around the old fortress of Modlin, twenty miles north of Warsaw in the direction of East Prussia, where several important roads converge on the junction of the rivers Vistula and Narew. We managed to scrape together enough cement to build a few pillboxes for machine guns or observation posts at intervals along the dirt trenches.

I was continually around the area supervising and directing my officers. One day I found a civilian car parked at a cross-roads directly overlooking some of my defence posts. I ordered my driver to pull in in front of it and block the road. Walking towards the men grouped around it, one of whom was taking photographs, I said:

"It is well known that photographs are forbidden in this area. Consider yourselves under arrest."

They agreed with remarkable equanimity. I sat in the back of their car, ordering my driver to precede us and prevent them escaping, but they caused no trouble. At Divisional Headquarters in Modlin I handed them over with a written report on the circumstances of their arrest.

Within a few hours they were free. They were members of the German Military Attaché's staff and the Polish Government did not even ask for their withdrawal as undesirable. Pressure from the West had been brought on the Government not to cause any incident. One of the men was Captain von Mackensen, Assistant Military Attaché and nephew of the famous German Marshal.

Our preparations continued. Earthworks were being built all over the country, not only by the troops, but also by civilian volunteers. Every hamlet, every village prepared to defend itself. Even schoolchildren turned out to help erect air-raid shelters.

At the end of July 1939 I left Warsaw and took my brigade on manœuvres. On August 22nd I received urgent orders from my Divisional Commander to return to barracks in the Citadel. On arrival in the capital, I soon realised from the preparations that the Government expected a German attack. I received my mobilisation instructions on 23rd August to take effect as from early on the 24th. General mobilisation was not proclaimed until the 29th, to be effective on the 30th; but under pressure from the West, this was delayed for another twenty-four hours. Some secret moves were however authorized and on the 26th and 27th we marched north towards the East Prussian border to take up battle positions.

Polish infantrymen had to rely on their feet to get them from place to place, as we had no columns of fast-moving trucks. To transport the medium machine guns and mortars we had a few horse-drawn wagons. Food was carried in field kitchens and cooked as it travelled by means of wood fires underneath large boilers.

My regular troops were trained to march sixteen to twenty-two miles a day, but with general mobilisation many of my soldiers were taken to build up other units. I was given reservists who had been called up only two days before: they were in poor physical condition and at first the battalion commanders could not force the pace. We marched from Warsaw through Modlin to the Opinogora area—a distance of over sixty miles—by easy stages. We arrived during the night of 2nd September and dug in some thirty miles from the East Prussian frontier.

As we marched through the night of 31st August, we listened to the drumming of massed formations of aircraft flying overhead and then the rumble and gentle shudder of the earth under us as German bombs found distant targets on Polish soil. We were getting very little news about the war and what was happening at the international political level was not clear to the troops at the front.

On 2nd September I attended a conference at Divisional Head-quarters and was ordered to take my brigade further east, positioning my troops near to the main route from East Prussia to Warsaw. We moved at night to avoid the searching eyes of German spotter planes and Stuka dive bombers, and arrived near the village of Koziczyn during the morning of September the 3rd.

The Divisional Commander called his commanders together and gave his final battle orders. Our information on the enemy was that lorry-borne infantry, supported by Panzer units, were driving south from East Prussia to Warsaw. The 20th Polish Infantry Division, which had been fighting on the border since September 1st, had been overwhelmed and partly encircled. My orders were to attack and stop the Germans by cutting across and blocking their lines of advance. We planned to assault from West to East. Another Brigade of the division was ordered to block other troops from the South.

There was a wide open gap between my units and the rest of the division, which made it all too disjointed for my liking. I told the divisional commander my objections, but he reminded me in no uncertain terms that I was under his orders and would do as I was told. I was angry yet—as always—I obeyed.

Back at my Brigade Headquarters I set in motion the war machine which I had been training for several years, just for this eventuality. Up at the front, patrols probed forward seeking and passing back information, which my staff plotted on operational maps. I stayed with the leading battalion commander. At about 2 p.m. I heard from the forward area the quick staccato chatter of a German machine gun, and immediately the battalion commander reported:

"We are in contact."

Shortly afterwards I mounted my horse and rode forward for a closer look at the battle. With the foremost troops, I saw through the trees and across a field the scuttling grey-uniformed figures of German soldiers with their bucket shaped helmets. It was there

I had my first experience of modern German mortars and fast-shooting machine guns. Once more I felt that thrill which comes to every professional soldier when battle is joined and he is doing the task for which he has prepared.

I kept a careful eye on the troops at this juncture, because many of them had never been in action before, and no matter how hard and well a man is trained, it is impossible to tell his reaction until he has had his baptism of fire and felt the nearness of death, the involuntary shiver of fear. I was pleased with what I saw. The officers and N.C.O.s exercised the right sort of control and gave the men the encouragement they needed.

German pressure increased against the battalion and, with the threat of being outflanked, I ordered my second battalion into the fight. This eased the situation and the sudden onslaught of fresh troops forced the enemy back about three-quarters of a mile, but the German commander soon counteracted my move. Finally I had to send in my third battalion. This seemed to do the trick, for the German advance was held and for the rest of the day both sides contented themselves with mortaring, shelling and patrol activity. At dusk I telephoned Divisional Headquarters and asked for another infantry battalion. One was promised by ten o'clock.

During the evening my battle patrols kept contact with the enemy, although I urged them to avoid any strong offensive action until I had a sizeable reserve to back them up.

Ten o'clock came and with it no troops. I waited impatiently. After half an hour I telephoned again. There was no reply. The signals officer reported the line was broken: I told him to keep trying. Radio contact was also impossible. I sent off several dispatch riders with orders to report for information to Divisional Headquarters. Not one of them returned.

Throughout that worrying night the bombers continued to thunder overhead. Sometimes because of our lack of anti-aircraft guns, the planes flew so low we could see them silhouetted against the sky. It was apparent that all around us small battles were being fought—we could hear the roar of tank engines and trucks, the sound of drivers' voices as they cursed their horses along the rutted roads. We could see the flash of shell bursts. We could sense the fighting and confusion, but had no idea of the true situation.

To my immediate front there was only the occasional burst of machine-gun fire, or a signal flare would hang almost motionless in the sky, illuminating the trees and ground for some hundreds of yards. Men froze in mid-step, even rabbits and horses stopped, instinct warning them that to move in the light was to invite death.

By 2 a.m. I was a very worried man. I knew that, without the reserve battalion, I had no hopes of attacking or holding the Germans. They would soon realize the situation and advance relentlessly. If I was to hold them with my present forces, I would have to give way slightly and retire to some high ground over-looking our positions. From there I would be able to dominate the lower ground with guns, mortars and machine guns and give the Germans a rough passage.

At 3.30 a.m. I decided to move. The troops had approximately a mile to go. I ordered the battalion commander to keep patrols out until the very last moment. I did not want the Germans to suspect the withdrawal or they might have assaulted during the confusion of the march. By the time a bright September dawn had broken, my units were busily digging fresh positions.

Unit commanders started sending in reports of burning villages and deserted posts. Contact had been lost with neighbouring units. Then inhabitants of local houses began returning home after a night spent in the fields and ditches, terrified of the bombs and marauding troops. They asked in amazement:

"What are you doing here? The Germans have got through to Warsaw. You are behind the German lines. You are lost."

I could see what had happened without waiting for my com-manders' reports or listening to the rumours of civilians. Not far from my headquarters I was horrified to notice a battery of aban-doned guns, with boxes of untouched ammunition lying around them. It was obvious that panic had sparked and spread through all ranks. The Children of Warsaw appeared to be the only brigade in the division to have stayed and put up a fight, remain-ing as an organized fighting unit. I knew, however, these things could happen in war and, although it was a bitter blow, there was nothing I could do about it. I shrugged my shoulders and turned to the problems facing me.

I was pleased with the way my troops had fought and with-drawn. They had proved themselves as good as the Germans and they were feeling proud that on the previous day they had met the enemy and, man for man, beaten him. Facing facts, however, I realized we were in a pretty hopeless position. If we stayed and fought, we would be up against the overwhelming might of the German Army. It would have been a stupid sacri-fice. My two thousand men, cramped up inside a small perimeter, would have been pounded night and day until all resistance ceased. Dive bombers would have played with us as hawks play with their prey. Tanks would have rolled over us, artillery decimated our ranks, mortars sought and found the cracks in our defences, while our food and supplies got lower and lower. It was a hopeless position and I determined to get my men out and somehow escape through the advanced German lines to Modlin, where I hoped to find Army Headquarters.

Behind and south of me lay an undulating plain sparsely dotted with trees. It was as bare as a desert, without cover for a truck or a horse, let alone several thousand men and vehicles. Six miles away was the lush, dense forest of Opinogora which could hide us, and thousands more, from the prying eyes of enemy pilots.

The Polish air force was so weak that I knew we could expect no help from them. They were, in any case, fighting a David and Goliath battle in the German-dominated skies above Warsaw.

So between us were six miles of very real danger. Once we left the shelter of our trenches and started the march, we would be exposed to every weapon the Germans liked to use against us. But what choice had I? It was a chance and I took it. Fortune smiled on us: we were neither attacked by aircraft nor by enemy troops.

The soldiers, after days of marching, counter-marching and fighting, were dog-tired. They were also ravenously hungry, as the Brigade field kitchens had failed to arrive on the previous day and they had been without food for twenty-four hours.

It was not a pleasant sight for any of us, as we marched towards the forest. Everywhere were the signs of panic. Horses with cut harness wandered in the fields. Wagons blocked the way, their contents strewn on the roads and in the ditches. Official papers, maps and military orders festooned the hedges and wire fences. At artillery sites, guns lay abandoned, many of them still with breech blocks in position. Something had obviously happened during the previous night. Not only had platoons and companies panicked, but battalions and brigades. Small wonder I had never received a reply to my messages.

The effect upon the soldiers, when they saw what their comrades had done, was immediate and morale shattering. I talked to as many as I could and told them how well they had done and how proud I was; I told them all Poland looked to them for victory and deliverance. Because of good training and sensible officers, their morale went up again.

25

Shortly after midday we approached the forest, keeping watchful eyes on the sky in case dive bombers should appear. Massed along one road, we would have made a horribly easy target, but the men were too tired to disperse and it would have delayed us considerably. The closer we got to the trees, the more relaxed the men became—but it was too soon to thank our lucky stars.

From a village ahead we heard the sound of shooting, and shells came from the forest. I ordered the leading company commander to push on and find out what was happening. I soon received a message, asking me to go forward. At the entrance to the village, I was saluted by a staff officer.

"Sir," he said, "you are the senior officer present and now in command of the remains of the 8th Infantry Division."

The few Polish troops were fighting a small group of Germans who had chanced on the village, but were now pulling out. Organizing headquarters, I checked on the number of men I now had under me. In addition to my three battalions, there were two other battalions from the 8th division, plus two from the 20th division. There was another battery of guns and two companies of light tanks: a total of six battalions with supporting arms, about five thousand men in all. But we were all alone, with no idea of the whereabouts of the rest of the Army and out of contact with any senior formation.

Around us were German Army units. Most of those we saw were intent on pushing ahead, without looking too closely at their flanks. The Blitzkrieg theory was being put into practice for the first time and, so far as we could ascertain, it was working well.

My chief problem was, before anything else, to see to the comfort of my men. They needed food and sleep. We managed to scrape up sufficient food for a small meal for every man, and I ordered as many as possible to rest, with a few sentries patrolling the edges of the forest. I went round giving words of encouragement and praise.

Our position was very insecure. It was impossible to say when the Germans might turn on us, but it seemed to me that my duty was to get this force back under the Polish Army Command, where they could perform a useful task in conjunction with the main units of the country. There was no point in fighting small and costly battles along the route, or staying to fight the Germans around us.

As soon as the subordinate commanders had had a short rest, I sent for them and told them my plan. The whole force was to move back to Modlin; splitting into two columns, it would move only by night. By day we would hide in the forests and woods— at dawn we would always vanish.

Each column was about three miles long, and included guns, tanks and wagons. The tank commander informed me that he had only enough petrol to drive half his vehicles. I ordered him to fill the tanks of one squadron and destroy the others. He obeyed reluctantly, but it was our only hope of getting away.

In the hope of letting the Army Commander know of my intentions and the fact that there was still a fighting force north of Modlin, I sent for two of my dispatch riders. I wrote a report, giving details of my force, for them to carry in their pockets. They also took separate messages written on lightweight paper, on which was indicated our route, with an urgent request for food and petrol. If captured, they were to swallow them. They were well aware of the fact that five thousand men depended on them for their lives. They were good fellows—I sent them by different routes and wished them luck, as they rode off on their cycles.

By dusk the men had been roused and were ready to march. Strict orders had been issued that rifle bolts should be removed and carried in the trouser pockets. Bayonets were to remain in the scabbards, so they would not glint in the moonlight. All pieces of metal equipment had been bound with rags to cut out rattle. The horses' harness was blanketed. All ranks were warned not to shoot, even if fired upon, as I had no intention of fighting the Germans, nor did I want to see frightened men firing at comrades. The old saying "All cows are black in the dark" applies only too well to confused troops at night.

Ahead and on either side of the columns were mounted patrols. They were armed and swept the ground well ahead, guiding us along the route and across main roads. For we had to march by lanes and across country, as the roads teemed with German traffic.

That first night we made slow progress—but we kept clear of the enemy, although to me the noise of the troops was more like a fair ground in full roar, instead of a secret column marching through enemy-held territory. However, we made our destination and, after requisitioning sleeping quarters, I spoke to the mayor of the village. Explaining that the troops had not been properly fed for over forty-eight hours, I apologized for being forced to take some of the village stores. I gave him a signed paper for the amount delivered and issued strict orders that any troops found looting would be severely dealt with.

To the casual observer it was a peaceful village going about its everyday tasks, yet hidden in the shadows of rooms and doorways sentries kept watch in case of discovery and attack.

Much refreshed by the day's sleep, the men were in good heart when we set off again at last light. We had several brushes with the enemy that night, but the cavalry patrols successfully kept the main columns from getting caught up in a battle. Again we reached our destination. Before leaving, we blew up the two bridges leading from the town towards Warsaw. I was present when the engineers sparked off the explosives blowing the main spans high into the air, before they crashed to the bed of the river.

That night we were lucky to find two barrels of high-octane petrol on an abandoned airstrip, just as the tank commander announced that the tanks only had enough petrol for a few more miles.

On the fourth day my forward patrols nearly shot up a small convoy of trucks moving towards us. Luckily they held their fire and discovered them to be Polish lorries sent out by Army Head-quarters with the food and petrol for which I had asked.

Later an officer told me that some idiot had sent paraffin instead of petrol. Fortunately a trooper had smelled the difference and stopped filling the tanks.

The officer in charge of this relief party swore that the road between us and Modlin was clear and I decided to push on in daylight. To our dismay we found Modlin almost empty. Head-quarters had moved, leaving only a small garrison. General Zulauf was in command and overjoyed to see me; he had been given to understand he would never see my brigade or me again.

"The road to Warsaw is wide open," he said. "The capital is almost undefended. You will be very very welcome there."

I asked about one particular division and enquired what had happened to the commander and his staff. He confirmed my suspicion that they had panicked. News of the cavalry was also given me. They had fought long and valiantly against massive tanks; they had faced the armoured guns and machine guns with light arms. Finally, with most of the horses shot from under them, these proud and brave units were forced to retreat. Both flanks of our units had thus been left unprotected, allowing the Panzer units to roam at will, killing and destroying behind the Polish front, striking at our lines of communication and supplies. Tanks had smashed through without stopping, sweeping through wagon lines and smaller headquarters. Carrier-borne Panzer grenadiers had infiltrated between all units, cutting them up into small, easily overwhelmed pockets of resistance.

I saw the Divisional Commander in Modlin for a short time. He was a broken man and I felt sorry for him. Yet I feel that, had he kept his units closer and himself in more intimate touch, he would have had far greater control and obtained earlier information about troop movements and enemy attacks. Much the same thing happened to commanders of other formations, who were cut off from forward units and lost all control. This is exactly what the Blitzkrieg was designed to do and this was the proof the Germans needed; now they could carry out their grand design over the whole of Europe.

General Zulauf continued his preparations for defending Modlin. His small force blocked the main northern approach to Warsaw. If his troops could hold it for a day—or even a few hours—it would give the citizens of Warsaw that much longer to prepare. German bombers occasionally attacked the bridges across the Vistula near Modlin on their way back from the capital, if they had bombs left over after the main attacks on Warsaw. Our reconnaissance patrols skirmished with small Wehrmacht units, but we were not in the middle of a battle and it was comparatively calm. Looking back now, it was ominously so.

As soon as my troops had settled in Modlin, I took my car and visited Army Headquarters at Jablonna, reporting to General Przedrzymirski. We spoke for some time about the situation and of the troops under my command. He was very impressed with my brigade and hinted that he would probably move them to Warsaw for the defence of the capital.

From Jablonna to Warsaw it is only a matter of a few miles and I decided to take a chance and drive in to my barracks in the Citadel to see if I could find any more men or supplies. With my driver I set off along the main road. Even after all these years, I can see vividly the picture that unrolled as we went along. Bombs had torn up the roads in many sections, machine-gun and cannon bullets had marked the surface like stamp perforations. Damaged trees stood with tops snapped off, leaves wilted and brown, but the lower branches still lived and forced their greenery through the dying vegetation. Farm animals wandered across the lanes and through gaps torn in hedges. Cows bellowed in pain for their herdsmen to come and relieve them of the agonizing pressure of milk in untouched udders.

Horses, cows, pigs, goats and even dogs lay dead and rotting, gas ballooning their stomachs, transforming them into monstrous, swollen nursery toys. Farmsteads and cottages stood with drunken hanging roofs, and fires still flickered at the remains of foundation timbers. Often it was impossible to get the vehicle along the roads. German pilots, with bombs and bullets to spare, had been attracted by long columns of unprotected refugees heading for Warsaw. They had swooped down from the heavens to play with their toys of pain and death, life and hope. Prams, childrens' carts and wheelbarrows, piled high with homely belongings, lay abandoned and tumbled. Intimate personal possessions left exposed to the elements. The dead lay in the dust, struck down in flight in positions of self-protection. We were almost physically sick at the wantonness of destruction carried out by these Luftwaffe pilots. Death flew easily from their fingers. They struck regardless of justice. Good and bad, rich and poor, young and old, met the same unworthy end and now lay rotting in the dust of Poland, without knowing why or deserving such a casual end.

Sometimes family groups, seated round small twig fires, would shout out, asking for news. We gave them whatever information we could but, above all, warned them to keep off the main roads and, if possible, travel by night. It was no use telling them to go home; most of them had already seen their houses blown to pieces or consumed by fire; their belongings salvaged at the last moment were packed in small haversacks or hauled along in makeshift trolleys.

As we approached the capital, we saw a cloud of dark smoke hanging lazily over the whole of the city. It extended into the suburbs and surrounding country. Breasting a small rise, the silhouette of Warsaw was suddenly spread out before us. At once we could see something was different—something was missing. Apart from the clouds of smoke, the smell of burning and the flickering orange flames, the outline of the town had changed. The towers and spires of the churches, the well known landmarks, had toppled into piles of rubble and, even as we drove into the suburbs, we saw bombers with black crosses on their wings flying deliberately and steadily over the metropolis. They circled slowly, while the aircraft captains chose their targets and the small egg-like black dots came from their bellies to drop in angled flight into the over-populated centre. A few anti-aircraft guns opened up, but the bombers ignored them.

All the shops were closed, with windows barred. Few people walked the dirty littered streets. Only here and there did we see organized groups digging in the smoking ruins, searching for survivors. Police were few and far between, and most of the inhabitants were unshaven, dirty, ill-dressed, with blood-soaked bandages and the light of desperation in their eyes.

Quieting my fears, I drove over one of the bridges to the west side of the Vistula into the Citadel. To my relief and delight, there was still a sentry at the gate and, as he saluted, there was a most unmilitary smile of welcome on his lips.

In my office I found the Bandmaster. He was so pleased to see me that he forgot to salute and pumped my hand up and down with joy. He explained that the quartermaster's supply column had come back to Warsaw under an N.C.O. and that the Quartermaster had disappeared. They did not know where the brigade was at that time and had been unable to send out supplies. Parked on the parade ground, unharmed, was the column of field kitchens and supply wagons.

I told the Bandmaster that we would not need any music until the war was over and that he was promoted lieutenant quartermaster. He organised the column, got the wagons loaded and a meal started in the field kitchens; within an hour I watched them trot off with all the supplies and ammunition my units would need for several days.

The Citadel was a massive eighteenth-century fortress, situated near one of the main bridges. It had remained almost untouched by the bombing, apart from my own office, which had received a direct hit, resulting in the death of a major seated at the desk. A few windows were broken and the walls scarred with shrapnel. It was a wonder that it had been missed by the hundreds of bombs aimed at the bridge.

I asked one of the clerks what had happened in Zoliborz, where my house was; he said that he had been continuously on duty since the bombing started and did not know. But he did tell me how Warsaw had been heavily bombed within hours of the declaration of war; so soon, in fact, that the planes were dropping death before any warning was given. The streets were crowded, theatres and cinemas were packed. Hundreds died in the first few minutes. Stukas had machine-gunned the terrified crowds. On September 3rd, fifteen hundred civilians were killed. A girls' school was hit on the 4th. Warsaw Radio stayed on the air and in between news bulletins, the notes of Chopin's stirring *Etude Révolutionnaire* sounded through each wireless speaker in every house that still stood, as a sign to the rest of the world that Poland was alive and fighting.

At one time, it had been the Government's intention to declare Warsaw an Open City, but this idea was abandoned. At the first blow of the Blitzkrieg, the Polish Government left the capital, taking most departments with it. On September 8th the Commander-in-Chief decided to defend Warsaw and General Czuma took command of the city. The gallant mayor—Colonel-in-Chief of my Regiment—Stephan Starzynski, was appointed Commissioner for Civil Affairs and the citizens prepared to fight and set an example to the free world. It was also the desire of the Polish people. For hundreds of years bullying, conquering nations had carved Poland into pieces and tried to absorb her, but Warsaw, throughout all the wars, rebellions and battles had remained Polish and a symbol of our nationhood.

Without much hope, and with the continued terror of the bombing, the few civil authorities remaining in the capital could not, however, maintain law and order. With the news of defeat of the 8th and 20th Divisions and the subsequent rumours of vast German forces descending to butcher and rape, thousands had packed their belongings on their backs and set off along the roads, blocking them solid with miles and miles of humanity. They did not know where they were going, they made no plans other than to get away from the bombers and the threat of the enemy from the north. They fled to the east and shortly met up with refugees heading westwards. There was chaos and terror and the opposing columns fought to get past each other, bringing military traffic to a standstill. Luftwaffe planes, like vultures, swooped and struck, taking their pick at leisure.

With the refugees from the west came the evil men and women of the Fifth Column. They moved into action behind the lines, spreading panic and defeatism wherever they went. Like well-trained troops, they were invaluable to the invading forces. In Britain, there has been no experience of such people and their loathsome activities. I firmly believe that, had invasion come to Britain, a Fifth Column would have risen just as it did in every other occupied country. In Poland the insidious, evil influence of Nazism found a suitable breeding ground amongst the hundred thousand German-born Polish citizens, appearing in the most unlikely places. No organization, no strata of society was free from it.

With a deep fear in my heart I drove to my house. No street was without damage; often we drove on the pavements to get round bomb holes. Broken water mains spouted fountains into the air and the smell of broken sewage pipes pervaded every corner.

Miraculously, my home was almost untouched, with only a few window panes broken. The garden looked neat and the flowers reflected the autumn sunlight filtering mildly through the pall of smoke hanging over the city. I leaped from the car and, as I approached the front door, there came a deep-throated growl and an animal flung itself against the door as a warning to me to keep away. It was my Great Dane, Tom, almost crazy with anger in his urge to protect my home and those in it. I called to him, shouting his name, and the growls died in his throat. He hurled himself again at the door, trying to break it down in his joy at the arrival of his master. The maid opened the door and the hound threw himself at my chest, his tongue seeking and licking my face and hands. Standing on his hind legs, he was taller than I and almost as strong. From a murderous protective instinct, he had changed almost to a lamb.

Anne, the maid, welcomed me with relief and joy, explaining that she was alone in the house. I learnt that my wife had left Warsaw very early and gone to friends in the country, but Anne did not know her whereabouts. My son—a doctor in the Medical Corps—had also left with his unit and there was no news of him.

Gathering together a few extra belongings, I told the girl to let my wife or son know that I expected to return in a few days, should she hear from them. I then drove to the main Medical Depot to enquire after my son. I was told that he had been posted as assistant to the doctor in charge of a hospital train sent in the direction of Lodz. The Adjutant informed me that this train had been bombed and the chief doctor had returned to Warsaw with the news that everyone but he had been killed.

This news numbed me completely. My son and I had a close relationship, which was more than that between father and son. We had always been great pals, with a very deep affection and understanding. I comforted myself a little with the thought that it was most unlikely that everyone had died and that probably the doctor had fled in fright before finding out about the others. But it was with a heavy heart that I started back.

After some hours, the field kitchen arrived and my soldiers soon filled their stomachs. Fresh supplies of ammunition and petrol were issued and all ranks were shortly looking and feeling much more confident. Food is one of the greatest morale-builders.

Two days later, I was ordered to take my troops to the capital. My force was a composite one, consisting of my own Children of Warsaw and some field artillery. We were to prepare fortifications and await the expected German attack.

I was told to move fast and this meant marching by day, in full view of marauding enemy planes. I protested that it was better to get to Warsaw a day later with all my men than a few hours earlier with many casualties. I was over-ruled.

My fears proved right; Stukas spotted us near Jablonna. As the leading troops approached a wood, the first flight put their noses down and started their screaming, wailing dive before loosing bombs into our midst. Machine-gun bullets and shrapnel bombs killed forty men with one blow and wounded dozens more. The pilots circled and attacked, picking us off as they pleased. We dispersed under the trees, but even as we crouched, burying our faces in the roots and grass, the planes continued to rake the speckled leafy corridors of trees with bullets, filling the air with the smell of powder mingled with the odour of sap oozing from broken branches and holed trunks.

Early on 14th September, we arrived in the Warsaw suburb of Praga. As my troops marched through the ravaged streets, I saw looks of anger and sorrow cross their faces. Many, for the first time, were seeing what happens to civilians in total war. Whole families slept huddled in doorways, covered with paper or ragged blankets; the fronts of some houses had collapsed into the streets and we saw the pitiful remains of homes destroyed in the midst of life. Beds with linen on them hung drunkenly through holes in ceilings. Crockery and the remains of meals still lay on kitchen tables. I remember seeing the pendulum of a clock swinging on the one remaining wall of a gutted living-room. Not one of those soldiers ever forgot the little golden-haired girl who lay face down on a pavement, dead and finished, pressing to her chest a rag doll.

I urged the troops on as quickly as possible. In the area which we had been allocated there were a few badly dug trenches and several road blocks erected by volunteers, but the defences were very sketchy.

General Czuma, Operations Commander, Warsaw, had directed that the capital be defended sector by sector. Mine included the Paderewski park, a residential area, and the Warsaw East Station. This district faced east and north and had several main roads and railway lines coming into it. Already there were two battalions of volunteers, who had worked on the trenches. With my own three battalions, the force numbered five infantry battalions and a battery of mixed guns. I found more guns at the barricades.

After a preliminary reconnaissance, I allocated the troops to positions and told them to get on improving the defences.

I decided to defend every point. Soldiers were placed in the basements and cellars, in factories and houses. Every street corner was manned and machine guns covered every entry and exit.

34

On the main road we erected an enormous mound of earth, bricks and rubbish, which blocked it completely, providing cover for the defenders. At the one main cross road, we built a very strong redoubt.

For twenty-four hours, apart from the frequent visits of bombers, the men worked in comparative peace. On the 15th, the leading elements of the main German Army struck my forward units, but were taken by surprise and beaten back with murderous fire. This first battle was fought in the houses and gardens of Grochow. I ordered the artillery to shell the area to let the enemy know they had now met determined resistance. After a few hours of skirmishing and patrol contacts, the Germans settled down and dug in. Between us was a No-Man's-Land of deserted houses, as well as flat fields, up to a mile wide in places, but in others only a few yards.

Sector Headquarters was in the administrative building of the Motlot aircraft factory. Signallers laid telephone lines to all battalions and I issued strict orders about conservation of ammunition and the need for strong battle discipline.

Sitting in Headquarters, I casually picked up the civilian telephone which lay on the desk. Almost without thinking I dialled my home number. To my amazement, I heard the bell ring and then the voice of the maid. As shells burst around the factory and the rattle of machine guns chattered around me, I asked if she had any fresh news.

"Yes," she answered, "your son . . ."

A bursting shell drowned the rest of her words.

Urgently, almost pleadingly, I called into the mouthpiece:

"What did you say about my son?"

"Your son has been here," she called.

"Thank God, thank God," I cried. "Is he well? Where is he? How did he look?"

My questions were shouted without waiting for a reply. Finally she broke in and told me he had been to the house asking for me; if I returned, I was to go to the tunnel at Warsaw Central Station, where he would be with his unit.

I told her, if he called again, to tell him I would go there at the first opportunity.

During the next few hours, the Wehrmacht troops consolidated their positions. A tight ring of men and steel was drawn around Warsaw and we were besieged. German artillery and mortars marked the targets and ranged all their weapons. Every move brought down shells and all cross-roads were subjected to periods

35

of concentrated fire. One morning I was caught with my orderly, crossing a field. We were alone, going to visit one of the companies, yet a Stuka pilot decided to attack us. We threw ourselves in the nearest ditch and crawled away. We felt as exposed as targets on a rifle range.

By night Warsaw was a backcloth of flames, stench and noise. The water mains had been hit so often that it was impossible to get water. Fires blazed throughout the nights, providing markers for pilots; buildings collapsed without warning and burning gas mains lit up the debris-littered streets. Rats and half-wild cats roamed the ruins seeking food, while dogs fought each other over dismembered human limbs.

Warsaw was fast becoming a bloody jungle of lawlessness, where the strong conquered and the weak went under. Broken, oozing sewers and blocked drains slowly seeped poison into the air and the fear of typhoid and typhus was with us all the time.

Tracer bullets cut coloured lines in the night sky, death never stopped his search for fresh victims. Every cellar, every subway, every ditch and trench had its civilian occupants. Even in the front line there were women and children, who could not be sent away. The troops shared out their food and water and it was a great problem to produce enough for all.

I organised some civilian burial parties. We cleared most of the bodies in the open, but there were many, lightly covered with wreckage, that rotted unseen, a target for animals and myriads of flies.

One morning I was called to see a general at Warsaw Headquarters. This was located in the Post Office Savings Bank, in one of the few deep shelters built in the city. It had four underground floors and was impregnable. It survived then, and was also used in the 1944 rising.

Close by was the Central Station and, after completing my business, I went there. In the tunnel, I asked an Engineers captain if he knew Sosabowski.

"Of course," he replied. "He is my medical officer—and a wonderful chap."

He pointed out the carriage in which my son was working and I walked swiftly and silently to it. Inside, under a light, "Stas" was treating a lightly-wounded soldier. Taking him by surprise I roared:

"Stas, how are you?"

He whipped around, an expression of incredulity on his face. We rushed together and flung ourselves in each other's arms. We embraced and kissed a dozen times, crying unashamedly and repeatedly telling each other how wonderful and unbelievable it was to find the other alive.

As soon as his work ended, Stas took me to the sleeping compartment where he had his quarters and told me all his adventures.

Luftwaffe planes had deliberately bombed the ambulance train in broad daylight, in spite of the large red crosses painted on the tops and sides. It had been hit at one end and the chief doctor had run off in a frenzy and disappeared. A few of the staff, including some nurses, had been killed, but the train and medical supplies were mostly all right. The main difficulty was that the line on both sides of the train had been broken, so they were unable to move.

Some time later a party of Engineers found them. Stas explained their predicament, asking if the lines could be repaired. The Engineers' commander, a young Captain Moscibrodzki, agreed to do it and got them back to Warsaw, where they were giving urgently needed medical aid.

After this, every time I visited Headquarters, I managed to spend a few minutes with my son.

With the build-up of enemy artillery, it became increasingly difficult to cross the bridges and main road intersections. All the bridges from Praga across the Vistula to the centre of the city were overlooked by German observation posts and were littered with wrecked vehicles, which could only be cleared during the night. In daytime we ran a gauntlet of fire. I had several narrow escapes.

Life at the barricades was difficult. We had little ammunition to spare and for every hundred German shells we could return only one. My men were told they must never fire until they were certain of hitting a target. Enemy patrols were allowed to come almost into our trenches before we fired and, where possible, were killed with the bayonet, rather than waste bullets.

Early in the siege—on 16th September—I was standing with an officer near the great mound of earth which blocked the main road. He was describing a patrol sent out the previous night and I was looking at the ground through my binoculars. I suddenly noticed two German tanks appear along the road, preceded by an open car flying a large white flag.

Some of the troops opened fire and the anti-tank commander was about to give his orders when I told them all to stop shooting. The turrets of both tanks were open with the crews standing up, guns pointed high over our heads. It was obviously a party under a flag of truce; no fire came from the enemy trenches.

The tanks stopped and the car came on alone. I stepped out from behind the barricade and walked up the road with one of my company commanders. At our approach, the car stopped and, in German, I asked the enemy officer in it what he wanted. The officer, a young Staff colonel, saluted.

"I have a letter from my commander," he said, "addressed to the Officer Commanding, Warsaw. It is a demand for the surrender of the city."

Asking for the letter, I said I would send it to the General Commanding, Warsaw. I then blindfolded the German officer and made him sit in his car in front of the barricades.

The note was taken immediately to the Warsaw army commander. Within an hour, the answer came back saying that General Czuma would neither talk with, nor see, the enemy emissary. The car reversed and the German colonel saluted me. I returned his salute.

Twenty minutes later, I ducked as a mortar shell screamed down to explode in a nearby field. The truce was over.

My chief worry was the shortage of artillery ammunition. We had found small arms ammunition in a factory situated in the sector, but the supply for the guns was nearly exhausted. To our chagrin, we knew that, in No-Man's-Land, near the German forward positions, there was a train fully loaded with artillery shells. I often thought about this and tried to devise some way of getting it back to our lines.

Talking with my son and the Engineers captain one day at Warsaw Central Station, I told them of our difficulties. Turning to the captain, I asked if he could help carry out a daring plan which was slowly formulating in my head. Eagerly he said that he would help to the best of his ability.

My plan was to send a battalion out on an offensive patrol, which would attack the German troops entrenched near the ammunition train. They would make plenty of noise and I would supplement it with artillery and mortar shells. Under cover of this noise, the Engineers would drive a locomotive as quietly as possible towards the ammunition train—as far as I knew, the railway line was unbroken. When the engine was hooked on to the wagons, a final attack would be launched, and the train would run back at full steam into Warsaw.

A locomotive was driven into our area and kept out of sight from the enemy. As soon as it was dark, the battalion moved out with orders to approach slowly and listen for prepared signals controlling their movements. The engine driver quietly eased the locomotive through our lines into No-Man's-Land. Not a glimmer of light showed from the boiler, not a spark came out of the funnel; but, as it passed near me, I thought the noise would be heard for miles and every German gun would range on it, blowing it into small fragments.

The manœuvre took us almost all night. But it was successful; the Germans never suspected what was happening. My infantry kept up small raids during the approach of the engine. When it was within a hundred yards of the ammunition train, a platoon charged with bayonets. The driver pulled his steam lever and the machine shot towards the wagons. An Engineer dropped to the ground and quickly joined the couplings; then, with wheels spinning madly, the locomotive reversed at full speed. By the time the Germans realised what was happening, it was too late. As the driver re-entered our lines, he blew a defiant blast on his whistle. We had captured plenty of ammunition in return for only a few lives.

By day it was a one-sided battle. The German artillery and mortars never stopped. Machine gunners continually sprayed the forward areas and, of course, there was the unending stream of bombers and the hated Stukas. Apart from keen-eyed sentries, the men slept during the day in order to be fresh for night-fighting. Our guns were silent, unless they were certain of hitting a target.

By night, however, we came into our own. We knew every street, every back alley, every garden; we had maps showing plans of the drains and underground cables; we knew every entry and every exit; my men could go where they pleased. The Germans never knew where we would strike next. Sometimes the troops charged in from No-Man's-Land, but more often the enemy would find himself caught from behind, as men crept out of side roads and secret approaches.

Every night I sent at least one battalion to sweep the area and keep the Germans awake and guessing. They became so frightened that often we found their forward positions deserted and small units hiding in barricaded houses. Occupied buildings we set on fire or blew up. The main danger with these patrols came if they were caught crossing No-Man's-Land, as the Germans had covered the area with machine guns on firing fixed lines and with mortars and guns sighted onto pre-arranged targets. One false move—and dozens of men died.

At my Headquarters in the aircraft factory, life was very uncomfortable. The tall chimneys in the yard attracted too much attention from enemy guns and my casualties were mounting.

One night, after a heavy day's work, a shell hit the wall of the room in which I was sleeping. I woke to find the air full of dust, and several bricks on my bed. My staff came charging in to ask if I was safe. I assured them I was very much all right and as one shell had already landed in the room, it was unlikely that another would. I said I would stay where I was and I turned over and went back to sleep. My car and radio set had received a direct hit and the yard outside was dotted with shell holes.

Across the road from us was a smaller, stronger edifice, the city slaughterhouse. I ordered a move to it.

Strangely enough this building, so used to killing, never saw death throughout the whole of the siege. The horses put in the stalls remained unharmed and none of my men were killed.

After breakfast one day, I was looking over the maps and street plans, arranging night patrols. The Germans were shelling a sector some distance away and, apart from an odd mortar bomb, my part of the front was comparatively quiet. I had been scanning the reports sent in by unit commanders, which nearly always made depressing reading. The casualty lists increased daily; I kept seeing the names of soldiers with whom I had marched and fought, and the ranks were getting thinner and thinner.

I was sitting at my desk, feeling rather depressed, when into my office walked an officer carrying a lion cub. It was hardly old enough to have left its mother and was not even weaned. It was most attractive and soon became the Headquarters pet. Bombers had wrecked the zoo, killing many of the animals, and the cub had been found mewing plaintively. We fed him on milk and he became the centre of attention, and gave us a lot of fun and pleasure by distracting us momentarily from the horrors of war.

Violent days followed—and even more violent nights. Old and trusted companions were killed and wounded; food was difficult and the water situation very bad. Hospitals overflowed with wounded and thousands lay on blankets on stone floors, waiting for attention which often never came, because a doctor would be killed on his rounds, or vital drugs destroyed.

All day on the 25th of September and again on the 26th, Nazi bombers came in their hundreds; the sky was almost black with them. By now, our anti-aircraft guns were out of ammunition; we could see the faces of the pilots and bomb aimers, glancing casually down as if we were ants to be crushed underfoot. These huge roaring machines circled the city and then in they came, in line astern, dropping their loads with deliberate precision. Those young Nazis were not seeking to destroy military targets, they were trying to destroy a nation. They knew that Warsaw was for Poles the true Poland. It represented everything good about our homeland. They were intent on destroying us body and spirit. That they never succeeded the whole world knows.

Warsaw became an inferno; in parts, it was hardly possible to recognize streets, as all the landmarks disappeared under the rubble. The inhabitants lived permanently in a twilight of dust, acrid smoke and gloom of underground basements, sewers, and shelters.

People died, men, women and children were torn apart by the blast of high explosive. Evil men preyed on the dying and dead, desecrating the bodies in search of gold, jewels and food. And in the midst of all the carnage and suffering, women gave birth to children, often to lose them immediately, even as they suckled life from warm breasts. The goodness and courage of people showed itself in this time of agony and terror. Men sacrificed themselves for their wives and children. Half-starved humans shared crusts with strangers. Priests, still believing in God, gave courage to the weak in the midst of sin and wickedness.

The following day the vast air armadas stopped their destructive labours, but smaller formations still came to keep the fires burning and the roads blocked. Patrols on the outskirts of the city met the fire of the German infantry and shells rained down on our positions.

On the afternoon of the 27th September the enemy guns stopped firing. It was uncanny; after days of violence, it was also ominous. We had heard that the Russians had entered Poland to come to our aid and I thought it possible that the Germans had retreated. I hurried out of my battered room into the corridor to find my staff with questioning frowns upon their faces.

Why had the firing stopped? This was a puzzle which had to be solved. I sent out a patrol, but it was met by German bullets.

I decided to go to Army Headquarters at the Post Office Savings Bank. It was a typical September day, the sort of morning when, in peace-time, I would have gone with my son and a dog for a gallop through the forests and returned home for scalding coffee and hot rolls, and the pleasures of a happy family life. But that morning the only normal things were the sun and the sky. Everything around me was destroyed or damaged, dead or dying.

I drove round gaping black bomb holes and carcases. A few dirty, bedraggled citizens came up from their underground homes and, recognizing my rank, called out:

"Sir, can you tell us what is happening? Is it peace? Have the Russians arrived and beaten the Germans? Is there an armistice?"

These and a dozen other questions had already been going round and round my head.

I said I did not know but was going to find out at Headquarters. If they liked to look out for me, I would let them know on the way back.

I drove on, deeply depressed by what I saw. I had seen death and destruction in many forms, but never had I seen such mass destruction, which had hit everyone, regardless of innocence or guilt. Gone were the proud buildings of churches, museums and art galleries; statues of famous men who had fought for our freedom lay smashed to pieces at the bases of their plinths, or stood decapitated and shell-scarred. The parks, created for their natural beauty and for the happy sounds of laughing, playing children, were empty and torn, the lawns dotted with the bare mounds of hurried graves. Trees, tossed into the air with the violence of explosion, lay with exposed roots, as if they had been plucked by a giant hand and negligently thrown aside.

Almost the only noise on this morning was the rumble of bricks as walls, weakened by bombs, finally subsided. The smoke of burning houses pillared into a windless sky and the smell of putrefaction lingered in the nostrils.

In the midst of an enormous area of rubble I saw a sentry standing at the entrance to the vast underground fortress of the Post Office Savings Bank. Inside, there was an air of depression and dejection. Old friends hardly spoke when they saw me, although one did say that an armistice was being arranged. I tried to see General Czuma but, as he was too busy, I saw his Chief-of-Staff. After wandering around, seeking information, I left and returned to Praga.

In the front lines, the troops were taking advantage of the cease-fire. They were sunning themselves on top of their positions, smoking and washing and eating in the open for the first time in 14 days.

The effects of a truce on soldiers are very hard to assess, but it is certainly bad for morale. Every man at the end of a battle says: "Thank God I am alive"—and is afterwards reluctant to re-enter the fray.

There was nothing I could do. I asked my commanders to keep the normal sentries posted to avoid any treachery on the part of the enemy.

On the 28th September I attended a conference at Army Head-quarters at which General Czuma announced the surrender terms. These had been negotiated with the Germans by General Kutrzeba.

These were the conditions:

1. *29th September: all units to lay down their arms in specified area.*
2. *Disarmed units to gather in indicated sectors.*
3. *Barricades, road blocks, trenches, etc., on the main roads to be destroyed and mines removed.*
4. *Polish units to march out of Warsaw along certain routes according to a programme, under their own officers, my sector being first to move.*
5. *Privates and N.C.O.s to be released from camps and returned home after a few days.*
6. *Officers to go to Prisoner of War camps, but to retain their sabres.*
7. *Officers not surrendering would, on capture, be treated as criminals and not accorded rights under the Geneva Convention.*
8. *Troops to carry enough food for three days.*

I went back to the ruins of Praga and our slaughterhouse with a heavy heart. I still felt confident that with help from both Britain and France, we could hang on and win through. But I had not all the facts; I only knew what happened in the capital, as Warsaw Radio, fallen into German hands, was silent.

It was dreadful to have to tell the troops, who had been fighting well with good morale, that they must lay down their arms and surrender.

My commanders came to a conference in my office. I was delighted to see one of them, Major Obrembowski, who two days previously had been badly wounded and sent to hospital on the other side of the river. When I remarked on his presence he said, with a wry smile:

"I could not stay away at a time like this and I wanted to know your decision. Whatever you do, I shall follow."

The loyalty of many of my officers and troops was very touching.

Having briefed my downhearted commanders, I put two alternatives to them.

"Shall we try and fight through the Germans and join up with the Russians—or shall we carry out the terms of the Armistice?"

We did not know then about the Ribbentrop-Molotov agreement and the treachery of Russia.

Turning to the commander of the 1st Battalion, I asked his opinion.

"There has been no fighting for two days," he replied. "The troops are mixed up with the civilians and the talk is all of peace. I don't believe more than half would follow me now the surrender has been announced."

The other officers were more or less of the same opinion; the rot had set in fast and deep, which was understandable. It is human nature.

I had no alternative; I told them to prepare for surrender.

One of the commanders stood up.

"Sir, I have served and fought under you and have been proud to do so—but even you cannot order me to surrender: that decision is mine."

I agreed and said it was entirely a personal matter and I would not order anyone into captivity. They knew the German conditions. My only stipulation was that at least one officer per battalion should march with the troops over to the enemy.

I then worked out my own interpretation of the Armistice terms and issued the following instructions:

1. Breech blocks from the artillery and the bolts from all machine guns and rifles to be thrown into the river.
2. Documents to be collected and the important ones buried secretly in the slaughterhouse.
3. Soldiers to be paid in full and any money left over divided equally among them.
4. Troops to be given as many rations as they could carry and the remaining food to be distributed among the families.

I knew full well I was disobeying the Germans, but the responsibility was mine.

Many of my officers, after saying goodbye, disappeared that night and were not seen again. The Germans had been very clever with their statement that soldiers and non-commissioned officers would be returned home. This meant that the bulk of them stayed in order to get a discharge certificate.

The Chaplain came to me that evening. He lived in Central Poland, in a small country village. Would I let him return home? I gave him permission. He asked if I needed the two horses which drew his wagon, so I told him to take them.

"Don't forget I shall be back to claim them when the war is won," I called after him, jokingly.

44

In the morning, I had the five battalions paraded in their sectors. I visited each one and spoke to them. I knew them personally—their faults and failings, as well as their good points. It was a solemn occasion. I addressed them with feeling and sadness.

"You have fought well during this campaign and I am proud of you. Warsaw will never forget your valiant and gallant struggle. The citizens will remember the blood spilt by your comrades. However, through no fault of yours, we have agreed to an Armistice. When you march off parade, you will leave your weapons behind. You will march into captivity—but only for a few days and then the Germans will send you home. Yet when you take off your uniforms and put on civilian clothes, do not forget you are still soldiers of the Republic. We cannot be broken by this passing defeat of arms; the time will come when we shall rise again. You should remain soldiers, ready to receive my orders or the orders of officers designated by me. Have no doubts that we shall meet again to fight shoulder to shoulder to victory. As it is impossible for me to say goodbye to each one of you personally, I should like the officer in charge of the battalion to come forward with one non-commissioned officer and two privates from each section. I am not saying 'Adieu'—only 'Au revoir'."

The men marched stiffly forward and I clasped each one by the hand. There were tears in our eyes and, through the mists, my mind flashed back over the years, to the wonderful times we had had and the good comrades I had known.

"Pile Arms."

As they marched off, I saluted them for the last time. Then I was alone, surrounded by the unmanned triangles of rifles which would never be fired again.

I turned from this desperately unhappy and desolate scene and walked away, trying to shake off my depression.

The idea of marching voluntarily inside the barbed wire of a prison camp was repugnant to me. I called one of my remaining staff officers.

"I am leaving," I announced. "If anyone asks for me, tell them I have committed suicide and my body has not been recovered."

None of my friends would believe this, so they would not worry.

I hurriedly bundled a few personal possessions into a knapsack and drove home. Stas was already there, eager to know my plans. I told him I was not going to a Prisoner of War camp and he immediately agreed to stay with me.

45

Needing much more information from Army Headquarters, I went off to the Post Office Savings Bank.

A dismal sight met my eyes. Nearly all the General Staff sat around on cases and kit bags, most of them staring blankly at their feet or the walls. Hardly a man returned my greeting—even old friends looked at me almost without recognition. An air of hopelessness permeated the atmosphere.

An old friend, Colonel Litynski, was sitting, like the others, on a suitcase.

"What are you going to do?" I asked.

"We are waiting to march into prison camp."

I was startled and annoyed that he should say this so calmly and protested, but he swept my arguments aside.

"You are foolish to think of escape. Nearly everyone in Warsaw knows you. Someone will recognize you and give you away. When you are caught, the Germans will treat you as a common criminal and you'll probably be shot. But in a few months, at the most, the British and French Armies will have beaten the Germans and you'll be needed again in the Polish Army."

How long we argued I do not remember. Other officers joined in against me, telling me repeatedly not to be a fool. I left Headquarters faltering in my original decision.

Back home, I looked at my son and thought about the problem. Then I said:

"You stay here in civilian clothes—I'm going to lead my soldiers into captivity."

"No, Father," he replied. "Where you go, I go too."

At 6 p.m. on 29th September 1939, I rejoined my troops. They were formed in column of march, ready to move from the Poniatowski Bridge. The Germans had given permission for some transport to be taken and for staff officers to keep their vehicles. I told the officer leading the column that I would drive just in front of him.

As we set off, I ordered my driver to go slowly and, with Stas, sat glumly in the back. We progressed gradually down the battered and scarred main streets. The few civilians we passed gazed woodenly at us, without praise or condemnation.

The troops kept good order and were well-disciplined. But as they walked through the ruins, I was disturbed to notice figures dressed in torn and dirty uniforms crawl out of holes and run to join the column. They were mostly men who had lost their units and their one desire was now to get into a prison camp and obtain a discharge certificate from the German authorities. They soon

46

caused trouble by demanding food, and even trying to steal it; it was with difficulty that the N.C.O.s kept order. Every Army has its quota of these criminals and we are all ashamed of them.

The column turned westwards into the suburb of Ochota. I glanced back out of the rear window and looked at the broken, battered skyline of my beloved Warsaw. The sun was going down in a September blaze. The city looked like a fiery furnace as the light reflected on a million pieces of broken glass.

At the sound of motor cycles, I dragged my eyes from the miserable scene. Two German despatch riders came up on either side of me as escorts. Down the road, I saw a group of grey-uniformed officers waiting to imprison us.

Chapter III

OCCUPATION

OUR column had just passed through Ochota when road-
side loudspeakers suddenly broke out noisily with Polish
national tunes. We had sung these songs in the peace of
summer evenings when work was done; we had merrily pranced
to them in warm halls on cold winter nights; they were reminders
of our youth and Polish heritage. It was awful to hear them being
played by the invaders. Automatically the troops stepped to the
beat of the music. The Germans laughed and sneered as they
saw what, to them, was virtually a corpse dancing at its own
funeral. Stas and I sat in the car looking straight ahead, trying to
shut the noise from our ears. How we hated the Germans at that
moment!

Throughout the night we marched and not until dawn were
we permitted to stop. As we halted, tanks circled round, making
escape impossible. We were offered a barrel of salted herrings,
although the armistice terms had specifically stated that no food
would be issued. I warned the men not to eat them as, with water
rationed, it would be difficult to slake their thirst, but many of
the stragglers who had joined us did eat them and later there
were fights over water. On reflection, I think the Germans produced the salt herrings out of pure spite.

There followed another day and night of marching, and the
morning of 1st November found us trudging through Żyrardow.
Thousands of women and children lined the streets, silently
searching with their eyes for loved ones. German sentries prevented anyone approaching. The Armistice terms later proved
to be a hollow mockery; a few soldiers and N.C.O.s were in fact
released after a few days, but their freedom was shortlived; the
majority were arrested again and sent to forced labour in
Germany.

The troops marched into the yard of a tobacco factory surrounded by a tall brick wall. The vehicles and horse-drawn
wagons were allowed to stay outside. I heard a German N.C.O.
order a batman to drop his officer's kit and tell the officer to carry

48

it himself. The same instructions were given to all the Polish officers. I shouted to them not to carry the baggage. I had already made up my mind to complain to the German Commandant because officers were expected to sleep on the ground, mixed with all the ranks; this last insult decided me. Pushing aside the guards, I strode off to see the German Colonel. I saluted and he responded very stiffly.

"Colonel," I said in German, "it is not right that the officers should carry their own luggage: it is bad for discipline and morale. It is enough that they have to sleep with the troops in the open."

"We didn't start the war," was the sneering reply.

What an idiotic remark, I thought, but refrained from voicing my feelings.

"The officers will not carry the baggage," I said.

I saluted, turned on my heel and, expecting any moment to be arrested, walked away. My troops had stopped and stood watching. I joined my aide-de-camp and Stas, and we sat in the car. Shortly afterwards, a lieutenant came to say that batmen could carry the luggage. I had won my first moral victory over our captors.

This incident decided me. I was not going to march meekly into a prison camp. In my mind, I began to turn over plans for escape. For some reason, the Germans left me with my car outside the wall, where quite a number of civilians mingled among the guards and ourselves. Explaining my change of plan to Stas, I told him to change quickly into civilian clothes and wait in the car. I then walked up to two young lads and asked:

"Are you boy scouts?"

"Yes," they nodded.

"Well, in a moment, another scout will join you—my son. I want you to take him away from here and put him on the road to Warsaw. Can you do that?"

"Yes, sir."

"What is your name?"

"Leonard," said the elder.

"You must let me know when my son has reached safety," I ordered. "I shall give you three bicycles. Wait here."

I had noticed some cycles leaning against the wall, with no apparent owners. My driver fetched them and a few minutes later we watched as the three cycled past the guards to freedom.

It was time for me to look around and plan my own escape. Night was obviously best and I waited impatiently for dusk. Unfortunately, however, the Germans erected searchlights and

49

machine-gun posts and, although I was allowed to sleep in the car outside the walls, no opportunity arose. The following day it was worse, because we were ordered into the compound.

Around midday I was told that someone wanted to see me at the main gate. It was Leonard.

"He's all right," he whispered.

I had already evolved my scheme and asked the boy:

"Can you get hold of a suit, take it to the hospital in the town and get it hidden?"

"Yes, sir"—and he marched off like a soldier.

He treated the whole thing as a joke, disregarding the danger. I later heard that the clothes had been given to the senior doctor.

When a Polish medical officer came round the compound treating the sick, I had word with him: "Tell me an illness which is painful and hard to diagnose," I told him.

He glanced at me, saying: "Lumbago."

"Well, I have got a very bad attack right now; I must be sent to hospital."

The doctor objected, but I brushed him aside:

"Write a false name on the sick list—no one will be any the wiser."

Some time after, my officers and soldiers watched in amazement as, with my hand on my back and groaning slightly, I limped into a German ambulance. Ten minutes later, I was in hospital, in the efficient hands of a Polish nurse. A sentry counted the heads and disappeared.

Noticing my insignia, the nurse was all attention.

"Can I help you, sir? What is the matter?"

I put my hand on my back and grunted: "Lumbago. I must see the senior doctor."

"Unfortunately, sir, he is not due for another hour. I will give you an injection, which will take away the pain."

"Oh no," I said, looking with alarm at the hypodermic in her hand, "I would much rather wait."

Hastily withdrawing from the outpatients' department, I wandered down the corridors searching for the doctor. I found him. He told me the clothes were in the loft and was considerably put out when I said I was leaving that night. He was a harassed and overworked little man, with tousled hair and worried eyes.

"Please wait until tomorrow," he pleaded. "The Germans will then be in full control and I will not be blamed."

I was adamant, however, and eventually he agreed to bring

the clothes and help me. He directed me to the caretaker's room, which was being used for the officers' sick quarters. I undressed, got into bed and snatched some sleep. At evening inspection, the doctor dropped the parcel at the foot of the bed and I slid it under the blankets.

Before the dawn light filtered into the room, I was quietly dressing underneath the bedclothes. I had just struggled into the trousers, when the voice of the caretaker's wife startled me:

"Can't you sleep, sir?" she asked.

It was obvious what I was doing and our voices awoke the others.

"I'm sorry, I have enjoyed your hospitality, but now I must leave you."

I shared my uniform among the officers and then finished dressing. The kindly wife, all hairpins and motherly fuss, noticed I was without hat or overcoat. She dug her husband in the ribs:

"Give the Colonel your best coat and hat." He started to protest, and so did I, but she paid no heed and I was soon helped into a warm coat and snug cap.

We were on the ground floor and, opening the window, I glanced out to find it all clear. I hissed a quick farewell, stepped over the sill and, as dawn lit the sky, I joined the early morning workers on their way to the factories.

I looked for Limanowski Street where, at number 27, lived Mrs. Chotum, Leonard's mother. It was a second floor flat in a working-class block and the hall echoed emptily as I strode up the stairs. I knocked and, after some delay, knocked again. There was a scuffle of slippers, the door opened on a safety chain and a grey-haired woman stared suspiciously out at me.

"Does Mrs. Chotum live here?"

"Yes, what do you want?"

"My son came here yesterday with Leonard."

"Nobody came here yesterday."

She was terribly frightened and was about to slam the door.

"Don't be afraid," I said quickly. "I am not a spy; I am the boy's father and your son should have told you to expect me."

Her face lightened and she almost smiled. Releasing the chain, she invited me in, and within minutes I sat in the plain, drab parlour drinking a cup of coffee. Stas had already cycled off to Warsaw and I learnt that Leonard was at the Registration Office, trying to get some papers for me. I stayed at the Chotums' flat all day. The boy obtained a set of documents and discovered that the earliest train for Warsaw would leave at 7 p.m. With grateful thanks I said goodbye to my hostess and went with Leonard to the station. While we were waiting, a German patrol entered and commenced a check. I did not want my papers scrutinised too closely and decided a little impudence might help. I walked as close as I could get to the sergeant-major in charge of the squad. Staying at his elbow the whole time, I even talked with him while he inspected the others. Somehow or other he never questioned me.

At 9 p.m. the train steamed in and the usual mad rush followed. The carriages were without windows and the wooden benches splintered; I was lucky to get a seat. Thirty of us sat or stood in a compartment designed for twelve. Conversation was very limited as we were suspicious of each other; if we did speak, our misty breath hung in the air until whisked away by an icy blast from a jagged window. Hours later the train stopped at Pruszkow, a Warsaw suburb. Most of us stayed aboard because of a strict curfew, but as early as I could I started to walk the few remaining miles to Zoliborz.

My knock at the front door was answered by a familiar bark, and I was soon greeted in the open doorway by Stas, while Tom leaped and jumped between us. We were together again.

"Where is Mother?" I asked, but he did not know.

We had been chatting about the world-shattering events of the past few weeks and trying to look into the future, when there came another knock at the door and we opened it to find my wife and sister-in-law staring incredulously at us. After a month of wandering about, avoiding the Germans and the Bolsheviks, they had finally managed to get home. It seemed impossible that we should have all survived.

The following morning I went to see Major Thun, one of my former battalion commanders. He worked in a big publishing firm and knew everything that was going on. He said he might arrange a job for me with his firm or, alternatively, under a false name, get me into the Citizens' Guard which, with German sanction, was doing welfare work in the city. Most important, he put me in touch with the Underground Movement.

As soon as Warsaw fell, General Karaszewicz Tokarzewski, using the code name "Michael" organised a force which went immediately into action It was called the Association for Poland's Victory and formed the basis of the Home Army. Directed to a secret office, I met the Movement's Chief-of-Staff, an old friend —Colonel Rowecki.

My first task with the Underground was to get cover jobs for as many of our men as possible. I went to see the Lord Mayor of

Warsaw, Stephan Starzynski, who, I knew, would help to the utmost. Colonel-in-Chief of The Children of Warsaw, I had known him for many years. In answer to my request for bogus papers and cover jobs, he shrugged his shoulders.

"I would help if I could, Sosabowski, you know that. But nowadays I am only a figurehead. The Germans control all the offices."

I did succeed, however, in getting a few men placed in city departments. Shortly after this, Starzynski was arrested by the Germans and disappeared.

Stas, as a doctor, found no difficulty in getting a job in the isolation ward of the former Military Hospital.

I found it impossible to get employment. The job with the publisher as editor of a weekly paper never came off. I tried to form a Labour Brigade, consisting of some of my old troops, to clear rubble from the streets, and applied to the City Hall for a licence, but it was not granted. Everyone told me I was too well known and certain to be arrested. My lack of employment papers was very dangerous. All I had was a phoney identity card in the name of Sozanski.

Notices went up on city hoardings, warning all former officers to register at specified centres. Anyone failing to do so was threatened with imprisonment. The Germans said those who complied would be allowed to go free, but I was suspicious of their motives. I hung around the registration office and when a man came out, I followed him, asking to see his new card. It bore the simple statement: "Herr X has reported to this Command"—and nothing more. I smelt a rat. The next day I went inside the registration office, where I found two queues, one for Reserve Officers, the other for Regulars. Joining the one for Reservists, I noted carefully as I neared the desk that the clerks were only taking down the simplest particulars: there seemed no point in it. German forms normally require the minutest details and this was too simple to be true. When my turn came, I put on a vacant expression and asked for a travel pass. The German cursed me for a fool and directed me to another office.

I did, in fact, need a travel document. By then I had obtained, through the Underground, a set of papers which described me as a motor salesman, employed at Lodz. The reason was simple: the Movement had ordered me to go to Lodz and start an Underground unit.

These passes were issued at an office in Pilsudski Place. I joined the end of a long queue and slowly entered the building. I had been waiting patiently for about two hours, when I heard a loud voice:

"Oh, Colonel Sosabowski—how nice to see you!"

The hair on my head rose in alarm and with a great effort I refrained from turning. I expected any second to be arrested. A hand fell on my arm; I looked up with a start, expecting to see a German soldier, and stared into the face of a complete stranger, but he was not wearing uniform.

"Colonel Sosabowski, surely!" he said.

I could have strangled him.

"It must be a mistake," I muttered. "I should like to be a Colonel, but I don't happen to be one."

"What an amazing resemblance," said the stranger as he walked away.

I felt very conspicuous and, shortly afterwards, I looked at my watch, grunting something about being late for lunch, and left. It had been a narrow escape. Never again, I resolved, would I risk standing in a queue.

But the pass was vital, if I was to get about the country and carry out my Underground job. I decided to bluff my way in. The next morning, ignoring the queue, I went to a side entrance. To the sentries I announced "I have an appointment" and, walking up to a German sergeant-major at a desk, I asked for a travel pass. He glanced at me:

"Travel passes are no longer required."

"Yes," I replied, "but you know how it is, every area has different rules and it would be much easier if I had one."

"All right," he agreed, and picking up a form asked: "Your name, please?"

With a broad smile I interrupted:

"I have one of those Polish names that are so difficult to spell; it would be easier for us both if I filled in the details."

With a shrug, he passed it to me. Using the false papers of the motor salesman, I answered all the questions. The hours that I was permitted to travel, I filled in very lightly, so that I could change them later. I handed the form back to the sergeant-major and, without even glancing at it, he entered an officers' room and returned with it signed. I was lucky and, with an original set of German papers, much safer.

I made a habit, at this time, of never returning home until evening, so that neighbours would not recognize me. My wife and I arranged a secret sign: I always cycled past the house before entering and, if a pot of flowers stood on a particular window sill, it meant there was an ambush or search in progress. In spite of my failure to go to prison camp or to report for registration, German agents never visited my home or interrogated my family.

Within a few days I set off for Lodz. It was the 21st of October, and very cold. But a damned sight colder in the open coal wagon in which I had to travel! About forty of us crowded together, crouched on our haunches, trying to escape the icy blasts of wind which stabbed at us from every direction, threatening to paralyse our limbs.

Lodz—a heavy industrial city—always had a large population of Jews and German-speaking Poles. As a result, I found the city being rapidly transformed into a German town. The names of streets were already being changed; I noticed an Adolph Hitler Platz and a Hermann Goering Strasse; some shops had large portraits of the Fuehrer, and many youths walked the streets wearing Swastika armbands. Garish posters declared the inhabitants to be *Volksdeutsch*.

I needed accommodation for the night, but all the ordinary hotels were full. Undaunted, I went to the most exclusive hotel, the Metropole. The foyer was full of German officers. Walking to the desk, I asked the receptionist for a room, at the same time handing over my pass which enclosed several banknotes.

"The rooms are mostly taken by German officers," he smiled, "but I think I can find you a small one."

I was shown into a small back room and in a very short time was sound asleep. In the early hours, there came a loud knocking at the door and in walked a German patrol, complete with dog. Peremptorily they demanded my papers, and, after peering at them and finding no fault, they left and went to batter on the next door. I went back to sleep.

Altogether, I spent a week in Lodz, but found very few people suitable to put in charge of resistance units. Most of the prominent citizens had left; the town and people were in a turmoil. One did not know whom to trust and it was best to keep one's mouth shut. Generally, the German troops were well-behaved, but even so one residential quarter had been evacuated with only twenty minutes' warning and the houses taken over by the occupying army. The rate of exchange was one Deutsch mark for one zloty; this made goods very cheap for the Germans and terribly expensive for the local population. Special shops, with luxury goods and food, were open only to Germans and collaborators.

At this time, the Jews were not being persecuted, although shortly after their homes and belongings were commandeered.

On return to Warsaw, I found large posters announcing the annexation of part of Poland into the Reich and the formation of the General Government. Dr. Hans Frank, appointed Governor of this new State, told us to forget our national heritage and do exactly as we were told. Any resistance would be met with severe reprisals. It was a deliberate attempt to wipe out the nation.

Domestically, life was easier. Piped water was available and electricity soon followed. Food remained in short supply, so Stas and I made frequent foraging trips into the countryside avoiding control posts on the main roads.

The German authorities were still registering all officers, and had pasted up further warnings. Chancing to meet one of my former captains, I asked if he had reported. He showed me his card which, like the others I had seen, only recorded the fact that he had registered. I was in a complete whirl, not knowing what to do. But I bided my time.

November the 1st is Polish Remembrance Day, and in 1939 the streets were filled with mourning men, women and children, dressed in black, taking wreaths to graves scattered in parks and even in the city squares. The flowers were incredibly beautiful and their colours shone brilliantly in the midst of the drabness of the partially wrecked city. Precious candles were also lit over the graves. German troops trampled on the wreaths and patrols dispersed the crowds, but again and again they returned silently to their dead and, without force, the Germans were powerless to stop them. As dusk fell on the city, thousands of little pin points of light from the candles lit the open spaces of Warsaw telling the enemy that the spirit of Poland was not crushed.

Colonel Rowecki, the Underground Chief of Staff, ordered me off on another trip to Lodz and, at the same time, revealed a plan he had to send me through the Russian Zone to Roumania, where I could collect Government funds to finance the resistance movement.

This trip to Lodz was almost as unproductive as the previous one, and I stayed only a couple of days.

The train taking me back arrived in Warsaw many hours late at 2.30 a.m., well after curfew. I could have stayed the night on the Central Station or walked home. Either way I was liable to be checked by patrols, so I decided on the latter course. The travel pass had been extended by me and allowed me to be out until midnight.

I strode off into brightly lit streets, deliberately walking in the middle of the roadway, as if I had every right to be out. Crossing Pilsudski Place, I was accosted by a lone Polish policeman.

"Have you a pass?" he demanded.

I knew these policemen were unarmed and naturally nervous.

"Oh yes," I answered, and plunged my hand into an inside pocket, just as if I was reaching for a pistol. Hurriedly the man said:

"Oh well, that's all right, then"—and walked off without waiting.

The final stretch of the route home lay across a viaduct. As I approached, I noticed at the opposite end a German patrol. There was nothing for it but to go straight ahead. A corporal demanded my pass and I gave it to him.

"This pass expires at midnight. It is now 3 a.m. Why are you out?"

Knowing how Germans react to a loud bullying attitude, I raised my voice:

"Is it my fault the train from Lodz was four hours late? You cannot hold me responsible for the railway's inefficiency!"

I showed him my ticket to convince him and launched a tirade against the railways. The corporal, probably an Austrian, was sympathetic, and chatted away, appearing to forget that I had broken regulations. Then he said:

"Well, you had better get off to bed."

Five minutes later I was home.

Shortly after this I discovered how right I had been not to register. On the 11th of November, German police arrested hundreds of officers and sent them to Germany. The pretext was that they had plotted violence.

Colonel Rowecki's plan was taking shape and I was warned it would not be long before I left for Roumania. It was important to get as many supplies as I could into the house, and, with Stas, I visited neighbouring farms in an intensive search for potatoes and other basic foods, which would help my family during my absence. On the black market I bought fat and flour and left as much cash as I could.

Staff officers briefed me and I committed to memory all passwords and code names of contacts I would be meeting. The Paymaster gave me a certain amount of money, including seven lonely American dollars, the only foreign currency he possessed, which I hid at the back of a small hand mirror. A former Member of Parliament, Mr. W——, who had escaped from the Russian Zone, advised me how to dress.

57

The night before my departure, I went secretly into the garden and buried my sabre with other weapons and personal papers. Early on the 21st of November, I left home and, accompanied by Stas, went to the station. My wife was very relieved to see me go, as she had worried continually about my safety in Warsaw and had no idea of the dangers facing me on my journey.

Travelling under the name of Emil Helm, I was dressed in a leather jacket, a pair of boots one size too small and an old ski cap. In a rucksack I had a change of linen, shoes, toilet articles, bread and pork fat.

Stas did not say a word about my leaving. He never asked if he could come with me, although I knew he wanted to. I thought it might prejudice the success of my mission and was too dangerous. He would find it easier to escape later over the Slovakian border. He never succeeded and fought bravely in the 1944 Warsaw rising. During the battle, a shell exploding nearby blinded him—we were reunited in England after the war.

Lublin was the first stop and my arrival coincided with a wave of arrests in which many contacts and organisers disappeared, leaving large gaps in the Movement. I passed on the information and orders from Warsaw and quickly left the town.

The next few days were spent going from place to place, seeking a safe route over the demarcation line into the Russian Zone. Before the war I had served in this area, but none of my friends were able to help. I ended up at Belzec—the last railway station before the Russian Zone—where I went to see the station master, whose name had been given me as a contact. When I approached him, however, he hurried off saying:

"I know nothing about such things. Go away!"

I suspect he was being watched. Disconsolately, I wandered into the station café, where I was surprised to find several Bolshevik officials and a crowd of travellers waiting hopefully for the border crossing to be opened. Picking on the restaurant manager as a likely man to help, I spoke quietly to him asking if he knew anyone who could act as a guide. He said he would let me know later and at dusk a peasant sidled up and whispered that for fifty zlotys —about two pounds—he would take me across, on condition that another refugee could go with us.

After dark I was joined by the guide and the stranger; without a word, hoisting rucksacks on our backs, we set off. It was quite obvious what our intentions were and if we were seen by German or Russian Frontier Guards, we would be shot or arrested. Leaving the road, the guide led us across a meadow and made us lie low behind a dyke. Some minutes later we heard a patrol coming and we crouched, scarcely daring to breathe, waiting for it to pass; then we mounted the dyke and followed the guide across a bare field into the Russian Zone. A bright moon shone down on us as we marched in file hoping to be mistaken for a frontier patrol. Reaching a village, we were led into a cottage owned by the guide's uncle. He left us to fetch a horse and wagon to take us to Werchrata Station, from whence there was a train service to Lwow.

An old man, bent with years of physical labour in the forests, grunted a welcome and invited us to sit on a wooden bench near the vast tiled stove, which still gave out a touch of warmth. He looked at us out of deep-set incurious eyes and in a monotone said life was hard under the Russians, with food getting increasingly more difficult to come by. With an odd politeness, not normally found in a peasant's manner, he regretted his inability to offer us refreshment. The room contained the bare minimum of furniture, but the table was scrubbed white and the few pots and pans glinted in the light of the oil lamp.

After these few brief words, we lapsed into silence, the old man's eyelids slowly fell and he slept peacefully, stubbly chin resting on gnarled hands. My companion soon followed suit. Left alone with my thoughts, I was beginning to doze, when I was startled to hear the tramp of feet and Russian voices coming near the house. I prodded the old man and my companion, but our host, seeing my quizzical look and hearing the sounds shook his head and with the vague glimmer of a smile he reassured us: "Don't worry," he said. "Patrols change at this hour every night."

I looked at my watch and realised that our guide had been gone over an hour, and I had the conviction that he was not going to return. Having received most of his money, he had probably slipped back to the German side.

"It looks as though your nephew has done a bunk and left us stranded," I said to the old man.

"I would not be surprised," he murmured. "But I may be able to help."

Without another word, easing himself on to his legs, he disappeared through the door into the back regions of the dwelling and we heard the whisper of voices in conversation. He returned with a sleepy-eyed youth of about seventeen who, without pause for introduction, demanded:

"Give me four hundred zlotys and I'll take you to Werchrata."

This was equivalent to sixteen pounds and with my meagre

59

resources, a large sum of money. After some haggling, he agreed to accept about half that sum, fifty per cent to be paid in advance. We were on our way again.

He was a very nervous guide and his gestures were quite theatrical, as he glanced over his shoulders or hissed us to a halt. Just about dawn, we arrived close to another village and telling us to stay in a copse he went forward to investigate. An early morning mist had come up and under its mantle we felt secure. Half an hour passed, and once again I was certain we had been deserted. I stood whispering to my companion, trying to decide the next move, when I heard the sound of footsteps coming towards us. Grasping my companion's arm, I urged him to stand perfectly still. The steps came on and out of the mist, through the trees, loomed a figure of a Russian soldier with rifle and fixed bayonet. He came straight at us—I held my breath. Ten feet, six feet, five, four, and he walked straight past. I could have touched him; yet we were only partially hidden.

There was no point in hanging around and, stepping out from the copse, we boldly walked into the village. It was thronged with Russian troops, but they ignored us and we passed safely through into open country again. Not knowing the area and without a compass, I soon lost all sense of direction and after some time, noticing footsteps in the snow, I discovered to my chagrin that we were walking in circles. Depressed and tired, we sat down on a kerb-stone by a wayside shrine. Bad luck was certainly dogging our efforts, but I was determined not to turn back. I opened my rucksack and, taking out a crust of bread, sat nibbling and thinking. Fashioned from unpainted pinewood, the shrine, with its shrivelled offerings of wild flowers, stood at the brow of a slight hill in a forest clearing, where several tracks converged. Round a bend, I suddenly saw a peasant woman walking towards us: was she, I wondered, a Pole or Ukrainian? Her long skirt swung with her stride and she wore a shawl pulled tightly over her head, almost obscuring her face. I smiled up at her, giving the customary greeting in Ukrainian:

"Christ should be loved." Smiling back, she replied in Polish: "Always."

I sighed with relief; had she been a Ukrainian, she could have easily reported us to the Russians.

The country woman indicated the correct route and we set off, just as a light powder of snow began to fall. We had not gone far, when a horse galloped out of the mist and the rider reined in, blocking our path. He sat looking down on us, his large moustache elongated and swollen with frozen snow. I took him for a militia-man and presumed that he would apprehend us. Instead, he spoke in Polish:

"You are wasting your time going to Rawa-Ruska this way, as you will certainly be caught by patrols. I am prepared to take you by another route tonight, and all I ask is fifty zlotys and some razor blades."

I had to accept his offer, our safety depended on his honesty, but I hastily explained my lack of razor blades. He shrugged his shoulders.

"I had hoped to get a decent shave for once," he said. "But never mind!"

We rested in his house until midnight, when we were awakened and given a quick meal, before stepping out into the freezing dark-ness. I well remember that night, because my boots, which were a size too small, started to pinch and squeeze my feet, until even-tually I had to stop and change into thin town shoes. Within minutes, my feet were soaking wet and very cold, but they were considerably less painful.

Dawn found us at our destination at the first house in the town. It was a cobbler's and I took the opportunity of getting my shoes repaired. He gave us tea and we sat talking. As usual, he told us the only way to be sure of getting a train was to camp at the station. We shortly joined a thronging mass in the station hall. The smell of stale human bodies was almost as thick as the moisture covering the windows. Many were Jews who had fled across Europe from the Nazis, seeking sanctuary with the Russians. There were Poles, Ukrainians and Russian troops all mixed up. Unlike the Germans, the Russians fraternised with the people and allowed the Ukrainians a much freer hand in government.

There was a two-hour wait and, when the train arrived, the scramble started. Even Bolshevik officers were pushed and shoved in the melée. With a bit of shoving and pushing on my own account, I found half a seat in a third-class compartment. The corridors were jammed tight. How the inspector ever fought his way through, I do not know, but he checked all tickets and with a knowing look and voice full of meaning said that some passengers might prefer to get off before the main station to avoid the crush. Taking this to mean there was a pass control at Lwow Central, I alighted at Podzamcze and, with no trouble at the barrier, set off in search of my contact's address.

I soon realised that my clothes were all wrong for the Russian Zone, and I stood out in the crowds like a pea in a bowl of rice.

Unshaven, leather jacket and ski cap, I looked what I was, a refugee. My Member of Parliament friend had been hopelessly wrong with his advice. To avoid attracting too much attention, I jumped on a passing tram.

There had been little fighting in Lwow and no general bombing. The first difference I saw was that the conductor was accompanied by a People's Policeman, who kept a watchful eye on the passengers. Red flags, decorated with the hated hammer and sickle, flew from many flag poles and pictures of Stalin and Woroszylov were displayed in shop windows. On the walls, big posters bore slogans: *Long live Stalin* and *Long Live the Western Ukrainian Republic.* It was, however, all a big bluff; the people had been forced to put up the decorations and signs.

I got off near Malachowski Street, where the parents of a friend to whom I was taking messages lived. When I rang the bell of the apartment, it was answered by a most suspicious young boy.

"Does Professor L—— live here?" I asked.

"Yes," was the laconic and uncompromising reply.

"I have a message for him from his eldest son in Warsaw. May I come in?"

"Wait"—and the door closed.

Soon it re-opened, however, and a lady asked me to enter. I gave them news of their son and they offered to put me up. In fact, I did not stay, as their youngest son, who took a letter for me to another friend, Mrs. W——, returned with an offer of a permanent bed. Very soon afterwards, I knocked at Mrs. W——'s door and was warmly welcomed. She warned me, however, that the house was full of Russian officers, whom I would probably meet on the stairway or in the bathroom: if asked, I should say I was a cousin. At first, it seemed a little alarming, but few would think of searching for me in such surroundings.

As in Lublin, I found that many resistance workers had been taken away. Their leader, General Januszajtis, had been imprisoned and General Boruta Spiechowicz had set off for Hungary as an envoy to contact General Sikorski's government and had failed to return. All my contacts had gone. The only others I knew were two ladies, but I had no password or signs by which they could recognise me. I pondered this problem during the evening, while I sat talking with Mrs. W——. Noticing my extreme fatigue, she retired early, leaving me a large soft settee, where, after my various hard beds of previous days, I slept soundly.

Early next morning, I went to the bathroom and there, shaving at the mirror, I found a half-dressed Russian officer. I bade him "Good morning" and received a grunted reply. He tried to be friendly, but my Russian being limited to *Nyet* and *Da*, we did not get very far. I silently hoped that all my contacts with the Russians would be similar; but on second thoughts it would be better to have none.

Later, drinking ersatz coffee with Mrs. W——, I decided to take her partially into my confidence.

"I am in a spot," I announced. "You have probably guessed I am working for the Underground, but my contacts have all been arrested or gone. Can you help me?"

There was no hesitation in her voice:

"Certainly."

"Do you know a Miss Halina Wasilewska? Is she free?"

"Oh yes, I know her well. I am pretty sure of where I can find her quite easily. Leave it to me. I shall see her this morning and arrange a meeting."

I occupied myself during the day, firstly delivering a bunch of letters to the Red Cross, which was still working unobtrusively although banned by the Russians. I was told by their Chief that General Anders was in Lwow hospital and would be delighted to receive a visitor from Warsaw. I did not visit him, however, as I thought he was probably under Russian supervision and it might draw attention to me and affect my mission.

I then spent a few hours wandering round Lwow, visiting old spots well known to me. It was odd to see them again under enemy occupation. I always find it difficult to explain to others, especially the British, what foreign occupation means. Imagine then that the Battle of Britain had been lost and Operation "Sea Lion", the invasion of Britain planned by Hitler, launched successfully. The Royal Family and the leaders of the Government had fled to Canada to carry on the war from overseas.

Foreign soldiers patrol the streets of all towns and villages. British police are banned. The House of Commons and House of Lords turned into offices. Anyone can be arrested at any time without a warrant. Houses searched and plundered. No right to appeal. Guilty and not guilty transported to labour or concentration camps.

Loudspeakers on every corner broadcasting instructions and martial music. Flags and banners on every building, flaunting the victorious crooked cross. Imagine Trafalgar Square at Christmas. Instead of a tree, in its place a giant wooden statue of a Nazi

63

soldier. Burlington Arcade, Piccadilly, turned into a Petticoat Lane, where people sell their treasures for paltry sums in order to buy bread. The pound sterling has been valued as worth one Deutsch mark, resulting in prices ten times higher than normal.

This was the picture that unrolled before me in Lwow. The one bright spot was that the citizens did not look upon that state of affairs as permanent. Their spirit remained unbroken; they believed that soon General Sikorski would return with a Polish Army a hundred thousand strong, supported by British and French troops, and clear the Russian and German invaders from our country.

The Russians had orders to be friendly and in clumsy ways they tried to be nice. I listened in one arcade market to two traders, poking fun at a Soviet soldier. "Why do you have to buy everything here?" they asked him. "Why cannot you buy it in Russia?"

"Oh, in Russia we can wait—it will all come in time."

"Will you get fountain pens and fur coats?"

"Oh yes, all in good time."

"Will you get watches and clocks?"

"Oh yes."

"Will you get typhus and cholera?"

"Oh yes, plenty of it in time."

I remember too a stall selling ladies' nighties, which were bought by the soldiers as evening dresses for their wives and sweethearts.

At 5 p.m., accompanied by Mrs. W——, I knocked on the door of Miss Wasilewska's house. Our conversation started with generalities and we were both very guarded about what we said. After some time, with more confidence in each other, I must have raised my voice with eagerness, for she raised her forefinger and pointing at a door murmured:

"Don't talk so loud—there are other people in that room and they may be Bolshevik spies."

I sensed the shame in her voice and felt keenly the strain my country must have suffered with its split loyalties.

I made a mental note of all the information she gave me, and arranged to meet another contact the following morning. Punctually at 9 a.m. I gave three short and two long knocks on the door of an insignificant suburban house. A hard-faced young man let me in and blocked the passage.

"East Wind," I said.

His face relaxed slightly and, standing aside, he pointed to a door at the end of a corridor. Seated at a desk, I found Mrs. Wladyslawa who questioned me for some time. Satisfied at last, she described in detail the organisation, giving me the names of its leaders. I told her to expect a courier in a few days from "Michael's" organisation, who would want to take particulars back to Warsaw Headquarters. I then requested her to plan an escape route for me. As recent arrests had completely disorganised the contacts from Lwow, she suggested that I might travel through Stanislawow.

The following day I met Major D—— chief of a fighting section. From him I gathered that offensive action was out of the question —too many fighters had been arrested—and I reached the conclusion that ineffective acts against the Russians would only bring heavy reprisals. I advised him to wait until he was stronger and could receive orders from General Sikorski.

On the eve of my reconnaissance visit to Stanislawow, I asked the leader of the local Boy Scouts—an escape expert—to plan another route through the oil mining area of Drohobycz.

It was Sunday, 3rd December 1939, when I stepped off the train into my hometown. It was almost noon and, realising that everyone would be at mass, I walked to the Church of Jesus Christ, my old church. I found it packed and slipped unobserved into a niche. Listening to the service, I recalled another visit I had made there when, as a youth, I prayed to Saint Joseph to help me in the work I was doing for my family. The pious people were praying to God for help and aid in their time of misery with such feeling in their voices that my eyes misted and my heart rose in my throat. I left before the end of the service, as it would have been unwise to make my presence generally known; too many people would remember me.

But this trip was a waste of time. The escape route was closed; most of its contacts arrested. The one good thing that came out of my visit was that I managed to change my boots for a pair of right size, which I still have to this day.

A lady courier from Warsaw arrived in Lwow on December 6th. To her I gave detailed information about the Underground set-up in all the places I had been. From Mrs. Wladyslawa I received the ciphers and wavelengths of clandestine broadcasts. Unknown to the Russians, one of our best contacts was a Polish radio engineer in the Lwow Broadcasting station, who broadcast under the Communists' noses. Mr. C——, who was a student and a member of the Underground, was to accompany me to Budapest to establish an escape route and return to Lwow with information.

Another officer, Captain D——, was sent by a completely different route to Budapest with an identical set of memorised ciphers and code words: the duplication was in case one of us failed.

I fixed a rendezvous with C—— at the station, telling him to follow me, but not make contact until I gave the sign. He should travel in the next compartment and watch me closely.

Once again, I changed my identity and became a Post Office clerk. He was an engineer. On the morning of 7th December, we boarded the train from Lwow to Drohobycz. I looked my part in a working suit and overcoat and, instead of a rucksack, I carried a brief case.

It was a short journey and as the train steamed into the station of Drohobycz, I peered out of the window, anxiously searching the platform to see who was to meet me. As I got down from the carriage, a young girl stepped out of the crowd.

"How nice to see you, Uncle!" she said. "The present was marvellous."

She stretched up, kissing me warmly on both cheeks and turning to C——, who had hurriedly joined us, bestowed the same show of affection on him. Taking our arms, she walked us off the platform, chattering merrily, treating us as Uncle and Cousin arrived for a visit.

She led us straight to the house of a Post Office clerk, our first contact along the escape route. Travelling as a Post Office official, I had every reason to call on him. I remember how desperately poor they were; the rate of exchange made his salary worthless and already both he and his wife were showing the haggard look of half-starved people. Their children still looked fit, obviously through the sacrifice of the parents. I was loath to accept their hospitality, but they insisted and refused all payment. All through my journey I was impressed with the tremendous bravery and patriotism of the working-class people and how they put themselves out to help in every possible way.

We had planned to move on almost immediately to Boryslaw, but the Bolsheviks started a wave of arrests among the oil-field workers and several of our people were lost. In order to protect my hosts we moved, in spite of strong protests, and went to live with an N.C.O. of the local organisation. We did not have to wait for long. One morning two young girls, about sixteen, very pretty and pert, both members of the local Girl Guides Association, called to tell us to be ready to move that same afternoon. They knew very well the risks they were running, yet they faced all difficulties with cheerfulness and courage. After a meagre lunch of vegetable soup and ersatz coffee, the girls marched us to the station. To the casual onlooker, we were a happy laughing family group saying goodbye for a couple of days. We stood at the door of the compartment, waving to the girls until out of sight.

At Boryslaw the meeting and recognition were similar to previous occasions and that night we were guests of an oil-well owner, whose business had been commandeered by the Russians, but who considered himself lucky to have been appointed manager, with a Russian overseer. Part of his large house had been taken over as a Communist Youth Club and as we lay on beds trying to snatch a few hours' sleep, we could hear the laughing and horse-play of young people and the sound of music and singing. It was an ideal hide-out.

Our next guide, a milk-maid, was due to arrive in the early hours of the next morning. At dawn we were ready, waiting and anxious to be off, but there was no sign of her. Not until after lunch did she arrive and explained it had been impossible to get away and we had better get started, as a three-hour journey lay ahead of us. Quite openly we walked through the oil-fields, passing close to the derricks and storage areas; had we been saboteurs, it would have been easy to wreck them and escape in the confusion. The oil-fields were working to capacity and supplying the German army across the border. They continued to do this until war broke out between them.

We reached our destination, Schodnica, about 7 p.m. and she introduced us to her father, the local butcher. He and his wife were very kind, they fed us well, moved out of their own room and placed everything at our disposal. Hardly had we sat down to supper, when we heard the sound of voices in the street and then the tramp of footsteps up to the door. The butcher hissed for silence, beckoned us out of the room and upstairs. Whispering that it was a Russian patrol which often called, he shoved us into an attic cupboard and indicated a hiding-place behind some suitcases. We stayed sweating in the cupboard for nearly a quarter of an hour, listening to the Russian voices from the parlour below and wondering if we would be caught. There was a clink of glasses, a shout of Good Health and at long last the unwelcome visitors departed. Our host, beaming broadly, released us from the cupboard and handed us a glass of schnapps to cheer us.

But it was too dangerous to live there, so next morning we moved to the house of the local priest. A young miner named Peter called during the day saying his sister would collect us that night. Maria was her name and, although she worked in the local Communist Youth Party Headquarters, she was completely trustworthy. As he was about to leave, he turned to say:

"Excuse me, sir, but are you armed?"

"No," was my reply. "It was too dangerous to carry a gun on my journey."

"Well, you are now very close to escape," he argued, "and it would be a pity to get caught so near to your target. I have a pistol and ammunition at home; Maria will give them to you."

I thanked him profusely and offered money, but he got very angry:

"There are more important things than money at a time like this." It was a big sacrifice for him, as a pistol was considered a very valuable article.

Maria arrived at 7 p.m. She was blonde, with her hair neatly plaited, piercing blue eyes set above shining pink cheeks. She was gay and lively and not at all the sort of guide we had expected. Before leaving, the priest blessed us and asked God's guidance for us. Once again we walked quite openly through the oil-fields, even saying goodnight to police and army patrols. Late night shifts of workers still toiled at the wells, and the flames from burning waste flickered in the darkness, casting weird shadows across our path. It was midnight by the time we reached Maria's house at Majdan where we had a quick cup of coffee and she handed me her brother's pistol. She also produced two bed sheets.

"If you have to hide in the snow, these will be perfect," she explained.

There was a further eight miles to travel and much of our route was along a forest railway used for carrying logs down to the railhead. We had gone about halfway, when Maria stopped in her tracks and, standing motionless, we heard distinctly from behind the sound of footsteps. Maria led us on at a slightly faster pace and, leaving the rails, walked into the forest. Hiding behind tree trunks, we waited silently; after a few minutes a group of men in single file walked past along the lines without looking left or right. Was it a patrol or another group of escapers? We never found out.

Giving them ten minutes' lead, we set out again, keeping a careful look-out in front. It was 3 a.m. when our journey ended at a forestry house at Malmastal. Maria said she would have to start immediately on the return trip, as she had to be at work at 9 a.m. so that no one would suspect she had been out all night.

I offered her money for her great help, but she started weeping, saying she did it for love of country, not for gain. She even refused to be paid for the sheets and yet she was of a poor family to whom a few zlotys would have made a world of difference. All I could do was to give her a few sweets that I had in my pockets and an old electric torch, which she accepted as a memento of our acquaintance and with which she was delighted. I watched her slight figure trudge off through the snow back to Bolshevik slavery.

We stayed hidden in a forester's house until midday, when two new guides marched us back into the woods. During the night one of the guides complained of pains in his stomach, which grew steadily worse, until he eventually said he could go on no longer. His companion was all for leaving us stranded and lost in the middle of the trees. I had a long argument before he agreed to take us further. We rigged up a rough log and brushwood shelter for the sick man and, promising that help would be with him early next day, we set off again, the guide complaining and objecting almost every yard of the way. In a couple of hours we neared the village of Smorze, lying in a pretty valley close to the Hungarian border. Here the guide refused to go further and no amount of persuasion or money would make him budge from his decision. He said he had no intimate knowledge of the border. I paid him his due and he quickly retraced his steps.

We found ourselves, C—— and I, on the edge of a wood looking down on the village, with only the vaguest idea which way we should go. I decided it was far better for us to stay on our own. I had a hand compass given me by the forester in Malmastal, and, taking a route going roughly in a southerly direction, we started trudging through the snow. It must have been 2 p.m. when we realised that the border was very close. A broad tarmac roa㇄ ran straight across our path; beyond it was the river Stryj and Hungary. We could see the border area quite clearly from where we lay: the ground was as flat as a table for about half a mile each side of the river and it was easy to discern the odd patrol and the crossing points. I walked forward carefully to get a better view of the flanks, hoping to see an easier approach; as I was about to return, I noticed a man walking up the hill towards me. I hastily retired into the wood and indicated to C—— that he should hide and keep quiet. I put my hand in my coat pocket and grasped the pistol, determined not to be caught so near to freedom. I tried to look as unconcerned as possible and gazed around, as if on a job of work. The man came towards me quite deliberately; although he was dressed in country clothes, he bore

69

himself more like a soldier. Stopping in front of me, he removed his hat with a military flourish and a torrent of words:

"Good day, sir, can you help me? Yesterday I was with a party which tried to cross the frontier, but we were caught by the Bolsheviks and fired upon—I was the only one to escape."

"I am not surprised," I responded. "It is illegal. The Bolsheviks were quite right."

The man's eyes twinkled.

"You can't fool me: you are also trying to get into Hungary. I should like to travel with you."

I started walking slowly deeper into the wood and the man followed. If this was a trick, I was certainly not going to be caught in the open and would shoot at the first sign of trouble. I questioned him carefully, but he could have made up any story. Had I refused to take him, he could have reported us out of revenge or he could have followed us. Curtly, I told him he could come but he must do as he was told, without argument. C—— came out of hiding and the stranger was quite startled to see him. Jokingly, we told him how near death he had been, but he did not seem very impressed.

Worried that someone might have seen us entering the woods, we moved to the far end and settled in the snow, waiting for nightfall. December in Poland is very cold and as we had been climbing gradually all day, we were more exposed to the elements. A freezing wind whistled round the trees, playing in the folds of our clothing, driving what little warmth we had left away. My feet and legs were wet through; taking off my old pullover, I put my legs through the arms and drew the body up over my stomach. It probably made only two degrees difference to my warmth, but I welcomed it. To put a few calories into our bodies, we nibbled small pieces of dried black bread with a little pork fat and washed it down with a few handfuls of snow.

When it was dark, we left the shelter of the wood and the wind that had been an annoying breeze in the trees, tore into us with hurricane strength. Yet it was a good thing, masking a lot of the noise we made as we marched across frozen snow which cracked and snapped under our feet. One hundred yards and we were in the pines bordering the road. I motioned the others to stop and went forward cautiously to see if the road was clear. Standing in the drainage ditch, I looked left and right and, seeing nothing, I beckoned my companions on. With a swift rush we ran across the road and into cover.

I shall never forget the ordeal that faced us when crossing the river Stryj. It was only partially frozen; close to the banks it was frozen over, but in the middle a torrent of water still flowed free of ice. There was only one way to get across; without a word to my companions, I took off my trousers, pants, shoes and socks, tied them round my neck, hoisted my shirt high up my chest and stepped on to the ice. After a few slippery steps, the ice broke with the crack of a rifle shot and with my shins scraping the razor edges of the break, I dropped into the agonising cold of the river. The water came half way up my thighs and it felt as if a thousand needles were being forced into the pores. Gasping with the shock, I strode out firmly through the running stream and broke through the ice near the opposing bank. Then I climbed out onto the thicker ice. Behind me, I could hear the splashings and heavy breathing of my companions and after a quick backward glance to see that all was well with them, I ran as fast as I could over the two hundred yards open gap that separated us from cover. I dragged my clothes on over my wet slippery body, but they gave no relief to my aching limbs. In spite of the danger of border patrols I jumped and ran and threw my arms about in an effort to get the blood circulating again through near-frozen veins. The others suffered the same agonies and went through the same contortions.

In the meantime, with the coming of night, the wind had dropped and a fitful moon lit the landscape between the clouds; in the vast silences around us, the sound of our movements could have been heard for hundreds of yards. Twigs cracked with surprising violence, branches scratched our clothing like rasping files, but we had to push on; Hungary was still a hundred yards away. Our path led up a steep wooded hill and on the brow, about nine hundred feet up, a break in the trees and a line of stones marked the frontier. With hardly a pause, we ran across the line and down the slope, continuing a mad rush until I tripped, falling headlong into a snowdrift. I knew that a few hundred yards south of the frontier was another river, the Latorcza, and decided that we would not stop until we had reached it. Sure enough, we came upon it and then we did not worry about concealment any more; we talked and laughed with each other— freedom felt good.

Nearby was a haystack and young C—— suggested we should sleep in it. We all needed rest very badly, but our stomachs also cried out for sustenance. We lit a fire and drank some boiled snow. It was the first hot drink we had had for days and it tasted almost as good as hot mulled wine, as it warmed our insides with its scalding heat. We consumed the last of our meagre rations of bread and lard and, with an illusionary feeling of fullness, we burrowed three separate tunnels into the hay and slept warmly and soundly until dawn.

I was the first to wake and, rousing the others, suggested we should push on to the nearest village and get some breakfast. According to my reckonings, we should go downstream along the banks of the river and that would lead us to the village of Latorcza. We had walked for about fifteen minutes, when I suddenly recognised the place and realised with horror that we were standing in the loop of the Stryj. We were still in Poland.

Without a word to my companions, I led them straight back the way we had come. It was full daylight and it was incredible that we had not been picked up in our wanderings or during our camp-fire roisterings of the previous night. I charged along and the other two followed automatically, although C—— did voice a protest. Not until I had slogged a good quarter of a mile beyond the river, did I finally stop and tell them what had happened. We stood laughing hysterically for five minutes, wondering at our luck.

But at last we were in Hungary. Ahead was the village of Latorcza and, as we approached, I could see to the west men in Hungarian uniforms at the border check-point. In the village, passers-by greeted us and, just as we were looking for a café, a small boy ran up saying we should report to the border post. I had intended reporting to the police later, preferring to get deeper into Hungary, but we had no choice now so we followed the lad. An N.C.O. welcomed us and, guessing we were illegal immigrants, offered us coffee and breakfast and afterwards hot water for washing and shaving. Much later, he asked for our papers and I also handed over my pistol as a gesture of trust, hoping I would have no further use for it. Straightway, he offered to buy it, but I refused, saying he could keep it until I came back that way on my return to Poland.

He explained that I must report to a police post further on and apologised that we had to walk. Accompanied by two friendly Hungarian soldiers, we strolled along the lanes to the bigger village of Verecko. Once again, officials started putting us through the list of questions, to which we gave our usual false replies. But in the middle of the questioning, I got fed up and, standing up, said to the police officer:

"This is all a pack of lies. My real identity is Colonel Sosabowski of the Polish Army. I am on important business and it is imperative that I get to Budapest to see my Ambassador."

Impressed by my urgency, the police officer picked up the telephone and spoke to his superior. Half an hour later, we were in a bus under escort, speeding along the road to Budapest. On our way, we stopped at the town of Volovetz, where at Police Headquarters I was told that regulations insisted that all escapees had to be security vetted. I was promised, however, that I would be in Budapest the following day.

I thanked the police for their courtesy and asked them to direct us to a comfortable hotel, but was told that the only one was full. We were offered the hospitality of the police barracks, where they turned all the prisoners out from one large cell and had it cleaned up. The bed was a hard board, but it had plenty of blankets and a wood fire blazed in a great stove. There was a guard at the door, but it seemed only a formality. I soon had the staff running around, doing little jobs for us, and when supper-time came I asked the guard to accompany us to the best restaurant in town. He looked a bit surprised, but after a muttered conversation with the guard commander he returned with a look of even deeper puzzlement on his face: he had obviously never guarded prisoners like us before.

Although we had shaved and washed, in our old, worn clothes and scarred boots, we looked a pretty rough bunch. Into the restaurant we marched and, leaving the guard at the door, sat at a table. A waitress hovered undecidedly nearby and I demanded drinks and the menu. Her glance swept over me.

"And have you money to pay for them?" she asked.

It was not really surprising, but I was angry. She was much abashed by my outburst and, after apologising, produced three large steaks and a carafe of red wine. Two hours later, with distended stomachs and full of well-being, we woke our dozing guard to escort us back to the prison cell.

We were woken at 5 a.m. and put on a train to Munkacevo. In the barracks to greet us was an impeccably dressed lieutenant-colonel of the Hungarian Intelligence Corps, his boots and brasses shining with a parade-ground gloss. He oozed charm and good manners and, as we reached his office, he sent out for breakfast. While we ate, he sat back in his armchair, smoking a cigarette in a long slender holder, and chatted with us. I told him that C——— was my aide-de-camp but, when asked the name of the third member of our party, I had to admit I knew nothing about him; he had always evaded our questions—I did not even know his name. The colonel must have pressed a hidden bellpush, for almost immediately the door opened, letting in a soldier who, without even waiting for the third man to finish his meal, escorted him from the room. He left as he had arrived: a mystery man.

As we talked, I noticed my pistol lying on the colonel's desk, but I pretended not to see it. As I swallowed the last dregs of my coffee, he asked:

"Is this your pistol?"

With some trepidation, I replied in the affirmative—there was no point in lying.

"Take it back. It is yours," he smiled.

For about two hours we discussed the war situation and he was most despondent about the possibility of Hungary having to follow the dictates of Germany.

Getting back to our current problems, I asked if I could telephone to the Polish Embassy in Budapest. I was connected almost immediately and enquired for Colonel Emisarski, the Military Attaché. He was out, so I left a message announcing our arrival that evening and a request that we should be met. Our host accompanied us to the station and, giving an elegant wave, wished us good luck as the express drew rapidly away from the platform.

What luxury it was to lean back in the upholstered seats feeling warm and relaxed behind a newspaper. An attendant served coffee and soon I was forced to remove my leather jacket. But we attracted little attention—we looked just as if we had returned from a ski holiday.

We were due in Budapest at 7 p.m. It was December the 16th and Hungary was still at peace. As we approached the city, we saw brightly lit suburban streets and the hustle and bustle of homeward-bound workers and late shoppers. Dead on time, the train squealed to a halt in Budapest Central.

I hoped that my message to the Embassy had been acted upon, but what a staggering surprise it was to see my brother standing only a few yards from my carriage door.

"Andrew!" I shouted, and he came running forward.

Another well-known face appeared behind him, Major Klemens, who had served in my old regiment. Without explanations, they hurried us to a waiting Embassy car and we were whisked off to my brother's apartment which overlooked the Danube.

A hot bath, dinner and several bottles of Tokay—then Andrew and I exchanged the news of all our adventures since the war began. He had been captured by the Russians in South East Poland, but had escaped across the Carpathian Mountains and was working in the Military Mission in the department responsible for arranging the passage of people on their way to join General Sikorski's forces in France.

Early next morning, I reported to the Embassy, after a visit to a clothing store, from which I emerged as a smartly dressed civilian. I spent several hours closeted with Colonel Emisarski, giving him all the details about General Tokarzewski's Underground Army, and passed on the codes, ciphers and wavelengths with which Lwow was operating. I impressed on him how urgently we needed the money in Warsaw and asked that he should arrange as soon as possible for me to collect the cash, so I could return to Poland. He said he would report to General Sikorski in Paris immediately and let me know in a few hours his decision.

After lunch, I put in a check call to the Embassy and Emisarski told me that I was not to return to Warsaw, but must proceed at once to France. This was the last thing I had expected; I had set my heart on completing my mission and returning to carry on the fight in Poland and it also meant that I would be separated for longer from my family. I did not know then that I would never see my homeland again.

The Embassy booked me a seat on the Simplon Express on the 19th of December. Officials did their best to get a passport and all necessary visas. Andrew and I spent the remaining two days exploring the city, seeing the sights. With only a few days to Christmas, Budapest was at its gayest. There was an undercurrent of fear, but the people hid it with laughter and bright words. The shops glittered with decorations and were full of peacetime extravagancies. The markets were heaped high with Christmas trees and bright-berried holly. The city rested under a mantle of snow and from the open windows of over-heated restaurants came the sound of sentimental gipsy music. Beautiful women clad in expensive furs and escorts in white ties danced and sang, drank and ate; it was difficult to imagine that a few hundred miles away people shivered and starved, suffered and died under a savage regime.

The Simplon left without me, as my Jugoslavian visa had failed to come through. The only chance of getting to Paris was to join the train in Milan and the Embassy arranged for me to go by air as far as Italy. At 10 a.m. on the 20th, having said goodbye to Andrew and my young travelling companion C——, I took a taxi to the air terminal. The Embassy cashier had warned me that the Customs would not allow me to take more than thirty Pengoes out of the country; as I found fifty in my wallet, I left twenty of them on the back seat of the taxi. I was most surprised and slightly disturbed when the taxi-driver searched me out in the terminal and handed me this money. A most unusual taxi-driver.

The flight was full of excitement. First stop was Venice and to cross the Julian Alps we had to rise to over ten thousand feet. The plane was unheated and we were offered oxygen masks. Visibility was down to a few hundred yards and as, at long last, we came down to land, the pilot overshot the runway and we finished up with the plane's nose embedded in the ground. Luckily no one was hurt and we were soon taken by coach to the terminal buildings. There was an hour's delay until the next flight to Milan and, while drinking a cup of espresso coffee, I was intrigued to see several Nazi officials strutting importantly through the crowds. I wondered for how long Italy would be able to resist Hitler's pressure to enter the war.

The flight to Milan was uneventful and I had three hours to spare. I wandered to the Piazza del Duomo and, from a café window, watched the crowds flowing in every direction. It was a happy, laughing Christmas scene, but I was alone.

I went to the station early and settled in my sleeper. To the conductor I handed my passport and asked that, if possible, I should not be disturbed until we reached Paris. I got into my bunk and lay back on the pillow. Yet even with a riot of thoughts about the future going through my head, I was asleep before the train left the station.

CHAPTER IV

FRENCH INTERLUDE

THERE was an insistent tap-tapping at the door of the sleeper and the attendant's voice informed me that Paris was twenty minutes away. I drew the window blind and looked out into the Paris suburbs. I watched the houses hurry by; women with bags gossiped outside shops and workmen puffed at Gauloises as they leaned on shovels. France, outwardly, looked peaceful enough.

I was acutely aware of what lay ahead. I had to report to Sikorski and give him all the information I had gathered about conditions in Poland. In the forefront of my mind was the big question: "How are we to continue the fight against Nazism?" I was impatient to get back to my country and take an active part in the resistance. With these thoughts running through my mind I shaved and washed, swallowed a quick cup of coffee and a croissant and, as I snapped the lock of my briefcase, the train gently bumped and rocked as the brakes eased us to a halt in the Gare de Lyons.

It was December 21st, and I looked anxiously at Paris for war scars and misery. I could see no change, I could feel no change. I saw the Paris I had known over the years, a city at peace, gay and pulsating with excitement. With precious few francs in my pocket, I dived down the subway and bought a Metro ticket for Place de la Concorde. But there were a few changes: the ticket collector was a woman and amongst the passengers was a sprinkling of military and naval uniforms.

As I mounted the steps and emerged into Place de la Concorde, I paused for a brief moment to take a quick glance at the city. I have always found Paris exciting and on that occasion, after my escape, particularly so. At the end of the broad expanse of the Champs Elysées, my eyes caught the Arc de Triomphe and swept over the statues and fountains in the square. It was a pleasure again to see chic women and to watch the inevitable bereted figures that sit gossiping interminably over *café filtre* in the restaurants. Cab drivers cursed at each other and gendarmes gesticulated with their usual violence at one and all; for Paris, it was almost Business As Usual.

It was only a short walk to the Rue de Rivoli and the Regina Hotel. General Sikorski had been given this building by the French Government, in which he had installed the Polish General Staff. In the foyer of the hotel, all was confusion; civilians and soldiers mingled together; a hubbub of voices filled the air; it looked more like an auction sale than the entrance to a Head-quarters. Military Policemen argued with civilians and lounged against the desks. Going up to a Military Police sergeant, I said: "I am Colonel Sosabowski. I want to see General Sikorski."

He stared at me, not even saluting, and shrugged his shoulders. "So does everybody else."

I flushed with anger and ordered him to stand to attention and address me according to my rank. Nearby civilians looked on in amazement. I told him to telephone the aide-de-camp to announce my arrival and he was told to send me up to the General's suite immediately.

There were various reasons for this undisciplined state of affairs. Coming straight from battle and the misery of an over-whelmed and occupied country I was, not unnaturally, feeling a bit heroic and could not help looking down on my countrymen in Paris, who had either been in France when war was declared or who had quitted Poland early in the battle; some of them had never fought. Yet these people were full of blame for the Government and Army in Poland who had, in their opinion, not fought or prepared sufficiently to stop the Germans; they blamed people like me for letting them down. I resented this attitude.

Politics now played a large part in military affairs. Sikorski had been out of favour in Poland for some years and, when called upon by President Raczkiewicz to become Premier and Com-mander-in-Chief, had surrounded himself with friends, many of whom had also been out of office. These men had no conception of how valiantly the army had fought in the September cam-paign. They did not know about the Blitzkrieg or of the resistance being carried on against the enemy. But there were also some first-class staff officers, including many ex-professors of the War-saw War Academy. To top it all, there was also the resentfulness of the French, who blamed the Poles for losing the campaign; some French newspapers were taking a hostile attitude and an extreme minority in Paris was very antagonistic.

The sergeant escorted me to the aide-de-camp, who told me that Sikorski would see me immediately. I was the first senior

officer to come straight out of occupied Poland, and the only one
to have a fairly complete picture of what had gone on during the
campaign and subsequent events in both occupied zones. Mine
was the first on-the-spot report that Sikorski received. The aide-
de-camp ushered me into a luxurious room: rich curtains edged
tall narrow windows, the carpet was soft under foot, and delicate
chairs and occasional tables dotted the floor. The Commander-
in-Chief, tall and elegant, shook my hand politely, but was
barely friendly. He gestured towards a chair.

"Now, Sosabowski, make yourself comfortable and tell me
about your experiences."

He listened intently, nodding occasionally in approval and, at
other times, shaking his head in amazement or partial disbelief.
I talked without interruption for about an hour and a half, and
then the General, with more warmth in his voice, thanked me for
the clarity of my report. He told me to go and see General
Sosnkowski, Deputy Commander-in-Chief, who was organising
communications, supplies and contacts for the Underground
Movement. I was to join his staff. I was also instructed to write
a full report of the campaign, which would be considered by a
Commission investigating the reasons for defeat. Later I discovered that everyone who came from Poland was required to
write such a report and give opinions as to whom they thought
responsible. I wrote mine, restricting it to facts and made no
allegations. It was not very well received by the officer in charge
of the Commission, but I refused to alter a word.

The Caserne Bessier had been turned into an officers' depot
and most officers lived there while awaiting postings to units
that were being formed. They spent most of the time arguing
about reasons for defeat and the atmosphere was not at all to my
liking. I did not stay, but moved into a small hotel in Rue Boissy
d'Anglas between the Madeleine and Concorde.

Christmas came, and General Sosnkowski came to a Christmas
Eve dinner organised by his staff officers. I was guest of honour.
We had the traditional fish courses and we tried, with several
bottles of good wine, to raise a festive spirit—but for most of us it
was a time for thought and contemplation. Outside, Parisian
streets were gay with coloured lights and Christmas trees. Happy,
smiling last-minute shoppers hurried home burdened with parcels,
ready to celebrate the birth of Christ in the happiness of the family
circle. Light-hearted Paris forgot the war. But our minds wandered back to Poland, across the hundreds of miles separating us
from our loved ones. Would our wives and children have sufficient

to eat? Would they have wood for the fires? Had they warm clothes? I thought of my wife and Stas—I knew they would worry about me, as they had no idea if I was dead or alive. In spite of our efforts, the party broke up early and everyone, each with his own thoughts, went to bed.

A few days later I was called before the Polish Council of Ministers at Angers, where I repeated the report I had already submitted to Sikorski. Several Ministers questioned me on the state of the political parties, but I replied:

"I am a soldier—I have no opinions or politics."

Full of determination I set to work in General Sosnkowski's department, in a secret office near the Madeleine. I prepared a detailed report on the Underground Movement in German and Russian occupied territory. Our task was to work out ways and means of helping the Polish Home Army, arranging couriers and contacts; but nothing was easy and plans had to be continuously changed to replace those lost in action or on whom suspicion had fallen. Our chief difficulties were with supplies and means of getting them into the country. We badly needed aeroplanes for dropping parachutists and small, long-range aircraft which could land and take off in fields. Pilots were ready to go, but there were no planes capable of the long return journey.

In January, after many fruitless searches, we at last located in London a Polish civil aircraft and with high hopes we sent mechanics to check it over. Unfortunately, their report was unfavourable. Then, completely out of the blue, a fighter plane was found and by almost filling it with extra petrol tanks, it was adapted for the flight to Poland. One day in January I happened to go into Notre Dame Cathedral; in the shadows of that vast and beautiful church, I found the pilot Captain Wyrwicki and his co-pilot on their knees pleading for guidance and a safe return. The following morning we gave them final instructions and bade them good luck. They never came back and to this day nobody knows what became of them.

Comparatively speaking, we were well off in Paris. On full colonel's pay, I had more than enough for my basic comforts. There were plenty of temptations, restaurants, theatres and night clubs and it was easy, if one so desired, to lead a riotous life.

Hundreds of us put ourselves into the hands of Paris money merchants, believing their promises that they could easily transfer money to Poland. Too late, we found that this money never reached our families. When my wife finally joined me after the war, she revealed that not one penny of the sizeable sum I had despatched ever arrived, although they were perpetually near to starvation.

Officers and men were still escaping from Poland and finding their way to Paris. Unfortunately, most of them were officers, but we were not over-worried, as Sikorski relied on getting recruits from the half a million Poles who worked in the coal mines and heavy industry of northern France. The French Government had agreed that they should be made available and, on the strength of this promise, two Polish Infantry Divisions were formed; the 1st Division at Coetquidan, Brittany, and the 2nd Division near Tours.

Fed up with Paris, I was overjoyed to be appointed Deputy Commander of the 1st Division. It was a great honour to be chosen from the hundreds of officers who also had perfectly good claims to the job. Delightedly, I hurried off to a little Polish-Jewish tailor, who fashioned me a uniform modelled on the official Polish style, but with French variations. It was good to get into uniform again.

Hardly had the Division started to assemble, when four battalions were withdrawn, formed into a Mountain Brigade and sent to Norway with the British Expeditionary Force. Our Divisional Commander, Colonel Maczek, was posted and a Colonel Duch was appointed, but as he was attending an artillery course, I found myself in command. Our units were formed on French lines, with French instructors. On arrival, I found that the Polish troops had acquired all the bad habits of the *Poilu*; untidy, ill-disciplined, they spent most of their time in cafés, wasting their money on the numerous prostitutes who walked the village streets. Most of my officers and men had been living and working in France at the outbreak of war. They were unused to Army discipline—in fact few of them, apart from some Reservists, had ever been in uniform.

I was horrified at the bad discipline of the French troops and the effect it had on my men. Everyone knows the heroism of French troops, and the example of Verdun in the First World War will never be forgotten. But in 1940, the French Army was one of the worst I have ever seen. The war was unpopular and their discontent had started to spread to the Poles, many of whom had only the vaguest idea of what had happened in Poland, and with the French all round them blaming us for losing the campaign, they were bewildered and ready to believe anything.

Conditions in the camp at Coetquidan were so bad that a question was even asked about them in the French Parliament.

81

The wooden barracks had few panes of glass in the windows and there were many holes in the walls. Only iron stoves were supplied and these merely warmed the surrounding area for about two feet and were virtually useless. There were no made-up paths and the men walked in unrepaired shoes up to their ankles in mud. The French would not supply the leather to repair our boots, nor would they give us more than one blanket per man in these primitive conditions in mid-February.

I was pleased to meet the Chief French Inspector of Training, General Faury, who had been an instructor at the Warsaw War Academy. Unfortunately, my pleasure soon gave way to serious misgivings, as he blamed us entirely for losing the war. With no conception of the Blitzkrieg, his instructors were teaching First World War tactics, the same as they were putting into practice on the Maginot Line. I tried explaining to him modern German methods; I argued and argued—but the fact that we had lost carried more weight with him than anything else. The accent of his teaching was defence. To my every argument, he curtly replied;

" *Vous avez perdu la guerre—nous allons la gagner.*"

General Faury was a good and just man; a true patriot, who cried like a child when France collapsed, but he never believed he was wrong.

The promised recruits from the coal mines never materialised, because the French Government stepped in to keep them on priority work. We found ourselves with far more officers than necessary and nothing like enough men. With such a surfeit of senior ranks, the French, who were paying us, decided that only those on the War Establishment of units would get full pay: all others were put on half salary, which made it very hard, particularly on junior officers.

During the last days of February, General Sikorski came to visit the Division and almost the first thing he asked was how soon would we be able to go to the front? I said that, even if we got all the replacements we needed at once we could never be ready before the middle of June.

"The French Government," he said, "are pressing me hard and for political reasons you must have the Division ready by 1st April. I will try and arrange that you get the chance of further training behind the line."

In fact, the Division went to the Maginot Line on 15th April, four weeks after the first recruits arrived and eventually fought valiantly, covering the retreat of the French Army in May-June 1940. But my luck was out; I never went with them. Just before the move, I was sent on an artillery course, which was deemed necessary for all Divisional and Deputy Commanders.

Once again I came up against French instructors with out-dated ideas of warfare. They were convinced the Germans would never break the steel and concrete Maginot Line; they even tried to prove their theories by charts and graphs. When the course ended, I was posted as Deputy Commander to the 4th Infantry Division, then forming. The Divisional Commander was a cavalryman, General Dreszer, who lived in a *pension* in Rue Jean Bart, Paris. I called on him and he told me he had no idea how to run an Infantry Division, that anyway we had no men, and he suggested I had better go to Les Sables d'Olones and organise the staff.

I arrived on a bright warm April day. Some officers were already there and, while they were waiting, I found they were leading a pleasant life of wine, women and song. Here was a repetition of the difficulties I had already experienced with 1st Division. No men, no arms, no equipment, and French instructors well versed in the 1918 methods of fighting. Divisional Headquarters was located in the garage of my Chief-of-Staff, Colonel Lowczowski; our Chief Clerk was his wife, and she brought her own typewriter. Out of my own pocket I paid for stationery, which was not very convenient, as I had been down-graded to half pay until the Division was formed and placed on the establishment.

I remember one Divisional Study Centre, where the instructor could only speak French. He was very forthright in his condemnation of how our Army had fought the September campaign. I took advantage of his lack of Polish and translating his 1918 ideas into Polish 1939 methods, I overcame his defeatist attitude.

We were at last reluctantly issued with a few rifles by the French and I was amazed to see they were models that I understood were last used in the Franco-Prussian war of 1871. One instructor was blessed with the same name as the rifles, Gras, and he had his leg pulled unmercifully.

As part of our training, we sent several officers to the Maginot Line for experience. They returned very indignant, telling of a French order which forbade Polish units making fighting contact with the Germans or going out on patrol. They felt this was the result of a general unwillingness by the French to fight at all.

On May 10th, Hitler's offensive opened. German bombs fell on French cities and towns and, for the first time, many French-men realised they were at war with a strong and ruthless enemy.

Blitzkrieg tactics breached the Maginot Line and a flood of evacuees started their search for a haven along the military life-lines of metropolitan France. Civil authorities in many centres turned Poles out of houses and hotels in which they were billeted to make room for refugees. In one town, the inhabitants got so angry with Polish troops, believing that they should have been fighting at the front, that the unit commander voluntarily took his men into the country. On May 24th we received orders to move to Partenay, where we had been told we would find our reinforcements. But when we arrived, we found we had been let down again. A few days later, I went to Polish Headquarters. It was a very different Paris to that I had seen earlier in the year. True, many people still behaved as if there was no war, but the atmosphere was one of hollow gaiety and forthcoming defeat.

Our recruits eventually arrived on the 15th June, mostly from the Lille and Calais areas. The following day, we received fresh orders to move further south to Saint on the Bordeaux road. We could not go, as we were without transport. Anyway, the roads were packed solid with civilian refugees and soldiers heading for their homes. Everything I saw convinced me that France was beaten.

We were still without weapons apart from the Gras rifles and the French were increasingly hostile towards us. We had no news about operations at the front, we were out of touch with Head-quarters and the position was very obscure. We had no infor-mation or orders, because Headquarters had evacuated from the capital and was believed to be heading for Saint. Confusion and uncertainty reigned. My subordinates kept asking for orders, but I had none to give. General Dreszer went to Saint to try to get instructions but he returned without any. We drafted orders for the evacuation of all troops through the port of La Rochelle; but before putting them into effect, I suggested to the Divisional Commander that he should let me have a final try to speak to Polish Headquarters. He agreed and permitted me to take the car to seek out the Commander-in-Chief or General Kukiel, the Deputy Defence Minister. When I went for the car, I was told by the driver that it had been stolen and only after a long search did we discover an old broken-down Citröen which, with a lot of encouragement, reluctantly started and chugged off with myself and three officers aboard. We had considerable difficulty getting through villages and towns. French guards were loath to let us pass and, to make matters worse, rumours of German para-chutists in disguise made us most conspicuous and suspect.

It was after midnight when we arrived at Saint to find most of General Headquarters bedded down for the night. I was informed that General Sikorski was at the front and General Kukiel's whereabouts were unknown. As I could not sleep, I walked around the deserted streets, my boots rattling on the cobblestones. Suddenly a window was thrust open and an angry voice demanded in Polish:

"What the hell is all the noise about?"

I recognised it as that of a staff officer from Headquarters.

"What are you doing here?" I asked.

In a bad-tempered tone, he went on: "I'm trying to sleep; I have only just returned from General Kukiel."

This was a wonderful piece of luck and I hurriedly extracted from him the whereabouts of the General and learnt he was at Libourne with the President.

I rushed to the local Garrison Headquarters and woke up a very angry French Duty Officer. I told him I had to phone Libourne. He protested and proposed that I should return in the morning, but I overcame his objections and got through. An old acquaintance, Colonel Sulislawski, answered the telephone at Polish Headquarters, but deprecated my request.

"I daren't wake the General; he has only just gone to bed after two days without any sleep. Have a heart, ring back at eight."

But at 8 a.m. the French staff was wide awake and adamant in refusing me the use of the telephone. However, I did obtain a travel authority which permitted us to drive to Libourne. We encouraged the ancient old car to start and set off on the two-hundred kilometre journey. Soon we ran into the huge straggling columns of refugees; their carts, cars and prams plodded along at about two miles an hour. If anyone tried to go in the opposite direction, the steady unending stream consumed them. I had seen panic in Poland, but that was nothing compared to this. Yet by using side roads and really forcing the crowds out of the way, we reached Libourne at about 2 p.m., where I found General Kukiel and obtained permission to evacuate 4th Division from the nearest port.

With hardly a pause, we set off on the return route to Saint. The antique vehicle, with careful encouragement from our driver, went humming along at a remarkable speed, but the roads proved too much for one of the tyres, which burst, sending us into a ditch at the side of the road. By good luck, a car shortly came along going in the same direction and we managed to get a lift into Saint. There I found one of my officers with a motorcycle and, handing him the signed order, told him to go quickly to Divisional Headquarters at Partenay and tell them to move to La Rochelle, where there were believed to be several boats.

Without the car, we were forced to spend the night in Saint, hoping that it would catch up with us in the morning. During the evening I met a French colonel attached to the Polish Mission, who told me to be careful and produced an official cable in which the French Government forbade the evacuation of Polish units from France. I think there must have been a secret clause between the French and Germans that the Poles would be handed over. He also warned me that the French admiral in charge of Rochefort could easily stop us, if he wanted, and we should avoid the place. He then asked if I would take with me his driver who was a Pole and I agreed with alacrity. Our Citröen arrived shortly after lunch, the driver having found, goodness knows where, a new tyre. As we drove out of Saint, I noticed we were being followed by another vehicle containing Polish officers and civilians whom I did not know, but who were obviously hoping we would lead them to safety.

We had only gone a few kilometres, when I noticed a group of uniformed Poles sitting in a ditch and I saw to my surprise that one of them was Captain Jachnik, who had been my Chief of Staff during the Warsaw siege. It was a most amusing coincidence, as I had discovered him quite by chance in Warsaw sitting on a fence and here he was again, this time in a ditch. We squeezed him somehow into the overloaded car and proceeded.

The most direct route led us through Rochefort and, as I did not want to waste any time, I decided, in spite of the warning, that I would go through. It was dark when we approached the outskirts and I told the driver to "step on it". French Military Police did try to block the road, but we drove straight on, ignoring their signals and scattering them as we passed.

The driver maintained his speed and we were driving fairly fast along the deserted night-time roads; it looked as if we would get to La Rochelle in a fairly short time. Then, as we tore through a deserted village, a car coming in the opposite direction screamed around a corner straight into us. We finished up, the car on its side in the middle of a field. One of the officers was unconscious and bleeding profusely from the head but, apart from the shaking, the remainder were unharmed. Out of the other car scrambled several panic-stricken youths and girls. The vehicle following us had stopped and I asked them to take the injured man on with Jachnik and return for us. We were lonely after it left and, as time went by, we felt very cut off. We started walking towards La Rochelle and, when the first glimmer of dawn lit the sky, we became desperate. Suddenly, out of the darkness behind us, loomed a truck. Staying in the middle of the road we forced the driver to a halt and, as we climbed aboard, told him to drive to La Rochelle. It was almost full daylight when we arrived and in the market place we saw the car and our wounded comrade surrounded by several French officers. The lorry pulled up with a jerk and we hurried across to them. They looked at us in surprise.

"*Vite, vite, depechez-vous!*" they gesticulated.

We gathered that there had been some trouble in the small port and a Greek ship, on which the troops had originally planned to sail, had been bombed and was still burning in the harbour. There was, however, a British collier, the *Abderpool* which had already embarked the Division and the Captain intended sailing at first light—there was little time to spare. We quickly jumped into our car and a French staff vehicle and set off on one of the maddest drives of my life. With no idea at which quay the ship was tied up, we drove crazily from one dock to the next. Finally, we skidded round a corner and there we saw her, gangway up, and only a rope ladder dangling down the side. Troops were lining the rails and as they saw us, started cheering us on. Scrambling out of the vehicles on to the quayside, we ran to the ladder. As I waited for my comrades to climb, I turned to the group of Frenchmen.

"Come with us to Britain," I urged.

But not one came.

"*Non, nous n'avons pas les ordres,*" they said.

We were forced to leave them there on the cobblestones, a forlorn looking group, without orders, with an unknown future; it seemed to typify the French nation and the lack of decision and uncertainty which had hung over the whole of the French campaign in the face of the overwhelming Blitzkrieg.

CHAPTER V

ENGLAND

I CLAMBERED, hand over hand, up the swinging rope ladder, bumping my knees and grazing my knuckles against the dirty black sides of the ancient collier. Welcoming hands reached out and hauled me to the deck.

Standing at the rail, I gazed at the slowly widening gap of swirling, frothy water between the ship and France. Two burly, silent sailors shouldered me aside, hauled up the ladder and neatly coiled the rope hawsers. My eyes glanced again at the small group of Frenchmen on the quay, and I regretted the indecision and uncertainty that had brought them to such circumstances. A pall of grey smoke drifted across the harbour, but there were no other signs of war. A bright sun gave promise of a hot day which, in normal times, would have been welcomed by farmer, fisherman and holiday-maker alike. Yet to our shipload of refugees, it was but a façade covering the fate of a great nation. It was the thinnest veneer, hiding a country in suspended animation, not knowing which way to turn or what to do. A nation divided in itself.

My thoughts were rudely interrupted by the roar of aircraft engines, and a twin-engined Focke Wolfe, with its underside decorated with black crosses, shot out from land to lazily circle us. The twin Vickers at the stern of the ship chattered noisily as its barrels squirted bullets at the unwanted visitor. It must have been a reconnaissance plane, for it left us unmolested and flew off. We all visualised a wireless operator, tapping out our position to headquarters, which would bring the bombers to ravage and sink us. But our luck held; we never saw another enemy aircraft.

Turning from the rails, I stepped carefully through the crowds, which sat, lay or lounged upon the deck. I spoke to many and greeted old friends. I searched out General Dreszer and found him on the forecastle, gazing ahead. What he was thinking I never knew but, like us all he had turned his back on defeat and was looking into an unknown future. He told me to assume command of all troops on board so I climbed the steps to the bridge and reported to the Captain. We looked down to the crowded decks, a mass of helpless men, women and children—mostly Poles, with a small sprinkling of British Tommies, Dutch, French and other nationalities.

They were frightened people. Thousands of miles from home, they had been upheaved again from temporary abodes in France and, without knowing the real reasons, they were at sea heading into a doubtful future, with an equally unknown people, and with a very great possibility that the same enemies who had chased them out of Poland and France would also chase them in Britain. They were almost without hope.

Through an interpreter, the stocky Captain told me that he was steering for Britain but, until orders came from the Admiralty, he would not know in which port we would dock; we might be at sea for many days. He ordered water to be rationed and added that there was little food aboard and we would be wise to conserve what supplies we had. Using a megaphone, I told the troops the situation and called for strict obedience. The Captain kindly offered the use of his small cabin to the ladies and, as is usual with the ladies, they were soon squabbling amongst themselves over peculiar feminine problems.

With over three thousand people on board we were very cramped, every inch of space above and below deck was occupied.

It was aboard the *Abderpool* I learned my first English word and acquired the queue habit. As soon as a water point opened, a queue formed and it remained almost constant throughout the voyage. Another file formed at the lavatory door. This was the first English word that I understood. "La-va-to-ry"—I used to murmur it syllable by syllable, until I had it perfect. As soon as a man had collected his water, he would join the lavatory queue, and woe betide anyone who did not wait his turn.

We spent two nights on board: two nights and three days of worry and inactivity. The smell of sea-sickness hung everywhere, mingling with the odour of unwashed human bodies. Unshaven faces were the order of the day. Morale was at a low ebb. Men looked aside if you gazed into their eyes, or glared accusingly back seeking someone to blame for their plight.

On June 21st, the Captain told me he had been ordered to Plymouth. Early on June 22nd, standing on the upper deck, I got my first sight of England: the beautiful Plymouth cliffs.

Everything looked peaceful, quiet and settled, almost a story-book view of England. Lazy-winged gulls flew out to greet the vessel and escorted us screeching into the crowded harbour. The grass was so brilliantly green and, somehow, the sight of boys and girls swimming near the harbour entrance was very comforting. Brightly painted houses sat in small neat gardens smiling at us from the surrounding hills. What a contrast between frightened, burning France and the soothing, soft naturalness of England!

A fussy, blue-painted launch shot out, bringing the inevitable Customs officials. I assumed the responsibility for all Poles and formalities were soon completed. A staff officer told me that trains awaited us at the station to take us to Scotland. We walked ashore to be met by green-uniformed, brightly smiling ladies of the Women's Voluntary Service, who offered us tea, buns and cigarettes from trolleys. The men were so excited, particularly over the cigarettes, that I had to remind them of their comrades still to come. Then it rained and we were glad to get under the cover of the station. This was how we had all imagined England to be.

The train journey was boring, uncomfortable and uneventful. We ground to a halt in Glasgow station at 10 a.m. the following morning and were met by a limping British liaison officer, who told me in French that billets had been arranged for us in the schools. We marched singing through the dirty Glasgow streets and were delighted when the dour working people stood on their doorsteps to clap and cheer us; it was in distinct contrast to our treatment from the French. We did not then know that we would be partly responsible for defending Scotland, but neither did they know that we were unarmed apart from our few old rifles.

My Headquarters I installed in one of the schools and, on arrival, I was greeted by a compatriot, a colonel who had returned with the Polish Brigade from Narvik.

"I arrived first," he said to me, "and I am older than you, so I have taken command of all Polish troops in Glasgow."

I didn't waste time arguing with him.

"I have my orders," I replied, "and you are to consider yourself and your troops under my command."

That was the last I heard of the matter.

The first instruction I issued in Scotland confined everyone, officers, soldiers, wives and children to barracks. The wives and children I sent to one school in the charge of an old and senior officer and had armed sentries stationed at the doors. I gave orders that no one was to enter—not even husbands!

This started a storm of protests from the officers, who objected strongly to being treated like soldiers. I think it also upset the Glaswegians, as they had more or less declared the town an open city. Travel on all public transport was free and the citizens arranged parties for the troops. But I had nightmare visions of what would happen if I let these men loose on an unsuspecting population, so I stuck to my order. I did not even know how many Poles were in Glasgow at that time.

Only recently, in London, a Polish lady recalled the event.

"Do you remember me?" she asked, and I was forced to apologise.

Smiling broadly she told me: "It was in Glasgow in 1940, when you were a colonel. You ordered all the wives to stay indoors and came round on an inspection late at night to make sure we were in bed and not up to any mischief."

The British District Commander helped to the best of his ability, having agreed that all dealings with Polish troops should be through me only. A cheerful Paymaster arrived, but left with an expression of complete astonishment and frank disbelief on his face, when told there were over two thousand officers, but very few N.C.O.s and men. I am sure he was convinced that the officers had deserted their troops! Some days later, I toured the countryside with quartering officers, looking for a camp. The tour ended at Biggar, where I was asked to choose a site. This was done in a typically British way: they had already decided that we should have Biggar camp, but were too polite to say so.

The camps were planned strictly according to King's Regulations and I was horrified to see tents laid out in straight rows, with no attempt at concealment and quite defenceless against air attack; nothing I said could get them to change it. We were even sent British Army cooks. After a few days, by which time the troops were almost on hunger strike, I asked if we could have the raw rations. We were not ungrateful, but my men just could not stomach British food cooked in the British style. To make matters worse, it rained continuously and we were all wet through. Compared with France, it was very cold indeed.

I organised rifle companies and battalions, some up to strength, but others comprised of officers only. I soon had them scurrying over the country on exercises which, if they did nothing else, made them dog-tired so they went to sleep with no energy or thoughts to spare for mischief. In other camps, not under my command, officers sat around, idle all day, playing bridge and gossiping. As a result they became lazy and increasingly reluctant to do anything. In comparison, I soon had the nucleus of a rifle brigade and was making satisfactory progress with training.

Quite unexpectedly one day, an order came from General Kukiel in London that the 1st Rifle Brigade, forming under

General Paszkiewicz, was to be given whichever men he wanted and all supplies and transport. This was blow enough, but on top of this, when the General's staff came to select the men, they were rude and high-handed; we very much resented their attitude. After their departure, I found the few remaining soldiers were all of low medical category; none of my N.C.O.s remained, but I still had plenty of officers. To top it all, General Paszkiewicz told me to evacuate the camps immediately.

The instant effect was a lowering of the officers' morale. They had done their best to bring their troops out of France, with high hopes that they would lead them in battle at a later date. At this juncture, they could only visualise sitting in Scotland playing endless games of bridge and chess, mere spectators of the world's struggles. I decided that it was up to me to produce a con- structive plan and get them all working again as quickly as possible.

I had hidden away a motorcycle when all the other transport was taken, and with my aide-de-camp driving and me on the pillion, we set off to Glasgow to see General Burhard Bukacki, Polish Commander in Scotland. Having told him the position, I suggested he should allow me to form an Officers' Cadre Brigade, which would supply fully-trained officers for future fighting for- mations. He readily approved the scheme and further told me that General Sikorski planned to recruit Poles in Canada and my cadre could take them over. Later I received official confirmation and found myself commanding the Canadian Officers' Cadre Brigade for eventual posting to Canada.

Off I went on another conducted tour of many grim and freezing castles in Dumfriesshire to find a new camp. I eventually chose one near Kirmanoch, called Eliock. Surrounded by a beautiful park full of firs, it was eminently suitable for training; it also had the additional advantage of being almost cut off from other Polish camps and well out of interference range. With British co-operation, the castle and grounds were requisitioned in two days, which was surely a record for the British Army.

As we had no transport, the British agreed to move us by lorry, but could not let us have vehicles for everyday use. Explaining the position to my officers, I suggested we should pool some money and buy transport. They looked at me as if I were mad, but some hours later, the owner of a car "cemetery" thought me even crazier when I bought from him ten old cars for about £5 each. Owing to petrol rationing, the bottom had been knocked out of the second-hand car market and the salesman was only too keen to get rid of them at any price. I obtained permission from Glasgow to draw War Department petrol and our transport troubles were over. We were back in business, with more vehicles than most other Polish units!

The move to Eliock took place on 20th July 1940 and our luck changed. It even stopped raining! There was a progressive training programme; with the Scottish Home Guard we had anti-parachute exercises. When I saw them with their claymores, sabres and spears, I was reminded of how Polish patriots had on many occasions fought the Russians with only spikes, sticks and stones. The prospect of going to Canada to form a proper fighting unit was a great incentive. However, in August came another blow: I was told the Canadian idea had been cancelled, another unit allotted the task and we were renamed 4th Officers' Cadre Brigade.

In September, a parade was held at Biggar, when the Town Council presented a battle pennant to the 1st Polish Infantry Brigade. General Sikorski and many of his staff officers came from London for the ceremony. During the visit, General Klimecki, an old friend, revealed to me confidentially that saboteurs were being sent back to Poland to help the Underground Army.

"I shall send an officer to your Brigade," he said, "to choose some suitable men."

I pleaded with him not to do this: "I know these officers better than anyone, I am in the best position to choose them."

He agreed and units under my command had the honour, during the following three years, to send about three hundred officers into Poland.

A special training centre for these men was set up at Inverlochie Castle on the West Coast. Without telling them what it was about, I sent twenty officers, forbidding them to say where they were going or what they did, and informing them that they would be cut off from their families. British Intelligence who, I think, at that time were a little suspicious of us, sent a group of attractive girls into the pubs and cafés round about. I understand that the girls had a good time, but they never obtained any of the information they sought.

The officers learned unarmed combat and all the methods of silent murder, sabotage, disguise and the artistry of professional "agents provocateurs". When the course ended, I interviewed each one, asking them to sign the following statement: *I am prepared to do everything and go wherever my commander asks me.* I gave them my assurance that a refusal to sign would not be held

93

against them and that no one but myself would ever know their decision. They were still kept in ignorance for what operations they had been trained. It was at the end of their training, at a final interview, that I revealed what they had long suspected, that they were going into occupied Poland.

Even at this late hour, they all had a further chance to withdraw. They were told the implications of what they had been asked to do: they would lose their uniforms and military privileges; gone, too, would be their identities and they would be suspected by everyone, Poles, Germans and Russians alike; torture and cruel death awaited them if they were captured; they would be cut off from friends and even if they saw a close relation they were forbidden to make contact. Hunted like animals, death would not bring recognition or posthumous decorations.

"This is your moment of decision," I told them, "for if you change your mind later, you may be the cause of other deaths and your training will have been a waste of time and money."

Out of the hundreds sent to their deaths in Poland, none failed in action. Even today I still hear of deeds of unrecorded heroism by individuals whose bread and butter in wartime was intrigue and destruction.

September 1940 brought the Battle of Britain. It is not generally realised or appreciated that Polish airmen fought valiantly side by side with "The Few". Lord Vansittart wrote afterwards:

We shall remember that in this decisive moment of our history, the Polish airmen were almost our sole ally—except the Commonwealth nations —to fight side by side with us. The Poles shot down and damaged over two hundred enemy aircraft.

In October, we moved from Eliock to Fife, took over a sector of the eastern coastline and prepared anti-invasion defences. It was there I first came into contact with British bureaucracy. Having laid my plans and issued orders about defensive localities, the officers and troops marched out to dig trenches and emplacements. It was not long before an enraged lieutenant and a furious Scottish farmer strode shouting and gesticulating into my office. I discovered that, even in wartime, with a German invasion reported imminent, I had to apply through the proper channels for permission to dig trenches on private land, in order that the farmers could get compensation and everything could be properly arranged. I soon found it was best to meet the farmers, have drinks with them and get the work under way while the papers and forms slowly travelled from department to department.

My headquarters on the Fife coast was at Leven, and I was

Major-General Stanislaw Sosabowski, photographed at Arnhem, while commanding the 1st Polish Independent Parachute Brigade.

Arnhem – A Dakota, damaged while dropping supplies, after a crash landing: it hit a knocked-out German tank and burst into flames.

The Polish Parachute Brigade and their Colours from Warsaw.

Field-Marshal Montgomery addressing the Polish troops before the Battle of Arnhem. The author is on the right of the picture.

General 'Boy' Browning, *centre*, and the author, *right*. Their character clash proved fatal to Sosabowski's military career.

The final preparations before Arnhem – General Sosabowski, *left*, at the airfield before the take-off.

Paratroopers dashing for cover on the landing ground after grabbing arms from the containers.

Left to right: Colonel Stevens, General Sosabowski and General Thomas.

The leading vehicle of the Household Cavalry troop just after it had reached the Polish position at Driel.

Members of the Dutch Underground bringing in German prisoners.

A German position near Arnhem.

A Polish Paratrooper checking a wrecked German car.

Members of the Dutch Underground with a female collaborator after she has had her hair removed.

Left to right: General Sosabowski, General Urquhart and Brigadier Hackett.

The return from Arnhem – the Polish Paratroopers embarking at Ostend.

most amused later to learn from the British liaison officers that the local inhabitants were much relieved about our good behaviour. They had been told that we were "wild uncivilised men"; they really expected slant-eyed Asians in long-haired sheepskin coats to ride through the streets flourishing sabres and spears. They had hidden their valuables and locked up their daughters.

We formed at this time the equivalent of a British infantry battalion, although eighty per cent of the troops were officers; visitors found it rather startling to find lieutenant-colonels and majors digging trenches and carrying out clerks' duties. However, we at last received an issue of up-to-date weapons, rifles, stens and bren-guns.

In February 1941, after a long frustrating winter, when our thoughts had been continually of the hardships our families were enduring in Poland, I was told by London that I could send twenty officers on a parachute course to Ringway Airfield, near Manchester. I was told to ask for volunteers and had no difficulty in finding them. On their return, I talked with them to find out what it was like. They were most enthusiastic, but admitted that the physical standard required was very hard, in fact—in many cases—beyond their strength. They had also been upset by the rudeness of British N.C.O. instructors. In amazement, they had listened when sergeants shouted at officers, regardless of rank or nationality. It was their first contact with the British system, where officers may be instructed by N.C.O.s and all students treated alike. What was to the British an accepted tradition, was to the Poles bad manners and ill-discipline. I carefully explained the different methods and asked them to spread it about that the British were not anti-Polish.

The reports brought back from Ringway interested me very much. Here was something definite, training that could be put to a positive use. I was very aware, at this time, that although my men were busy and training for the doubtful day when more troops would arrive—General Sikorski still hoped that thousands of soldiers would turn up—we were getting nowhere. There we were, sitting safely in Scotland, while troops of other nations fought the Nazis overseas. In Poland, men of the Home Army were actively opposing the Germans, keeping valuable divisions tied up, preventing them from fighting on other fronts.

It was the ambition of all us exiles to get back and fight for the freedom of our country. We felt guilty being in Scotland. "Were we relying too much on the help of others?" I wondered. We

95

alone could plan and make decisions about our country—we should get on with it. A quick glance over Polish history shows that success has never been found through sitting still and waiting. All our national heroes were men who pioneered and revolted against oppressive regimes, and small numbers worked miracles against vast armies. I remembered a sign that I had seen on the wall of a British Quartermaster's office: *The impossible we do at once; miracles take a little longer.* I decided to try and perform a miracle.

I made up my mind to form a Polish Parachute Brigade.

I was all alone in my office on the second floor of the Leven Y.M.C.A.; a small coal fire burning in an iron grate spread a meagre warmth through the stolid bare office. It was afternoon, everyone was out training, and I had several hours in which to pace the room and make plans. It was a long time before I sat down and committed my ideas to paper. It would not be easy, I thought, to train men, most of whom had never even been in an aeroplane, to suddenly change their nature and throw themselves out of one. But I have always maintained that a good commander can get his men to do anything. Human beings are normally divided in three groups: those who are dead against a project; those who are enthusiastic; and the bulk, who are neutral. I already had twenty enthusiasts back from Ringway—they were unit heroes—and boasting how easy it really was. They would start the ball of enthusiasm rolling through the Brigade. Enthusiasm, however, would not be enough; I had to have some means of toughening the men up and getting them a hundred per cent fit. I decided that everyone fit enough would become a paratrooper and I did not give them the choice of volunteering. This may seem strange to British readers, because in most armies parachute troops are all volunteers. It even seemed strange to General Kukiel for, some months later, after the Parachute Brigade had been given official blessing, he queried:

"Why don't you allow officers and N.C.O.s who don't wish to be parachutists to transfer?"

I had my answer ready.

"General," I replied with some feeling, "you are a soldier and an historian. You know that in all our wars and risings the cream of the nation was killed off. Those who were afraid to take part in the battles lived on. Can you give me any reason why only the brave should die? I can assure you that in my brigade everyone will not only fight, but fight well."

General Kukiel never thought of a reply.

However, that was months ahead. I took these initial decisions without consulting any of my senior officers, determined to overcome all opposition. I started by setting up a medical board and making friends with Squadron-Leader Maurice Newnham, the Royal Air Force Commander at Ringway, who helped by training instructors and lending equipment. I also looked around for a suitable training centre.

Facing me was the tricky problem of getting official support. As far as General Sikorski was concerned, he was very busy as Prime Minister and unlikely to want to be bothered with a comparatively trivial matter. I by-passed him and went to see the Chief of Staff, General Klemecki. Unfortunately, he was not very enthusiastic and thought the whole idea unrealistic, yet he promised not to oppose me. I went then to the Director of Operations, Colonel Marecki, an old friend, and there I received tremendous support. He was thrilled and I found two more enthusiasts on his staff: they promised every help.

At last, I was all set to go. I had chosen Largo House as our training centre. An old stone mansion, surrounded by a park, it had many outbuildings and rooms which were ideal for indoor instruction. At the end of February, I gave the order for parachute training to begin.

So started our double life. Officially we were the 4th Officers' Cadre Brigade, with the normal British Infantry establishment, assigned to defend the Firth of Forth from invaders.

Unofficially we started to organise and train a Parachute Cadre Brigade. The intention at the time was that we should drop into Poland as a cadre and collect our men on arrival.

I was determined to form a strong fighting unit, manned by men of courage and truth, with one object in mind above all others:

Poland and liberation!

CHAPTER VI

PARACHUTE PIONEERS

I STOOD with several soldiers and a parachute instructor in the swaying basket under a silver-grey barrage balloon, looking down at ant-like figures, five hundred feet below. Paratroopers who had already landed were folding their 'chutes and walking towards the Y.M.C.A. tea van. A small group of soldiers and air-men clustered around the winch lorry, to which we were attached by a very thin-looking cable. The breeze sighed in the wires overhead and the fabric of the balloon bellied and billowed like a pregnant elephant. Suddenly, I heard a voice shout:
"GO!"

My arms and legs pushed with a reflex movement and I found myself falling, feet first through the hole in the floor, down, down, down, falling helplessly and irrevocably.

Feeling a tug at my shoulders, I looked up to see a mushroom-shaped parachute canopy and heard a loud voice through a megaphone:
"You, up there, put your feet and knees together! Get ready for landing, bend your legs and roll."

I was not quite ready for landing. One moment I had been floating in mid-air, then all of a sudden the green grass rushed at me with surprising speed. Biff, bang, wallop—my first jump was over. There to greet me was Maurice Newnham, Commander of the Parachute School.

"Are you all right?" he gasped. "Are you sure you haven't broken anything?"

I assured him everything was fine and I felt very good indeed.

Newnham's anxiety was understandable. He had been very much against my making any parachute jumps at all. To make matters worse, on arrival that morning we had witnessed a fatal accident, when a 'chute failure caused the death of a British paratrooper. This was certainly not a pleasant occurrence, but it did not deter me. Newnham had a theory that older men's bones broke easier. Taking me aside in the mess, he tried to persuade me against parachuting; I was, at the time, fifty years old.

98

"Why," he suggested, "don't you do like most senior commanders: make just a couple of jumps—don't take unnecessary risks." I informed him that I had already made men as old as myself perform eight qualifying jumps and they just would not understand it if their chief only did two. To increase Newnham's anxiety, I did all eight in three days, as I was in a hurry to return to Scotland.

Maurice Newnham is a good friend of mine and in his book, *Prelude to Glory*, he wrote of me: *I was greatly relieved when I saw him off on a train, after he had completed the required number of jumps.* I am sure he thought me a little mad.

Largo House had been converted in 1941 into what some mild-mannered soldiers called "A Hell on Earth"; others were more outspoken. The engineers, with great ingenuity, had built a set of ropes, planks, jumps, walls, cat-walks and leaps in the park and through the woods, which had been christened "The Monkey Grove".

Many officers who joined my brigade had escaped from Poland and survived amazing journeys before reaching Britain. Some followed extraordinary escape routes, which are still secret today. Others came through Yugoslavia, some through Spain, where many were interned in appalling concentration camps. Yet others came via the Middle East and Portugal, and some even journeyed through the Sahara Desert.

One of them, a captain, wrote an amusing account of his impressions on joining the Brigade:

Posted to the Polish Depot at Dunfermline, I was left hanging around with little to do, except play interminable games of cards and gossip. I was offered two alternatives: to join either the Polish Army in Russia or the Parachute Brigade. I decided that each was as bad as the other, and applied for both. I was posted to the Parachute Brigade. My colleagues commiserated with me: "The Commander is Sosnkowski," they warned. "Don't you know him? Haven't you heard about him? He is a tyrant." They put the fear of God into me. I couldn't sleep for thinking about parachutes opening and shutting, and sometimes not opening. The next day I reported to Brigade Headquarters.

As I entered, the first sign I saw read "Silence". On another wall: "Don't talk—the enemy is listening." As I walked up the stairs, an officer told me to keep quiet. On the Commander's door there hung another notice: "Silence. No entry without permission."

All of a sudden pandemonium broke out: the door flew open and a middle-aged, strongly built man rushed into the room shouting:

99

"Where is the telephone?" He snatched up the instrument and yelled several words. He listened, scowled and threw it at his aide-de-camp crying:
"Take it—they can't understand a word I say in English."
Silence again descended. Ushered awestricken into the Commander's room, I saluted and introduced myself. A pair of fierce eyes, covered with heavy brows, glared at me.
"So you want to be a parachutist," he grunted. "You will have a medical and do your preliminary training, and we will see what we can make of you."
But the eyes twinkled and I emerged feeling a lot better than when I went in. I had my medical and on the following day reported to the Monkey Grove.
Like the sign that stood at the yawning gates of Dante's Hell, some macabre humourist had painted above the entrance: All hope abandon, ye who enter here.

An instructor told us the course lasted two weeks. "But," he added, "if you fail, you stay on for a further two weeks, and another two weeks, and another, until you pass."
For raw recruits, men whose feet had never left the ground, there came P.T.: Jump, skip, hop. Stand, lie, fall. Arms, legs, heads. Swinging, bending, stretching. Aching, sighing, moaning, groaning. Into a mad Monkey Grove, shouted at by monkey-like men. Jump from fallen trees; somersault forwards, backwards, sideways. Fall gently—GO!—use angle of bones and limbs, fall side of calves, side of knees, thighs, roll onto back of shoulders. Stand up, fall down, stand up and get knocked down. Jump from tree trunks, fall out of windows . . . swing from trees . . . get thrown from trees . . . play monkeys upside down . . . GO! GO! GO! Every other word is GO! . . . brings instinctive reaction . . . GO! means jump . . . we jump in our sleep . . . feet together . . . legs together . . . bend your knees . . . look up . . . bruises, wounds, hurt bodies, hurt pride . . . stronger bodies and stronger minds . . . better men . . . better morale . . . falling, falling, falling . . . keep knees together . . . what a wonderful thing to be a paratrooper!

The pièce de résistance of preliminary training was the Tower. This we had built with a £500 grant from Headquarters. That we managed to get steel girders in wartime was remarkable, but the Sappers got them and built it a hundred feet high; it was a very good way of simulating a parachute drop, without the dangers of the real thing. From the top protruded an arm and under it, hanging on a cable, was an iron circle upon which a parachute canopy was stretched. After climbing the long ladder to the top, a man was fitted into a harness and then hung under the stretched silk, the top of which was attached to a cable. At the press of a button, the cable ran out and the man floated down, just like a normal jump, but without the initial sensation of falling. The instructor could stop the cable halfway, or wherever he pleased, correcting faults during flight and preparing the men for landing. Many of the ideas produced at Largo House were later copied by the British and used with great success at Ringway.

In all the exercises and activities I took a prominent part, so that nobody could turn and say: "It's all right for him to give orders—he doesn't have to carry them out."

I clearly remember parading the officers and men of Brigade Headquarters for the P.T. lesson. We borrowed the local school gymnasium, and what a sight we were! Mostly in underpants, vests and socks. Even the Padre, the Quartermaster and the Administrative Officer were on parade. With stomachs sticking out and rounded shoulders, we slipped and slid on the polished floor like a scene from some comic ballet. I positioned myself in front, so that I could lead the class after being shown the movements by the instructor. After the lesson, however, I ordered them to get proper P.T. kit and said that they were never to turn up again in such an incredible variety of clothing. In spite of rationing, the Quartermaster found enough shorts, vests and plimsolls to go round. Every officer and man in the Brigade had P.T. once a day and, without a medical certificate, there was no excuse. I told the instructors to take it easy to start with, but we ached in every muscle for at least a fortnight and it was extraordinary how stomachs reduced and lungs expanded in such a short time. There was also a remarkable increase in morale; chests stuck out and shoulders were drawn back. Relationship between the officers improved and a greater spirit of camaraderie appeared.

The full pre-parachuting course in Monkey Grove was two weeks, and after that the recruits went to Ringway, where a separate section with Polish instructors had been established. Not only our own men were trained here; we also took on the training commitment for other foreign units, French, Norwegian, Belgian, Dutch, and Czech. I think they preferred being trained by other continentals, and by the end of the war over six hundred of them had passed through our hands.

A second lieutenant of the Brigade described his first impressions of Ringway.

We arrived in Manchester still smothered in bruises from Monkey Grove. A sergeant-major met us at the station and on the journey to the

Parachute School, in disjointed sentences, he revealed a picture of life at Ringway: "Breakfast 0700 hrs. . . . lunch 1230 hrs. . . . best beer is at the Charleston . . . supper 1730 hrs. . . . mustn't sit with W.A.A.F.s—against regulations . . . but if you want girls, plenty at the Charleston. . . . Number 64 bus . . . watch your step: you aren't the first troops at Ringway . . . there are more ways of getting into hospital other than breaking your leg . . . Besides, parachuting and women don't mix."

By the time we arrived at Ringway, we had a very mixed bunch of ideas. We gathered that parachuting from a bomber or transport plane was simple; the excitement came when jumping from a Spitfire. On the first morning, we divided into "sticks" of ten men (a "stick" is the number of parachutists jumping from any one aircraft). On arrival at the vast hangar, known as "Kilkenny's Circus" from the Squadron Leader who invented much of it, a British officer made a short speech and then left us in charge of the Polish instructors.

One of these, Flight Lieutenant Julian Gebolys, was described by Group Captain Newnham as "one of the best parachutists in the world". He was a pioneer in cutting down the oscillation of parachutes, the cause of many casualties. Briefly, this method, now used all over the world, consists of pulling down on the lift webs, thus changing the shape of the canopy and increasing wind resistance. It also has a considerable effect on the manipulation and speed of the parachute.

The same officer described his thoughts on the day he was paraded for the first balloon jump:

It is quite right to get our first jump over and done with . . . but isn't it a little bit windy? . . . why all this hurry? . . . We have only just arrived—there is plenty of time . . . Oh, for Pete's sake, let's get on with it . . . is this parachute all right . . . was it packed properly? . . . it feels heavy and saggy on my back . . . why is the release buckle under my chin, it should be on my belly. . . . Am I nervous? . . . I'll just go and . . . wash my hands.

Parachutes checked, and fitted, we carry them gingerly to the lorry and drive to Tatton Park where "Bessie" the balloon is stationed. The instructor stays in the back of the lorry with us. He tries to make us sing . . . to the tune of "John Brown's Body" "Glory, glory, what a hell of a way to die" he fails . . . he tells a funny story—nobody laughs . . . Perhaps I should not jump today . . . I have a headache . . . it's not my lucky day . . . I'll speak to the instructor and arrange to do it tomorrow . . . I'm sure there's something wrong with this parachute . . . it has a brown stain on the case: is it blood? . . . why on earth did I join the Parachute Brigade? . . . must be mad . . . human beings were made to walk on the ground . . .

if we were meant to jump in the air we would have wings . . . what's that? the wind is too strong . . . rubbish, it's as calm as anything . . . I must jump today—I can't go through this again.

The lorry pulls up with a jerk and, as we jump out near the Y.M.C.A. refreshment van, we see and hear laughing groups of British soldiers. They have reason to laugh: they have finished their jump. High overhead, I hear a voice shout:

"*GO!*"

Looking up, I see a man plummetting towards the earth. From his back streams a strip, then a sack and then a silk canopy, first a bud and then a full-blown flower, which opens, closes slightly as it breathes, and then opens fully.

We put on the 'chutes and our instructor checks us. We march towards the lorry, whose winch is whirring, bringing down the huge bulk of the balloon. Having all made jumps from the tower in Scotland, we are assured that this is much easier. Strangely, we believe it. We get into the basket, which is all hole, metal and canvas. The instructor fastens our straps to a strongpoint and secures each with a pin. At a signal, the winch operator allows the balloon to climb. It is a strange sensation, in spite of the cable one feels terribly insecure. It is ridiculous, because we have parachutes on our backs.

In the basket, all is silence; we avoid looking at each other, but we see the instructor leaning negligently against the cross bar over the hole, looking unconcernedly down. The fabric of the balloon flaps and flops, the air hums through the cables and ropes. A quick glance down through the hole, the figures are very small and the lorry is really only a toy, yet voices still sound remarkably clear. An unexpected bump and the end of our rise is reached; the basket lurches and almost at once the instructor shouts:

"*Action stations, Number One.*"

I hear this through a cloud of cotton wool—it isn't really happening. I see, as through a rain-washed window pane, Number One swing his feet into the hole and look up at the despatcher. Smiling confidently, the instructor holds up a hand yelling:

"*GO!*" and, at the same time, tapping the man on the head.

The basket swings wildly, the man is gone.

"*That was good,*" grunts the N.C.O. "*Don't forget to keep your knees together.*"

I personally can hardly keep my teeth together—they are chattering so much.

"*Actions stations, Number Two!*" is yelled out.

Again a man puts his legs into space and disappears at the command "*Go*".

"*Action Stations, Number Three.*"

103

This is me, my body moves before my mind, my legs dangle into thin air, my eyes fix on the instructor, and all of a sudden the word "Go" enters my body like an electric shock. My hands jerk, my body falls neatly through the hole—I'm falling, falling, falling, but my God, what has happened to the parachute? Then a gentle strain on the harness tells me it is my lucky day and a voice from the ground bellows:

"What sort of fool are you? This is no place for circus clowns: put your feet together."

I am not moving, I am suspended for ever between the green grass of Tatton Park and the blue sky; no, I am not moving, yet the earth is rushing up to hit me.

"Keep your knees together, pull up on the lift webs."

The ground hits me, I collapse and roll, I stand up.

"I've done it! I've done it!" I shout out loud.

But nobody takes any notice. They are all drinking tea and having a smoke by the Y.M.C.A. van. I roll up my 'chute and join them.

And so it was for most of us. All parachutists are afraid and, in my opinion, those who claim otherwise are either liars or very unimaginative.

We were terribly short of the ordinary equipment for infantry training. Ammunition and explosives we had to scrounge. Some of the officers acquired pistols by devious means and, in order to get ammunition, took out civil licences. Many years later, in 1948, a policeman knocked at the door of my London house to ask why I had not renewed my firearms licence. I told him not to worry, the pistol had long been an exhibit in the Polish War Museum. Yet, one way and another, by scrounging and indenting and buying privately, we managed to go ahead with normal training.

Some of our happiest times in Scotland, much of which reminded us of the Carpathian Mountains, was spent out in the wilds. At the end of a hard day's scheme, we would gather round a camp fire to sing old songs of Poland and listen to comrades give well-known renderings of poems and solos.

My men were kept busy and I had courses all over Scotland, climbing, ski-ing, shooting. On one of our expeditions, I remember offering to our British Liaison Officers one evening for supper a dish made from various types of edible fungi. They expressed considerable doubts about this, being under the impression that only mushrooms are worth eating but, fortified with a certain number of double whiskies, they sampled the tasty dish, enjoying it very much.

Some time later, they returned our hospitality, endeavouring to produce a similar meal. However, they got muddled between the various fungi and included several poisonous types. Luckily, whisky again came to our aid and, apart from mild stomach-ache, no ill effects were suffered.

In June 1941, Germany declared war on the Soviet Union. In a broadcast soon afterwards, General Sikorski offered to forget the past and come to an understanding with them. Long and protracted negotiations followed, until the Sikorski-Maiski Agreement was signed. One of the most important points was that a Polish Army was to be formed in the U.S.S.R. General Anders, held prisoner by the Russians, was appointed Army Commander.

Britain immediately despatched by convoy 100,000 uniforms and masses of equipment. The convoy docked safely at Archangel, but much of it never arrived at its destination. Also sent from Britain was a certain number of senior and middle-rank officers, to act as commanders and instructors.

About this time, we were granted the privilege of wearing a special parachute badge. This was in two styles: a poised eagle without a wreath indicated that the wearer was a qualified parachutist, whilst an added golden wreath meant he had jumped into battle.

September 23rd, 1941 was a great day for us. I had particularly wanted the Commander-in-Chief to see the progress made with parachute operations and techniques. I invited him to Scotland for the biggest exercise to date. I borrowed twelve planes from Maurice Newnham and invited several British Airborne commanders and others to come along; amongst them was Brigadier Richard Gale; Brigader Colin Gubbins, of the Economic Warfare Branch; Air Commodore Cedric Porter; and Lord Elgin. Lots of civilian friends gathered on the high ground near Kincraig to watch.

The day before the exercise, General Sikorski's Secretary asked if there was anything special I wanted the Commander-in-Chief to say. I asked him to give us official recognition as the 1st Polish Parachute Brigade.

The day for the scheme was perfect: the twelve planes came over in line ahead formation, dropping the men with great accuracy on the landing zone. Only one plane went wrong and ten men landed near the seashore. This caused consternation in the neighbourhood, as they were mistaken for German invaders because of the strange rubber training hats they were wearing.

The Home Guard turned out and it took the men some time to convince the police they were Poles, not Huns.

After the exercise, which greatly pleased Sikorski, he paraded my men and formally announced that we would be known as the 1st Polish Independent Parachute Brigade.

The 23rd day of the month has strangely cropped up in the life of the Brigade. September brings our Regimental Day; on that day in June we arrived in Scotland after our travels across devastated Europe. On the 23rd July we moved to Eliock and transferred to Fife on the 23rd September 1941. Three years later, on 23rd September 1944, we were fighting at Arnhem.

It was very gratifying to have had my work recognised by the Polish authorities. I had always felt that my unit was an Army bastard, born out of wedlock, unwanted and with most of the qualities and faults of a love-child—strength, stubbornness and determination. We were still desperately short of soldiers, but I would not allow this to depress me and I had worked out a plan whereby—if necessary—a complete Brigade Cadre of officers would be dropped in Poland to take over and command troops already on the spot.

In view of the subsequent friction between myself and other British generals, I would like to record here that for four whole years I worked in close contact with all sorts of British authorities, without any official blessing and never, not even once, did I have a disagreement.

We were granted Parachute pay in February 1943 of two shillings a day, the same as the British, and it was backdated to February 1942. This meant the troops received a sizeable sum of money and it also meant, in my opinion, that the girls would have a wonderful time and that the pubs in our district would do a roaring trade. The troops were paid every ten days and to start with the privates had plenty of girl friends, but as the days went by and money got short, the girls switched their attentions to the junior non-commissioned officers and, progressively, up the ranks to the sergeant-majors. I felt strongly that this money should not be squandered and I suggested they should all contribute to the widows and orphans of Home Army fighters, left helpless in Poland. I addressed them all and made my point:

"This money comes from Heaven [this was not strictly true—I had fought a long battle for it]. You did not expect it; you should not take it all for yourselves; I suggest you give one third of it to the women and children at home." Unanimously, they decided in favour of the suggestion and seven thousand five hundred pounds was sent via an agent, for which sum I later got a receipt from an Underground Commander, after the money had been distributed.

As foreigners in a strange land, we had various difficulties to contend with. I can hardly start to describe the trouble we had with women. At one stage, I sent my Padres and Security Officers round the churches, asking Ministers to warn the congregations that I would not hold myself responsible for what went on between the girls and my troops. I let them know I would not grant permission for marriage to every soldier who applied, not even if a child was born; although, in these cases, I would ensure that the father maintained it.

My mail contained many letters from girls, nearly all on the same theme:

Dear Sir,
I am expecting a baby; Stanley promised to marry me.

Goodness knows how many Stanleys there were in the Brigade; the name is almost as common as Tom, Dick or Harry and only seldom did the girls know a surname. I put a Welfare Officer in charge of the correspondence and he had a full-time job!

One case I remember well. I had given permission for a soldier to marry an English girl and I arranged to meet them both, to give them a bit of fatherly advice. I soon discovered that he spoke not one word of English and she spoke no Polish. After this horrifying revelation, I insisted that no soldiers could marry until they had successfully passed an English examination.

We formed close connections with various towns and eminent people. Lord Elgin had taken a great interest in us and had been very kind to the Brigade. We had wanted for a long time to show our appreciation, when we heard that he was selling a collection of rare coins to raise money for charity. I sent an officer to the auction sale to purchase them and we gave them back to him. He was deeply touched.

Many were the difficulties I had with other Polish Commanders, who were jealous of the success we enjoyed. Sikorski finally agreed that men of other units could volunteer to join my Brigade and instructions were issued accordingly to other formations. One day I received a note from General Kukiel, the Corps Commander, that he was sending me one hundred N.C.O.s. This was a pleasant surprise and I wrote a warm note of thanks. It was not until I started going through their papers that my thanks cooled: my hair almost stood on end as I read on. Nearly all had been found guilty of some offence, including civil crime. It left no doubt in my mind that their commanders had given them the option of joining the Parachute Brigade or going to prison.

Bad conduct sheets often indicate bad man-management, rather than a hardened criminal and, much against regulations, I found an answer to the problem. I had them paraded in the market square of Peetween and addressed them:

"I have looked at your conduct sheets and I know exactly the type of men you are. Yet I am prepared to come to an agreement with you. I am going to forget what I have read and nobody will ever see those conduct sheets again. You will be promoted on merit and treated as N.C.O.s as long as you turn into first class instructors and are a credit to the Brigade. One slip—and only one—and you will be sent to prison for the longest sentence I can obtain for you."

Less than ten per cent of them ever let me down.

We had a visit from the Polish President at the end of the year and he expresed great surprise at the high standard of training achieved. Speaking to one Cadet, he asked if it was too tough.

"No, sir," the youngster replied. "We know where we are going."

The main reason for the very high morale was the plan for us to fight for Poland's liberation. All other Polish units, Army, Navy and Air Force, had been placed under the Supreme Allied Commander for use as and where he thought necessary. We were the only unit remaining under the direct control of the Polish Commander-in-Chief and plans were being made for operations in our homeland.

General Anders visited Moscow at the end of 1941 and made a deal with Stalin, which resulted in some Polish units being sent from Russia to the Middle East. There were Polish formations in Syria, Persia and Palestine, some of whom were needed urgently in England as reinforcements. The British at this time were pressing for the 1st Polish Armoured Division to be brought up to full war establishment, but even so I managed to extract the promise of three hundred men from General Sikorski. When they arrived in September 1942, however, I was appalled by their condition. Many were unfit to be in the army, let alone in a Parachute Brigade. Their physical condition after months of starvation and lack of exercise in concentration camps had left them weak and skinny. Bad food had resulted in swollen stomachs, yet they were perpetually hungry. We gave them special rations and extra vitamins and slowly their health improved. In six months, most of them qualified as parachutists.

Shortly afterwards, the Brigade received official British recognition and we were put on the same war establishment for weapons, equipment and other supplies, without which we could not carry out proper training.

On 21st November 1942 at a parade on Edinburgh Airfield "Boy" Browning presented us with a maroon and blue pennant with a Pegasus on one side and the Polish eagle on the other, inscribed: *1st British Airborne Division to the 1st Polish Parachute Brigade*. It was a proud occasion for us and came, I think, in response to a large silver badge we had given them as a Christmas gift.

The last event of any importance in 1942 was an agreement between General Sikorski and General Sir Alan Brooke, the C.I.G.S., confirming that the Polish Parachute Brigade would stay under Polish command and be used only in Poland. This, as we shall see, caused considerable trouble later.

To close this chapter, I would like to recall one of the most amazing and miraculous parachute accidents of which I ever heard. It concerned one of my lieutenants, an instructor at Ringway, who wrote an account of his escape, which he called a "miracle".

He missed a bus which was to take him to Tatton Park, where he was on duty, but he heard that a group of British instructors was going to drop there. He obtained permission to fly and parachute with them.

The flight was short, he wrote; soon the green jumping light came on and the despatcher was urging the men out of the hole in the belly of the old Whitley bomber. I was number ten and last, and, as we were all instructors, it was our aim to get out and land in the smallest possible area. I followed almost on a colleague's head and, as I fell through the hole, I felt a static line wrap itself round my ankle, pulling me out violently. The slip-stream caught me off balance, whipping me round in a somersault, and my feet hit the rigging lines, which were just coming out of the bag. The lines wrapped themselves round it, preventing the canopy from opening. Looking up in horror, I saw a great long stretch of rigging lines, all tangled and jumbled, like a skein of wool. Desperately I pulled and jerked, but to no avail, I went on falling at increasing speed. The most ridiculous thoughts shot through my mind: I would break my legs and be unable to dance with the pretty girls at the Red Cross; I should never see my parents again and the Chief Parachute Instructor would be very angry with me. With all my heart, I prayed to God—Jesus, only You can save me.

This all happened in a couple of seconds, as I plummetted down, and then the miracle happened. A gust of wind blew me slightly to one side and I crashed into the branches of a tree—a lone tree in a huge wide open space —my body smashed through thick branches and twigs tore at my clothing and skin; I broke through the lower branches and then, with a violent jerk, I stopped just a few inches above the ground, the unopened parachute and lines entangled in the tree preventing me from smashing to a jelly on the hard ground.

Not a bone was broken and he soon returned to duty. Such accidents were luckily very rare and we all had great confidence in our 'chutes and the W.A.A.F.s who packed them.

Chapter VII

COLOURS FROM WARSAW

A MILLION stars twinkled in a vast midnight-blue sky, and a group of men and women in the deep shadows of a copse shivered and shook under the almost physical weight of the extreme cold.

It was December 1941: tree branches drooped heavily with the weight of snow and all round was virgin white, untouched by footprint, apart from the lone two-clawed trail of a hare. A thickly-built man, his face almost obscured by a fur cap, glanced at the luminous dial of his watch and in a quiet voice whispered:

"Take up your positions."

The group dissolved, each to a prearranged spot, with hooded torches ready to flash signals into the sky. Eyes and ears watched and listened intently.

They were members of the Polish Underground Army, waiting near Warsaw for the arrival of a plane from Britain bringing agents and supplies. The people on the landing zone had broken the German-imposed curfew, well aware that a house to house check revealing their absence would result not only in their execution, but in the murder of their families too.

Faintly, through the thin air, they heard the drone of heavy aircraft engines, but the sound passed and faded well south of them. After two hours, by which time their joints were stiff and fingers bloodless, they wended their way back to the copse. The leader grunted:

"Same time tomorrow. We must come every night until they arrive."

One by one, each in a different direction, they trod wearily back to their beds for a couple of hours' sleep before attending to their normal everyday jobs.

Operation "Jacket", as far as they were concerned, was delayed for another twenty-four hours.

Yet, unknown to them, Operation "Jacket" was well and truly launched. Even as they trudged homewards, German troops, and the Polish agents they had been waiting for, were fighting just on the other side of the demarcation line. The pilot had mistaken the area, dropped them into that part of Poland incorporated by Hitler into the Reich, slap bang into the midst of a German patrol. Six agents had jumped and got involved in the skirmish which commenced as they landed; two of them, Effendi—cover name for Lieutenant Swiatkowski—and Lieutenant Jurecki stayed on the spot to fight and ordered the others to escape over the border at all costs. The party was carrying secret documents and fresh funds for the Underground. Both Effendi and his companion were killed in the engagement which, for them, was preferable to capture.

Captain Kalenkiewicz, who took over leadership of the group, was wounded in the arm when they were ambushed by a border patrol, but they reached Warsaw and made their contacts, splitting up to carry out their assignments. Owing to his wound Kalenkiewicz remained hidden as the German police were on the look-out for a wounded man, having found blood stains in the snow. He stayed in the house of a patriot with several British airmen who had been shot down and were awaiting an opportunity for escape. A surgeon, brought secretly to the hide-out, treated him and set his arm in plaster.

Captain Kalenkiewicz had trained at the Monkey Grove and shared the fervent desire of all of us in the Brigade to have a flag presented by Warsaw City. Before he left on his mission, I mentioned to him the possibility of somehow getting one made and smuggled back to Britain.

During his period of enforced idleness, he was attended by a pretty young nurse who, from time to time, called to dress his arm. She worked for an Underground Medical Unit under the cover name Martha and her help was enlisted to trace the famous novelist, Mrs. Zofia Kossak, an ardent patriot. Martha did not know her personally but some days later she mentioned her quest to a Mrs. Maria Kann, who knew her whereabouts. By devious means, a meeting was arranged and one afternoon, taking strict precautions, the two ladies visited Kalenkiewicz who told them about our Parachute Brigade and that its task was to help in the liberation of Warsaw. He then revealed our most earnest desire to have a colour presented by the city.

These two women organised a collection throughout the capital; rich and poor alike were asked to contribute and it was amazing how everyone rallied round and how the secret was kept from the enemy troops and Gestapo agents, who swarmed like blue-bottles in the city. Well-known artists were invited to enter a competition for the design of the flag. We had indicated roughly the devices to be shown, but left the lay-out of the pattern to the competitors. They worked in private in their studios and final drawings were sent to a committee, which chose the one submitted by a young architect, Mr. Michael Nowicki.

His design followed the formal lines used for hundreds of years on Polish military flags and pennants. The main cloth was in crimson silk; on one side were the national arms of Poland with the eagle and crown and the Warsaw City Coat of Arms; in each corner was a parachute badge. The reverse side depicted Saint Michael the Archangel, patron saint of parachutists; above was the inscription *Warsaw 1942*, and below, expressing the desire of all patriots, the motto *Surge Polonia*.

The Colour Committee sat regularly in the nuns' quarters attached to the Church of the Deaconesses in Theatre Place. Extreme caution was necessary, as at this time the Gestapo was very active and hardly a day went by without some member of the Underground being arrested. Outside the building where they talked, passers-by were stopped and asked for identification papers; houses close by were entered and searched, but luckily the church and nunnery were left alone.

But the risks were great. One day, Mrs. Kann, returning from a visit to her brother, was carrying a plaster cast he had made of our parachute badge. With this in her hand and secret papers relating to Underground activities in her handbag, she was stopped in the street by a German patrol. Dropping the cast on the ground, she trod it into a meaningless pile of plaster and she put some of the papers into her mouth, but was unable to swallow them all. She was taken to a Police Station and interrogated by an officer. The sergeant in charge of the patrol handed over the remaining papers. After looking at them and asking her a few pointless questions, he tore the documents into small pieces, tossed them into a wastepaper basket and released her. She was very surprised, as the papers were highly incriminating and she could only presume that the officer was a member of the Underground Army who had inveigled himself into an official position.

The next problem was to get the materials—and nothing but the best was good enough. No cloth was available and clothing and material shops were shut. Gold thread and heavy embroidery silks were unobtainable. Professor Adamczewski heard of their plight and, from a large collection of historical gowns, presented the crimson robe of Cardinal Dunajewski, an eighteenth-century church dignitary. This gave to the colour a most unusual and historical background. A search was instituted to find Mrs. Madalinska, the old lady who owned the workshops which for years had embroidered military flags. The shop was closed because of the Occupation, but the old lady gathered together some of her seamstresses, discovered a quantity of gold and silver thread and secretly they set to work on the intricate artistic project. Eventually a work of beauty emerged from the silks and their devoted fingers. It was almost a year before the colour was completed and ready for handing over.

Consecration of the flag was arranged for November 3rd, 1942, in the Church of the Deaconesses at 6.30 p.m. The Guard of Honour consisted of Captain Kalenkiewicz and two other parachute agents who, under the Chicago-style pseudonyms of Little John and Stork, were members of diversion units fighting the Germans in Poland and Russia.

Polish military colours, following ancient custom, always have godmothers as a symbol of all the women who sacrifice their sons for their country. Godmothers to our colour were Mrs. Maria Kann and Mrs. Zofia Kossak, who had guided the plan through at great risk to themselves.

As the hour of the dedication service neared, solitary figures crossed Theatre Place, quietly making their way into the side entrance of the nunnery. Inside an unlit doorway stood one of the ladies, allowing in only those who knew the password. She directed them down a long dark corridor, which led to the church. A few candles lit the high altar, their bright haloes accentuating the pitch-black body of the church and shadowy figures, which crossed and recrossed the candle-light like black moths. Only a shuffling and rustle of clothing could be heard and odd whispered instructions.

Very few people were invited to the ceremony, but they represented all who had risked their lives in its preparation and the soldiers who were to carry it in battle.

The whispers and the shuffling died, as the robed figure of Father Krause appeared ghostlike at the rails of the altar. Climbing to the top step and kneeling with his face lifted to heaven, he cried to God for His infinite mercy on those assembled in His house and for the protection and furtherance of their plans.

The Guard of Honour and the Godmothers knelt by the colour laid out on a crimson satin cushion. It was a ceremony of high emotion: this colour in the midst of Warsaw, in a country occupied and divided by enemies, was a symbol of victory to come. It represented the feeling of all true Poles. The wavering light of the altar candles reflected blood red on the silken colour—perhaps as a sign of the blood that would be spilt in its honour. Father Krause, his hands in urgent supplication, asked God Almighty to bless and protect the colour, to guide the feet of its defenders and bring to a successful conclusion the high aims set by those whose only object was a free Poland.

As silently as it had come, the congregation disappeared into the blacked-out streets; a few only retired to the vestry to drink a glass of wine in solemn celebration of the event. Then they too dispersed. Little John and Stork went back to the Underground fronts, the others to less spectacular but vital tasks.

But how was the colour to be brought to London? A number of agents were entering Poland by air and other means, but few were leaving; those whose duties took them back to Britain were incapable of carrying the flag. So for months it lay hidden and many times the hiding place was changed. Finally, it was sewn into the cassock of a priest and hung in the vestry of the Church of the Grey Sisters, where it remained until the spring of 1944.

Then it was arranged to evacuate some important people from Poland to Britain in an operation named "Bridge". An airstrip was secretly prepared near Belzyce, about one hundred miles south-east of Warsaw. There were five passengers: three army officers, including General Tatar Tabor, and two politicians, Vice-Minister Stanislawski and Mr. Berezowski. The flag was taken to Belzyce and, when the plane touched down on the airstrip and the passengers hurried aboard, the colour was taken with them. Wrapped with the flag came a letter addressed to the Brigade, expressing the sentiments of the citizens of Warsaw and the eagerness with which they awaited the day when we would drop from the skies to liberate them.

Varying fates awaited those who had helped so much with the making and safe-guarding of the flag. Mrs. Kossak was arrested by the Gestapo when hawking Underground papers. Sent to Auschwitz, she was lucky to survive. Today, like Mrs. Kann, she lives in Warsaw. Captain Kalenkiewicz was killed in battle commanding a Partisan group. Little John was killed in the Warsaw siege. The Stork was arrested at Pinsk in Eastern Poland and brutally tortured in an effort to get him to disclose the names of his comrades. Frightened that he might give way under further torture, this brave man committed suicide just one day before Underground battle units attacked the prison and liberated all the inmates.

General Sosnkowski handed the flag over to me in London on the 29th April 1944 and ordered me to prepare a presentation ceremony. It was still incomplete, as in Poland they had been unable to put a fringe round the cloth, and the staff needed a silver eagle. The arrival of the colour was kept from everyone, apart from three of us who did the additional work on it. The main problem was the eagle. I then remembered that the colour from my old Brigade, the Children of Warsaw, had been brought to London and I thought it would be a happy union if I had the eagle from it copied and placed on the new colour from Warsaw. For me of course it was a very happy arrangement, symbolising my old and new commands.

On the 15th June 1944 the whole Brigade assembled at Cupar. Never before had they paraded as one body and with full equipment they made an impressive sight. I was very proud of them.

Seated watching was President Raczkiewicz with most of the Polish Cabinet and General Staff. Other visitors included high-ranking British and Allied officers.

It was a double occasion for me, because only the previous day my promotion to major-general had come through officially. The troops took this promotion to mean that they also were raised in official status. Quite spontaneously they cheered when I first appeared after the notice. That night, unknown to me, a group of them melted down silver coins to make badges of rank, which they presented to me prior to the dedication parade. If ever a commander needed confirmation of the love of his troops, that was it.

On the parade ground a High Altar was erected and the colour was laid on a table before it ready for the blessing and the handing-over. A priest pronounced the Benediction and celebrated High Mass; then my Order of the Day was read to all present. It closed with the words: *This colour signifies the start of our battles which will end on the fields of Poland; we shall not deceive those who made it, we shall bring it victoriously again to our beloved Warsaw.*

Vice-Minister Staniszewski then took up the colour from the table and, turning to the President, asked him to present it to the Parachute Brigade. Rising from his chair and receiving the colour into his hands, he turned to where I was kneeling with the Colour Party and passed it to me. In turn, I rose to my feet, handed it to the Guard of Honour and ordered them to troop it round every unit. As they marched along the ranks, the President with his voice full of emotion, proclaimed:

"This colour is a priceless treasure, which shows the union

existing between our beloved occupied country and you soldiers, fighting abroad for our freedom."

Then spoke the Commander-in-Chief:

"This colour is the measure of your obligations. This is a sign of the faith which the people of Warsaw hold in you. As you accept it, so do you accept the love and faith of your countrymen. Men of the 1st Polish Parachute Brigade, never let down the faith which has been entrusted with you."

The red silk fluttered in a light summer breeze and, as the colour approached each unit, the commander ordered the ranks to present arms. And so every man in the Brigade saw the colour, realised its significance and the greatness of the occasion.

CHAPTER VIII

TACTICS AND POLITICS

IN MARCH 1944 General Montgomery came to Scotland on his
pre-invasion tour of all fighting units. He particularly asked
to see the Parachute Brigade and we thought this most significant, as at that time we were under Polish Command and not
committed in any way to 21st Army Group.

I took three parachute companies to the 1st Armoured Divisional area. The senior officers, paraded in best uniforms, complete with our famous square hats, our boots and buttons shining
brightly, all felt a little odd when Monty arrived in a casual
battle dress, wearing his well-known two-badge beret. When
he inspected my troops, he looked at them closely, shoving his
sharp sensitive nose up into their faces, and then turned to me
at the end, saying:

"You have first class soldiers—they will kill everybody."

"No, sir, enemies only," I replied.

Monty laughed loudly in a high-pitched way and slapped his
hands together in glee. Then he asked the troops to break ranks,
gather round his jeep and sit on the grass. Standing on the bonnet,
he went off into one of his battle-rousing speeches in English,
which few of my men were able to understand. Some of them,
fresh from Russia, compared it to Commissars' meetings they had
seen and heard in the Red Army and puzzled what it could all
mean.

"Were these military or political instructions?" they asked
later.

But this incident was well ahead of our starting on the twisted
path leading to our readiness for battle. I had many other bloodless battles to fight before coming to grips with the Germans.

In 1941, when I was producing the nucleus of my Brigade, airborne operations were still very much in their infancy. The
Germans had used them with success, but their lessons were only
partly available to us. The Allies, working separately and
organising in their own ways, did not know what each other was
doing. Also in every Army there was considerable opposition

from senior generals who did not believe in airborne troops. These were similar to those in the First World War who did not believe in the tank and still thought that cavalry was the method of bringing mobility to a battle-field. An example of this neglect was that even in 1942 a Combined Operations pamphlet issued by Lord Louis Mountbatten devoted only one paragraph of four and a half lines to Airborne Forces; yet there were fifteen lines on ways and means of fighting sea-sickness.

A group of three of my younger officers, wrote a pamphlet at this time giving their concepts of parachute operations. I read it, found it full of sound ideas and allowed them to send a copy to Mr. Churchill. The Prime Minister acknowledged this later and I often wondered if it in any way influenced the great interest he always took in airborne operations.

On Salisbury Plain British Airborne troops were being trained and new techniques evolved. In charge was Major-General Frederick Browning, later to become Allied Airborne Corps Commander. Only shortly after I had started organising my parachutists in November 1941, my Army Headquarters suggested that it might be a good thing for me to go and meet him, as it would be a useful liaison. I wrote and was invited down.

In spite of his nickname—Boy—I was surprised to find such a very young-looking senior officer. He was impeccably dressed and not a crease was out of place. His welcome was warm and we had a long and friendly talk about mutual problems; when I explained that my parachutists would be used in the liberation of Poland, he later said he would also like to see them dropped in Northern France to encourage the Polish miners in revolt. I replied politely that this would please me, but the decision rested with my Government. As a result of this visit, we later obtained a lot of equipment and other help from Browning's organisation, with whom we established very friendly relations.

This liaison brought me into conflict with the 4th British Liaison Mission to the Polish Forces in Edinburgh, who complained to the War Office that I was by-passing them, leaving them in the dark as to what was going on. Browning persuaded Whitehall to let us deal directly.

The first time Browning came to see my units in Scotland was in September 1942 on the occasion of our First Anniversary exercise. He flew up on the day previous to the manoeuvres and I met him in the Leven Officers' Club. While we chatted over a drink, he asked if I was sure I would get all the reinforcements I needed.

"I don't know," I said, "but the Commander-in-Chief has promised them."

Then, turning to me confidentially, within the hearing of my aide, he made me an amazing offer:

"I would like you in command of an Airborne Division, which would consist of Polish and British troops."

It was a startling proposal and quite a temptation, although completely contrary to my plans. It would not be true for me to say that I was not honoured; yet I was forced to reply that the idea must be put before the Commander-in-Chief—such a decision was not for me.

Early the following morning, I made a point of speaking to General Sikorski about this idea. What ensued from this I never learnt, because the subject was never mentioned to me again. What is more, Browning did not attend the exercise: he only flew over the area in his plane and went straight back to southern England. There is no doubt in my mind that what he really wanted was to get the Brigade under British command.

At this time, Browning was very worried over the lack of British Parachute volunteers. They were not coming forward in the numbers required, in spite of widespread publicity and pay inducements. They were also having a constant drain of casualties, mainly through broken bones. In my opinion, the British carried out far too many training jumps. When I explained my point of view to Brigadier Richard Gale, telling him that Polish paratroopers only jumped when absolutely necessary, he replied that he thought that a lower physical standard should be allowed and that men could always be toughened up later. It was the plan to have three British Airborne Divisions, although in fact this target was never reached. Two divisions, 1st and 6th (which included a Canadian battalion), an Independent Brigade Group and the Special Air Service Brigade was the maximum ever achieved. There were also considerable difficulties with aeroplanes. The Royal Air Force, always reluctant to supply the Army with transport, had put at their disposal a limited number of aeroplanes, mostly old and largely worn-out, including at different times Whitleys (Old Cows), Albemarles and Halifaxes, all with different speeds and operating ranges.

In March 1943, I heard from my aide-de-camp, who was attached to Browning's Headquarters for experience of British methods, that Browning was thinking of writing to General Sikorski asking that my Polish units should be given to him for a single operation in France. The operation was to last only two or three days and my troops would then revert to Polish command. At the same time, he intended to express his disbelief that the Brigade would ever be able to fly direct from Britain to Poland. I do not know if this letter was ever sent to the Commander-in-Chief, but I do know that a special Parachute Company, completely separate from my command, had already been allocated for special use in France with the Resistance under the control of the Polish Ministry of Defence in collaboration with the British Government.

Relations between my Headquarters and Browning's set-up were first class and at all levels we made lots of friends, not only with the British Army, but also with the Royal Air Force. I was most surprised one morning at breakfast to be handed a telegram from General Browning, which read: *Hearty congratulations on your promotion to Major-General.* I was very taken aback, because I had no such information. There had been plenty of rumours, but I was well aware of the difficulties, one of them being that there were many senior officers with very few prospects of promotion; probably the biggest bugbear was the fear of some of the general staff:

"He is difficult enough as a colonel; God knows what he will be like as a general!"

However, I was not too worried; promotion does not come automatically in the Polish Army. There are no temporary ranks in our forces and it was quite normal to find a comparatively junior rank carrying out the job of a colonel or of a brigadier. In a perverse sort of way, it also gave me a slight hold over my officers who could be told, when complaining of lack of promotion:

"You are dissatisfied in your present rank—what about me?"

I was, however, concerned about them; some had been in the same rank for years and it was particularly galling for the cadets. General Sikorski later agreed that they could be promoted to second-lieutenant.

Promotion was better outside the Parachute Brigade, as we had more than enough officers, and many of the people I sacked as unsuitable were later promoted, whilst the officers I retained remained in their ranks. At a Promotion Conference at Corps Headquarters one day, I had recommended one of my Lieutenants to be raised to Captain, using the words: "He is a good officer." An elderly general read this and commented: "If he is only good, that is not enough."

I broke in angrily, stating that when I described a Parachute officer as good, it meant he was the equivalent of excellent or outstanding, as claimed by commanders of more orthodox units.

Two months later in May, General Browning flew up to Scotland to see me again. Within a very short time, he was back on his favourite subject:

"When will your Brigade join my Airborne Forces?"

I gave my usual reply: "It is up to my Commander-in-Chief."

Browning then informed me with a smile: "I am trying to persuade General Sikorski to cancel his agreement with General Alan Brooke, so that you and your men can fight with us on the Second Front. You don't really think—do you—that it is possible for the Polish Parachute Brigade to drop in Poland while the war is on? I don't think it is."

My retort to this was: "It's all very well your talking about using my Brigade in Europe, but from where will I get the reinforcements for an operation in Poland, which I shall most certainly need after fighting on the Continent? You know very well, General, that paratroopers aren't made in a day: it takes a long time to train them."

But Browning, confident and optimistic, broke in.

"Don't worry about replacements for your operation in Poland; I shall give you as many British paratroopers as you want."

I made no comment on this, thinking that he was just trying to impress me.

Then he added, almost as an afterthought: "If it were up to me, I should be delighted to carry out an operation with you in Poland."

During this same meeting, I learned that General Edward Grasett, Chief of the Liaison Mission to the Poles, had already asked General Sikorski to move my Brigade from Scotland down to Salisbury Plain. In some ways this would have been to our advantage: we would have been closer to 38 Group Royal Air Force, which supplied all the planes, and it would have put us in the centre of the British Airborne area. The 6th Division, under Major-General Richard Gale, was being formed there.

There were also disadvantages to the plan, which I explained to Browning:

"I am expecting reinforcements from the Middle East; all arrangements have been made and I have the equipment for training them. Apart from this, I also have men scattered all over Scotland on courses, so it is out of the question for some time."

General Browning was very disappointed, as this projected move was all part of his plan to get my units under his command as quickly as possible. Some time later, he wrote to the Commander-in-Chief asking again for the Brigade to be placed under his command, to which he received a reply to the effect that the Parachute Brigade was to remain under the control of the Polish General Headquarters, but advice and assistance would always be welcomed.

From then on, it seemed to me that our difficulties multiplied. Planes for exercises, which had always been scarce, became almost impossible to get. Accommodation which I needed for housing my reinforcements could not be found. I cannot dismiss all these incidents as imagined or coincidence; I am positive it was all part of a move to get us out of Scotland and under British command.

I feel that I should make it clear here that the whole of the Polish Army of a hundred thousand men in the Middle East and also those Polish troops in Britain were at the disposal of the Allied High Command. My parachutists were the only troops kept in reserve by the Polish Government for use in the liberation of our own country.

As part of progressive training, I arranged with Brigadier James Hill, Commander of the Third British Parachute Brigade, for a small exercise between a company of his troops and mine. The exercise was a disaster and everything seemed to go wrong. The British flew up from Salisbury in Whitleys to drop on Tents Muir on the tip of the Fife peninsular, adjoining the Firth of Tay. The date is engraved on my mind: the 13th of June 1943. It was a windy day and, because of high gusts, we almost had to cancel it, but it remained just within the very strict limits set by safety regulations. One of the aircraft, however, dropped most of the men into the sea, luckily in the shallows, and they were able to wade ashore. One man was seriously injured when a comrade dropped a kit bag on his head from a great height. Yet another plane let go all its paratroopers over the middle of the Firth of Tay: five were drowned and one lucky man, his parachute bellying like the sail of a yacht, was blown to safety on the shore.

I later heard of a sequel to this disaster which struck me as a case of carrying regulations a bit far. A British officer told me that in the aircraft from which the men had jumped to their death was a British paratrooper who looked out of the hole and, seeing water, said:

"Not bloody likely!"

He refused to jump, thus saving his life. I was told that, regardless of the untimely end of his comrades, this man later faced a Court Martial for refusing to jump.

The next time General Sikorski came to see how training was progressing, he arrived quite unexpectedly. I was quite pleased to show him how we were getting on. During his short visit, I spoke my mind to him. I had already received a few reinforcements back in August 1942, but we were still only a skeleton of a brigade.

"Sir, do you really want a Parachute Brigade Group that is fit and capable of going into Poland?" I queried. "Because if you do, I must have reinforcements—and the only place where I can get them quickly is from the General Depot. Will you give me permission to do this?"

He agreed and, although it made me very unpopular with other Polish commanders, I chose fit and healthy men at the Depot and was able to train them rapidly. They were not all volunteers. I saw no reason to have gaps in my ranks as, in my opinion, a pressed man could easily be as useful as a volunteer—just the reverse of British belief.

Shipments of thousands of Polish troops from the Middle East arrived in Scotland during 1943. I was not in the least impressed with those allocated to my units and I soon realised that half of those I accepted suffered from malaria. Half the others were starved and physically weak and a small number of pitiful human wrecks I had to reject as completely unfit and unsuitable. Even with these welcome additions, I was still several hundred men short in my order of battle.

One day, sitting in my office, I was surprised to hear strains of Polish military marches coming from a brass band. Looking out from the window, I saw bandsmen in Polish uniforms striding up and down a path. I sent the Duty Officer to find out what it was all about, as I had not been told to expect such a visit. Five minutes later he returned, grinning broadly, accompanied by the Bandmaster, whom he introduced.

"Sir," he said, "some of us volunteered to join the Parachute Brigade and rather than break up the band, we encouraged the other members to join too. So I have the honour to present you with a complete military band!"

It was a delight to have them and they played for parades and gave many concerts.

* * * * *

A most tragic blow fell on the Polish nation on the 4th July 1943, when an aircraft carrying General Sikorski and his party crashed at Gibraltar, killing everyone on board. Sikorski was not only

Prime Minister and Commander-in-Chief; he had our complete confidence and faith and had been a guiding star in the midst of all the chaos and disasters that had struck us. Killed with him was my old friend General Klimecki, the Chief of Staff, and Colonel Marecki, Director of Training, who had been such a wonderful help to me in putting forward my theories and plans on airborne operations.

General Sosnkowski was appointed Commander-in-Chief.

Visitors to the Brigade were sometimes surprised to hear American voices among the troops and would ask the reason. Before the United States entered the war, quite a few Americans volunteered to serve with foreign armies as soldiers of fortune. Some men in my units were Americans of Polish descent, with strong sentimental attachments to the "old country". When America entered the war, most of them transferred to the American forces. One, however, refused to go. His name was Richard Tice and he was not of Polish descent. As far as we could ascertain, he was a good character and not wanted by the American authorities for any crime or misbehaviour. Considerably puzzled, I had him brought to me for interview. I told him the various advantages of going into the American Army: better allowances, fantastic parachute pay, wonderful pensions and other benefits. His answer in a slow drawl quite took me aback:

"Sir, I learned at school that in the American War of Independence, many Poles helped us win our freedom. Names such as Kosciuszko, and Pulawski who fought and died in the battle of Savannah, are known to all Americans. In Washington there is a memorial to Kosciuszko close by the White House. I am not comparing myself to a national hero, but I would like to make a small contribution to your struggle."

I was deeply touched. He learned Polish—which was not easy for him—and was later commissioned. He dropped with us at Arnhem and was killed; I have no doubt in my mind that, in his own way, he had made a tremendous contribution towards peace and his heart was that of a true patriot.

After a trial period, while they watched and assessed us, the Scots in Fife took us to their hearts and in September 1943 the kind ladies presented us with a colour made by their own hands. On the 23rd of the month, which was the Second Anniversary of the Brigade, we paraded in the Leven Football Stadium and the colours were presented to us by Lady Victoria Wemyss, Lady-in-Waiting to Queen Elizabeth. Present at the parade was Lord Elgin, the Lord Lieutenant of Fife, local dignitaries and military representatives of the British and their Allies. It was a very heart-warming ceremony and gratifying that we had been accepted as part of the community.

Our life settled down into more of a routine and I recalled the experience of soldiers after the First World War and our own war with the Bolsheviks, who, because they had fought instead of staying at school, found themselves at a disadvantage with their civilian contemporaries and well down the unemployment list. With excellent co-operation, Edinburgh University opened a special faculty for Polish medical students, while Liverpool had a technical section for us. I started evening classes in the Brigade and it was very satisfactory when, in this spring of 1944, over three hundred Certificates of Technical Education were awarded to men of my Brigade by the Polish Ministry of Education.

There were Polish commanders who looked askance at this idea, as it had never been done before in our country. Yet I found it produced more intelligent soldiers and, when they were demobilised, often in strange foreign lands, their educational abilities put them ahead in the post-war rush for jobs.

In December I went to Buckingham Palace, and at an investiture I was made a Commander of the British Empire.

Christmas dinner, 1943, was for me luxurious and so enormous that I could not possibly eat all that was put before me. In spite of rationed Britain, as a first-class passenger on board the *Queen Elizabeth*, I was served with what seemed to be a full peace-time menu. We crossed the Atlantic at full speed, unescorted, avoiding the haunts of the German submarine wolf packs, which lurked in the icy waters, awaiting convoys which formed the life-lines between America and Britain.

Before he died, General Sikorski had arranged for me to visit the States, primarily to find out if they could supply us with planes to fly the return journey from England to Poland. It was also a good opportunity to see the latest advances in airborne equipment and tactics. I was delighted to find, on arrival, that the existence of my Brigade was not unknown in America, and I was very warmly welcomed. I was amazed at the advances the Americans had made in the dropping of not only men, but also heavy kit, such as anti-tank guns and field howitzers, using clusters of large parachutes. Back in England, we still flew our aircraft in line ahead formation, dropping men in lone groups of ten. Yet in America, I watched in fascination hundreds of planes in tight wing-to-wing formation drop thousands of men in a matter of minutes. They used giant aircraft towing two gliders each, which could travel for hundreds of miles. They were capable of carrying out all airborne operations by day or night, equally well.

I travelled the length and breadth of that vast country within a few weeks and was most impressed with American hospitality. One very disheartening thing I learnt—or rather, it was a strong impression I got—was that Europe had been divided into two distinct parts for operations: Britain and America were responsible solely for the Western front; Russia took care of the East. They were fighting one war, but in two completely separate departments. This was important, because it meant the Western Powers had no say about strategy in Poland.

Another picture of wartime America which lingers with me is a very domestic one. Often I stayed in bachelor officers' quarters and was horrified by the vast communal lavatories and washrooms in these camps; there was absolutely no privacy and the most private functions were carried out in full public view. I made a point of rising late—or very early—thus avoiding the back-slapping, chummy atmosphere of the rush hours!

After the States, I made a quick trip to Canada, where I spent a couple of days at the Canadian Parachute School at Camp Shilo, Manitoba. By the huge gateway, an enormous notice urged the troops: *Don't think about women—think about the war.* The sergeant instructor at Ringway would have heartily agreed: obviously here too they thought that women and war do not mix. I noticed, in spite of the warning, the walls of the Officers' Club were smothered with nude and near-nude pictures of girls!

The Canadians were also well advanced with airborne techniques, and I admired them greatly for jumping in sub-zero temperatures on to ground iron hard with frost. It was bitterly cold in Manitoba. Canadian hospitality is world famous: we seemed to consume quite a number of bottles of whisky during my stay.

The return journey to Scotland was in an unheated, unpressurized Liberator, flying at thirty thousand feet. It was extremely uncomfortable as we sat hunched up, shivering, sucking in oxygen from masks. We were also ordered to wear Mae Wests, which may have kept us a little warmer, but certainly would not have been much use in the icy Atlantic. The plane touched down at Prestwick on the 16th February 1944.

I was in a great hurry to be back: no commander likes to be away from his troops too long, particularly when great decisions are in the offing. There was still lots to do; I was still short of five hundred men, in spite of the Middle East reinforcements; I had men who had not completed the parachute course, because priority had been given to the British; I was not given any aircraft for combat training; I lacked supplies, especially heavy equipment and transport, and I had no artillery.

Before leaving for America, I had heard that pressure was being put on General Sosnkowski by the Chief of the Imperial General Staff, General Sir Alan Brooke, and in order to find out the latest situation I went down to London on February 20th to see the Commander-in-Chief and to report on my American visit. He told me that correspondence was continuing and he was expecting to get a letter from General Grasett in a few days, giving the British side of the question. With this information, I returned to Scotland.

Whilst in London, I took the opportunity to call at the War Office to see General Sir Kenneth Crawford, the Director of Land/Air Warfare. I had met him on several occasions and had been impressed not only with his extreme severity and dictatorial attitude, but particularly by the results he obtained. In America I had seen the paratroopers using the 75-millimetre mountain howitzer and I had determined that this was the best possible gun for use with airborne troops. It was easily air transportable and quick to bring into action. I asked Crawford if he could supply my artillery battery with these guns. None had yet arrived in Britain, but he said straightaway, in spite of my unorthodox approach:

"I shall let you have the very first which arrive—I cannot refuse you."

I had even more reason to be grateful to him in 1945, when I was trying to get my son out of Poland. Stas had been badly wounded and was gradually losing his sight; he was in need of the best possible medical attention. Crawford, then Deputy Chief of the Imperial General Staff, went to endless trouble to help in the negotiations to get my son to England and it was mainly through his efforts that Stas came to Britain, although it was too late to save his sight.

Early in March, Colonel Christopher Peto, newly-appointed Chief of the 4th British Liaison Mission to Polish Forces in Scotland called at my Headquarters to introduce himself and, during our conversation, he informed me that General Montgomery was very keen to have the Brigade in 21st Army Group. I really was getting a bit fed up with all the chatter as to where my Parachute Brigade should be used and where it should not be used. I spoke rather firmly to Peto:

"It is nothing to do with me where the Brigade is used. I am only the commander and it is my job to train my men for war; I will take them wherever my Commander-in-Chief tells me. Last year I told Browning that the best solution for him was to give me the supplies and help me to complete training. If my Brigade is not ready, it will be no use to anyone."

Two days later I went down to Salisbury Plain and saw General Browning. He informed me that he had heard "on the grape vine" that we would certainly fight on the Western front.

"After an operation in Europe," he said, "you will come back to Britain, collect reinforcements and go to Warsaw. But we must hurry. I am very keen to have you with me."

"Not me," I interjected, "but my Brigade."

I had heard all this before and, as far as I was concerned, nothing had been decided, so I said:

"Until I am told of such a decision, I shall keep my keenness for fighting in Poland." I then asked: "In what sort of organisation do you see my Brigade fighting?"

"As an Independent Brigade Group," he replied. "As soon as the decision is final you will get the full complement of equipment and material."

On March 11th, General Sosnkowski received a letter written on behalf of the Chief of the Imperial General Staff. It was a formal proposal from the War Office, asking to use the Brigade in Europe and laying down conditions which they thought acceptable to us. These were as follows:

(a) *The Brigade will be in reserve to the Allied Airborne Forces and will not be employed in the initial operations unless necessity demands it.*

(b) *Should the Brigade suffer severe casualties, which might be described as being of the order of 25%, it will be withdrawn and not committed to further operations until it has again been made up to strength.*

(c) *When an opportunity arises for employing the Brigade in Poland, it will be placed at the disposal of the Polish Commander-in-Chief. It is not possible at this stage to give a definite guarantee on the subject of aircraft, but every effort will be made to release aircraft for the transport of the Brigade to Poland.*

Two days later Monty visited us in Scotland and, as I said previously, we thought this most significant.

I was called to see the Commander-in-Chief. I pointed out that when a reserve unit is put into battle, it is normally thrown in where the fighting is heaviest. Secondly, we were already under our war establishment, and from where would come the twenty-five per cent reinforcements? The letter indicated that if we got them, and it was not then possible to fly to Poland, then we would again be used in Europe.

To General Sosnkowski I pointed out that the training of reinforcements, particularly specialist troops, would take six months. I gave examples of what had happened to British airborne troops: after Tunisia in 1942, the 1st Brigade was not used again until 1943 in Sicily. After the Sicily operation, the 1st Division did not go into action again until Arnhem. We would have to face the possibility of the Polish Brigade being used with many partially-trained troops. I reiterated my points and said that as my troops would not get to Ringway before April, the units could not be ready before August 1944.

On March 14th, the Polish Cabinet decreed that we could be used in Europe, under certain conditions. I was called in to plan details. The conditions put forward by the Commander-in-Chief were as follows:

1. *The Brigade should be used for only one large operation—or some minor actions.*
2. *It should be withdrawn after 15% casualties.*
3. *It should not be used in the early stages of invasion.*
4. *We should have a firmer statement about aircraft for Poland.*

I also asked that the Brigade should remain independent and not lose its identity in the midst of British units, as I felt it was important for our morale and for the morale of our people in Poland.

All this argument may sound very strange to British readers, but it must be remembered that the Parachute Brigade would never have been formed if it had not been our one main ambition to fight for the liberation of our own country. We wanted very badly to fight in Poland, and I knew only too well that large casualties on the Western Front might result in our being too weak ever to be able to fight in Poland. I also recognised the fact that if we refused to fight in the West and it was later found impossible for us to fight in Poland, then all our training would have been in vain. It was certainly a dilemma for the Commander-in-Chief.

On 15th April, Mr. Mikolajczyk, the Prime Minister, came to

Scotland with the Minister of Defence to see the commanders of units allocated to the Western Front. In an after-dinner speech, he explained the political set-up between the Allies and Russia, with poor Poland being blown backwards and forwards in the middle like a shuttle-cock. He said that his Government had tried to reach an understanding with the Soviet Union, but all the world could see that the goodwill was all on one side.

"As, however, we cannot fight against the Soviet Union," he concluded, "then we must fight the Germans wherever possible. There is danger in the fact that the U.S.S.R. and Hitler might come to an agreement to end the war in the East, which would be a disaster to the Allies. Therefore we must put all possible strength on the Western Front and help the Allies with their offensive."

Once again, on the 28th April, I had to report on the state of training in the Brigade. Being still short of three hundred men, I pointed out to the Commander-in-Chief that, if we went under British command and were short of men, they might tag a British battalion on to us and our independence would be lost. General Sosnkowski reported rumours he had heard that the British wanted the Polish Armoured Division completely up to strength. If we were too awkward, they might insist that the Parachute Brigade made up the deficiencies. I told him not to worry: they were far too keen to have my Brigade and I believed that, if they had to make a choice, they would choose the parachutists—it was all part of a plan to soften us up.

The diplomatic exchanges and polite letters were all brushed aside by Monty on 21st May 1944, when he refused to take the Parachute Brigade with any strings attached. This is the letter General Sosnkowski received from Lieutenant-General A. E. Grasett:

My dear General,

I write with reference to your letter No. 432-GM-44 of 1st May regarding the employment of the Polish Parachute Brigade. General Sir Bernard Montgomery does not feel able to accept this brigade under the conditions in your above-quoted letter. General Montgomery fully realises the shortage of Polish Reserves in the United Kingdom and the importance which you and your Government attach to this brigade. But General Montgomery considers that if the Brigade is to be placed under his command, he must be given a free hand to employ it in any manner that operations may demand. I am instructed to inform you that the British Chiefs of Staff, whilst unable to give any guarantee regarding the provision of aircraft to transport the Brigade to Poland or about replacement of equipment, will do their best in the light of circumstances existing at the time to meet the requirement of the Polish authorities in these respects. I feel sure you will appreciate the position of the British Chiefs of Staff and recognise their inability to commit themselves specifically at this stage of the war. The Chief of the Imperial General Staff and General Sir Bernard Montgomery both fully understand your wishes regarding the employment of the Polish Parachute Brigade. They consider that this Brigade being composed, as it is, of such fine fighting material, if available, might make a valuable contribution to the war at some stage in the operations. Field Marshal Sir Alan Brooke was under the impression, after your conversation with him, that you would be prepared to place the Polish Parachute Brigade unreservedly under General Montgomery's command and I would be grateful if you would inform me for the information of the British Chiefs of Staff whether you agree to do so.

Yours sincerely,
A. E. Grasett.

Montgomery was right. It was impossible to ask a commander to accept troops under the conditions which we had laid down. Although these had originally been suggested by Sir Alan Brooke in a letter dated 11th March, 1944.

The Polish Cabinet considered this request and on the 6th of June, when British and American troops stormed across the beaches and dropped from the skies to open the Second Front, a letter was sent to General Grasett handing over my Brigade, lock stock and barrel, with no conditions at all.

General Sosnkowski's letter read as follows:

My Dear General,
  I would be grateful if you will inform General Sir Bernard Montgomery that in agreement with my Government I place the Polish Parachute Brigade at the disposal of the Supreme Commander, Allied Expeditionary Forces. It is the most ardent desire of the Poles to contribute within the limits of their possibilities to the success of the most formidable war operation of all time which commenced today. With reference to your letters of 11th March and 11th May, the Polish Government and myself wish to express our complete confidence that General Montgomery in disposing of the Brigade will take into account both our difficulties in obtaining replacements and the importance of this Brigade for Poland. We are confident that the British Chiefs of Staff will do all in their power to facilitate at the right moment the employ-

132

*ment of the Brigade in support of the rising in Poland, particularly in
the securing of air transport for this purpose.*
Yours sincerely,
Sosnkowski.

The political battle was over—now followed the struggle for
readiness.

The Brigade was put on top priority for the issue of arms and
equipment, mobilisation to start on 19th June and finish by the
3rd July. The main reason for this priority was that General
Browning had only 1st Airborne Division and my Brigade under
direct command. 6th Division having assaulted on D-Day on
6th June, was still fighting in Normandy and being used—very
unwisely, I thought—as normal infantry.

All was going well and I was beginning to think that the British
were at last appreciating our difficulties and helping us to the
fullest extent. But this illusion was soon shattered by the unexpected arrival from Airborne Corps of Lieutenant-Colonel
Mackenzie, Browning's Operations Chief, in Leven on 22nd June.
He told me that the Brigade was needed for an operation on the
6th of July. I was aghast, particularly in view of all the previous
discussions and the agreement at all levels that we would not be
ready until August. In no uncertain terms, I reminded Mackenzie
of what had been said before and, in view of my attitude, he telephoned Browning, arranging for me to see him on the 25th. I
tried to get in touch with the Commander-in-Chief but he was in
Yorkshire watching the 1st Polish Armoured Division's final battle
manœuvres before they moved to France. I immediately drove
down to tell him that I was expected to take half-trained troops
into battle.

Sosnkowski agreed that it was entirely wrong and offered to
write to Browning. In my view, this was unwise and I told him so.
If Browning refused his request, it would put Sosnkowski in a
most awkward position. I maintained it would be best if I
reiterated our point of view to him and, if he still insisted on the
July operation, then the Commander-in-Chief could write direct
to General Eisenhower. I travelled by the night train to London
and reported to General Browning at Moor Park, the Airborne
Corps Headquarters near Rickmansworth, Hertfordshire.

He was very formal and had with him in the office General Eric
Down and Brigadier Walsh, the Chief of Staff. His greeting was
stiff and rather curt; our relationship had changed in any case,
as previously I had been independent and I was now under his

133

command. I think that our opposing views at this conference affected our attitude towards each other for the rest of the war.

Cutting short the preliminaries, he asked outright:

"Will the Polish Parachute Brigade be ready for action on 6th July?" Quite firmly, I replied: "No, sir."

In support of my words I handed him a written report on the state of training, mobilisation, manpower and so on.

He was not impressed: "In my opinion the Polish Parachute Brigade is considerably better trained than the 1st British Parachute Brigade was when it went into action in Tunisia."

I was surprised at his answer and refrained from giving my own views on what I thought about that operation, which was not successful; I also withheld a retort that he was in no real position to judge, as he had not been to see my units since early 1943.

Browning continued: "And if I insist that you go on this operation, will you report to your Commander-in-Chief?"

"Yes, sir. I shall report it."

He took up the telephone and asked for a number.

"Our friends from the North will not take part in this business," he said into the mouthpiece. "I shall see you this afternoon."

From this, I presumed that we would have fought in Normandy. Putting the phone down and turning to me, he added:

"Well, the Brigade must be ready by August 1st. I shall let you have General Down to help organise mobilisation, and he will see that you get everything you need."

I replied that in the opinion of myself and my Inspector General of Training, the Brigade would not be ready for two months.

"I don't care about the Inspector General of Training," he snapped. "I want the Brigade ready by August 1st."

I was most hurt, as I felt he was being unreasonable.

The conference broke up and Browning, in an effort at conciliation, said jocularly:

"You must remember, Sosabowski, you Poles are a nation of soldiers, we British are shopkeepers."

"Somehow, sir, I just don't see you as a shopkeeper," I responded light-heartedly.

Eric Down came to Leven on June 29th. He was tremendous: no one could have helped more than he. Our move down south to the Stamford-Peterborough area was set for 3rd July and, with hardly a pause, we went into strict training.

Company training with the new equipment took place until July 12th. It was followed by six days of battalion exercises and finally a full scale brigade exercise started on the 30th July. We were allocated American Air Force C.47s and it was wonderful to work to a timed programme with everyone giving full support. I cannot speak too highly of General Down; he tackled a difficult job with great enthusiasm and tact and we became firm friends.

Going back to our departure from Leven, I was later asked by a British brigadier if we had brought our families down from Scotland as he remembered the large crowd which had gathered to say goodbye at the station. I explained that we had no families in Scotland: those were just a few of the good friends we had made during our stay in the North. I had not taken into consideration the "unmarried families": two weeks later we were invaded by about a hundred women, some seeking paternity orders, others fulfilling promises they had made to the troops!

The decision having been taken that we should fight on the Western Front, the troops were keyed up for the day when they would be launched into battle.

All my life I had been taught and had learnt the responsibilities of a commander; that was why I fought so much to ensure that we did not find ourselves in battle half-trained, suffering the inevitable casualties that hit unprepared units.

I had instructed students at the War Academy that they should obey to the letter orders given by superior commanders, but always bear in mind that they should be carried out with the smallest possible casualties. I cannot remember a single case in history where a commander has been prosecuted for unnecessary loss of life: in fact, it is a common misapprehension that the bloodier the battle, the bigger the victory. I have often pondered the possibility of producing a code of laws to make generals responsible for unnecessary deaths, but I doubt if a reasonable system could be worked out.

A commander is the architect of victory in battle, all fame and honours go to him. The mass of the fighting soldiers who gain the victory remain unknown, so how grateful the commander should be to them and how careful in projecting them into battle!

These were the principles which guided me during my arguments with the British as to when my men should be used in action.

Even with the rush of training in which we were now involved, I issued orders that each man was to do no more than three jumps: I did not want unnecessary casualties, which would be impossible to replace. Yet we had one horrifying accident when two Dakotas crashed in mid-air with the loss of twenty-eight paratroopers and the American crews; only one wireless operator was thrown clear and managed to open his 'chute.

As I visited the scene of the crash, I heard talk among the troops that, if only I had been there, it would not have happened. They all had a strong belief that I led a charmed life, which was shared by those around me: I brought them all luck!

Marching played an important part in our training. One day, a battalion commander informed me that his troops could not march for a few days, as their feet were blistered. I went straight to his unit and held a foot inspection; to my horror, I found that some of the men's feet were very raw. I sacked the Commanding Officer on the spot—he was obviously unfit to occupy such a position. His men's feet should have been hard and clean and capable of marching at least thirty miles a day.

On July 20th, I went to see Brigadier Peto at the Liaison Staff's Headquarters to give him the latest information on the state of readiness. During our conversation, he asked:

"Do you think, General, that the question of the readiness of your Brigade is mixed up with the political situation in Poland?"

I was appalled at the suggestion and hotly retorted:

"I think, if that were the case, Brigadier, I should not be under British command at all, but fighting in Poland side by side with our compatriots."

Once again I was up against a complete lack of understanding of my problems. I had tried, and my senior officers had tried, to explain why we needed the training and—by God!—we did need it.

Brigadier Peto then said the Brigade was required for a small operation towards the end of the month: did I think we could do it? I repeated what I had already explained: we still needed training but, as we were under General Browning's command, the responsibility rested on him.

Soon afterwards, I received secret orders from the Commander-in-Chief to have one parachute company standing by for possible use in Poland. I ordered them to be at short notice to move, but they carried on with normal training. The political consequences in our struggle for freedom of using this company would have been important but, although the Polish Government fought hard to get permission to launch these troops, it was refused.

On July 25th General Bor, Commander-in-Chief of the Home Army, sent the following telegram to General Sosnkowski:

We are ready to start fighting for Warsaw. The arrival of the Parachute Brigade will be of important military and political value. Please arrange for the airfields in Warsaw to be bombed. I shall report when we start.

So about six weeks after we had been switched to British command, the call we had all been living for came. We did not answer it. It was not surprising that the whole Brigade felt very strongly over the political actions which prevented us carrying out our pledge. The whole world knows what happened in Warsaw: how Polish patriots rose against the Germans as the Russian troops approached the city and how the Russians deliberately stopped, leaving the Germans to wipe out the Home Army. Can you imagine our bitterness and our inner defeat?

CHAPTER IX

PRELUDE TO ARNHEM

TRAINING continued according to plan until the 8th August, when Browning decided we were ready for operations. Events then started to move quickly. Two days later, a telegram from Corps Headquarters put me under operational command of 1st Airborne Division and on the same day we were briefed for Operation "Transfigure" due to be launched on 16th August when, with 1st British and 101st United States Airborne Divisions, we were to have dropped south-east of Paris, in the Rambouillet-Yvelines area.

The Brigade was still three hundred men short, but we arranged accordingly to make-do where the gaps existed. My main worry at the time was to accustom the troops to their new battle equipment and a smaller problem was to discourage them from carrying too much gear in their keenness to make up for the holes in the ranks.

"Transfigure" did not take place, because the advancing American and British armies overran the area, making an airborne assault unnecessary. Yet it is interesting to look at this plan which was an altogether new idea in airborne tactics. At this time—early August—the Americans and the British were progressing swiftly and vigorously towards Paris. We were to be dropped in the gap between Orleans and Paris to prevent the retreating German divisions from escaping: the parachutists were to hold all the communication centres; the Polish Brigade was to jump near Rambouillet and seize landing grounds to permit 52nd Lowland Division to fly in.

It must be remembered that the Germans were in retreat and harried all the way by artillery and planes, but they were nothing like beaten. Most of their units were still intact, awaiting the chance of a good battle. When they brushed us in their retreat, they would have struggled valiantly, realising why we were there, and would have fought like rats to get away from the ever tightening net. As lightly equipped units, we would have faced severe odds and almost certainly suffered heavy casualties.

Never before had parachute troops planned to drop into a fluid battle such as that then raging and it is interesting to speculate what would have happened to us had the plan been put into action. I had a worrying feeling that we would not have been relieved anything like as quickly as forecast and, as soon as 52nd Lowland Division was put into the plan, I was pretty certain that some very heavy fighting had been envisaged. Thank goodness it was cancelled on 18th August, allowing the men a few days of comparative freedom.

This was the first occasion on which I met Major-General Roy Urquhart, Commander of the 1st Airborne Division. He came to my Headquarters at Stamford to brief me personally about "Transfigure" and my immediate impression was that he was a very pleasant man and easy to work with.

I was called to Corps Headquarters at Moor Park on 27th August, where Browning produced another operational plan, this time for using the Brigade in a partisan-type action on the Franco-Belgian frontier, where we were to assist the miners in revolt. This sort of operation had been suggested by Browning way back in 1941 and he had been told then that we were not in favour of the idea. There was, anyway, in existence a completely independent parachute company under control of the Polish Ministry of Defence specially trained for such work.

General Sosnkowski's view was that no partisan operation had been foreseen and, if we were not allowed to go to Warsaw, we were certainly not going to fight resistance movement battles in France or Belgium. What would be the effect upon our own people fighting to the end in beleaguered Poland? Two days later, I was told to forget all about it.

Hardly had a few hours passed, when I was asked to report to 1st Airborne Division Headquarters for another briefing on another scheme. This new plan bore the code-name "Linnet" and it followed very much the same lines as "Transfigure", although on a slightly bigger scale, three divisions and my Brigade being involved. Troops taking part were to be the American 82nd and 101st Airborne Divisions, 1st British and the Poles.

"Linnet" envisaged a landing in Belgium around Tournai to seize the railways and roads and block the German retreat. Local resistance units had been warned to stand by.

Although most of the Allied Airborne Army was to be used, it would have been spread over an enormous area, and we had been warned that our land units would not catch up with us for seven days. However, once again it was cancelled, but the same code name was retained for a similar operation near Maastricht, in south-east Holland, to capture the bridges over the Maas leading to Liége. Again, cancellation!

It would be untrue to say that I took all these projected operations and cancellations calmly. I did not—nor did my officers and men. Someone, somewhere, with a vivid imagination, optimism and little knowledge, was producing parachute battle orders with the same frequency and ease as a conjuror producing rabbits from a top hat. It did not exactly imbue us with confidence and we began to look askance as plan succeeded plan. I think it true to say that the British and American parachutists felt the same.

The next one popped up on 2nd September, when I again went to Urquhart's Headquarters. The start was not very auspicious, the initial briefing being delayed several times, until the next afternoon. "Fifteen" was its code name—not, as someone suggested, standing for the fifteenth abortive airborne plan! The name lasted exactly three days and was then changed to "Comet".

General Browning issued his appreciation of the situation. The object was for the British Airborne Corps to capture the bridges over the Maas at Grave, over the Waal at Nijmegen and on the Neder Rhine at Arnhem; we were to hold them and let the Guards Armoured Division through to form a bridgehead over the Rhine. 52nd Division was to be flown in to improvised landing strips to reinforce us with heavier weapons.

Browning laid down that 1st Division should concentrate in Arnhem and 1st Polish Brigade in the Nijmegen area. Corps Headquarters was to land by glider six miles south of Nijmegen at Knapheide.

The capture of the three bridges was allocated by Urquhart to his own three parachute brigades; it struck me that their landing zones were some miles away from their objectives; the Germans would therefore have plenty of warning of the attack and the element of surprise would be lost. But it was not my affair and none of the British Brigadiers raised any objections.

The Polish Brigade was given the task of dropping at Middelhaar and moving across the Maas-Waal canal to relieve Brigadier Hackett's 4th Parachute Brigade at Grave. If the bridge was still in German hands, we were to capture it.

On 8th September Urquhart and I had a talk at Wittering Airfield, where we discussed whether it might be necessary to hold the bridge over the Maas at Mook, in case the bridge at Grave was destroyed, as well as the crossings on the Maas-Waal canal

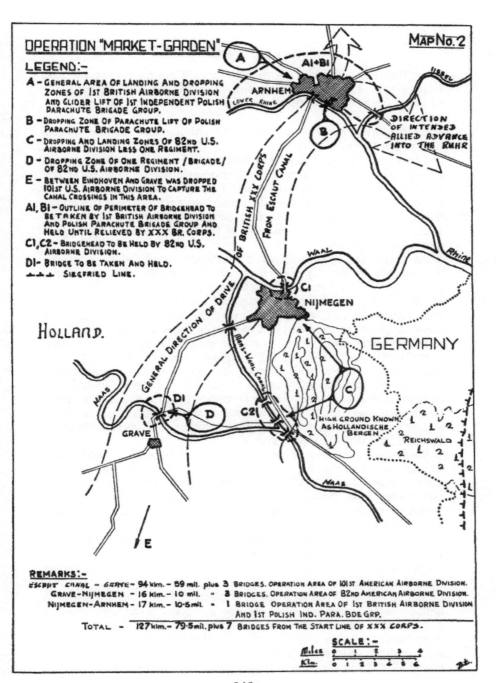

OPERATION "MARKET-GARDEN"

LEGEND:-

A - General Area Of Landing And Dropping Zones Of 1st British Airborne Division And Glider Lift Of 1st Independent Polish Parachute Brigade Group.

B - Dropping Zone Of Parachute Lift Of Polish Parachute Brigade Group.

C - Dropping And Landing Zones Of 82nd U.S. Airborne Division Less One Regiment.

D - Dropping Zone Of One Regiment /Brigade/ Of 82nd U.S. Airborne Division.

E - Between Eindhoven And Grave Was Dropped 101st U.S. Airborne Division To Capture The Canal Crossings In This Area.

A1, B1 - Outline Of Perimeter Of Bridgehead To Be Taken By 1st British Airborne Division And Polish Parachute Brigade Group And Held Until Relieved By XXX Br. Corps.

C1,C2 - Bridgehead To Be Held By 82nd U.S. Airborne Division.

D1 - Bridge To Be Taken And Held.

▄▄▄ Siegfried Line.

MAP No. 2

ARNHEM

A1+B1

LOWER RHINE

DIRECTION OF INTENDED ALLIED ADVANCE INTO THE RUHR

FROM ESCAUT CANAL

OF BRITISH XXX CORPS

WAAL

Rhine

C1

NIJMEGEN

HOLLAND.

GENERAL DIRECTION OF DRIVE

MAAS-WAAL CANAL

GERMANY

MAAS

D1

D

GRAVE

C2

HIGH GROUND KNOWN AS HOLLANDISCHE BERGEN

C

REICHSWALD

MAAS

E

REMARKS:-

Escaut Canal - Grave - 94 klm. - 59 mil. plus 3 Bridges. Operation Area Of 101st American Airborne Division.

Grave - Nijmegen - 16 klm. - 10 mil. " 3 Bridges. Operation Area Of 82nd American Airborne Division.

Nijmegen - Arnhem - 17 klm. - 10·5 mil. 1 Bridge Operation Area Of 1st British Airborne Division And 1st Polish Ind. Para. Bde. Grp.

Total - 127klm. - 79·5mil. plus 7 Bridges From The Start Line Of XXX Corps.

SCALE:-

Miles 0 1 2 3 4

Klm. 0 1 2 3 4 5 6

near Heumen Malden. I suggested to Urquhart that he had been given rather a big task and asked what was his estimate of the German strength. Spreading a hand over the map, he said:

"I shouldn't worry—according tó Intelligence reports there's no enemy there."

I was not really convinced: I had recently read in a Swiss newspaper an article by a military commentator on how vital the Arnhem area was to the Germans. I had a strong impression that the enemy was underestimated. I also had a feeling that Browning made these plans with tremendous, perhaps dangerous, confidence. I felt that Browning's assessment of probable German opposition was a bit optimistic.

As I saw the situation, my Brigade was required to jump on ground overlooked by the enemy in strongly fortified positions. This was the ridge on the Dutch-German border, including part of the Reichswald Forest, through which ran the Siegfried Line; this feature dominated all the crossings and bridges which we were supposed to capture; just to my rear was the river Maas.

In my estimate, enemy reaction would be swift and strong. Admittedly, 1st Air Landing Brigade was planned to put its gliders down on the high ground, but they would not stay there, as they had insufficient strength to take the bridges and hold on to the landing zone. I therefore reckoned that the Germans would be entirely free to attack my troops as we dropped and catch us at our weakest moment, either in the air or just after landing. I worried about it all that night.

Early next morning, I received a verbal message ordering me to hold the bridge at Mook and the Maas-Waal crossing. Picking up the telephone, I spoke to General Urquhart's Headquarters and arranged to see him at Cottesmore Airfield in the afternoon. When I arrived, I found Brigadier Shan Hackett with Urquhart. I came straight to the point:

"General, I received your orders altering the original plan and I would like you to confirm these orders in writing."

"Whatever for?" Urquhart asked with a look of surprise on his face. "Why is that necessary?"

"In my considered opinion it is impossible for any brigade to hold those crossings as long as the enemy occupies the high ground. I am under your orders and will carry them out, but I have a responsibility to my Polish leaders, and if my formation gets into serious difficulties with heavy loss of life, I would like them to know all the circumstances under which it happened."

Although we did not know each other very well, Urquhart and I had always been very friendly. We were of the same rank and he had always treated me like an equal commander. He was always most kind. It was because of this that I found it very unpleasant to have to speak to him in this way—but I felt that I had to.

Hackett had stood silently listening all the time, but at the end he agreed with my summing up of the situation and the probable action of the Germans. A little later he said to me:

"You know, it would be very difficult—if not impossible—for a British General to express his objections to a senior commander in such a forthright manner."

Urquhart suggested that we should go and see Browning. He had his Oxford aircraft on the airfield and in half an hour we were at Rickmansworth. Uruqhart saw Browning first and I was then invited to join them. I repeated my views and Browning agreed with me.

"But," he added, "I have no more forces available and the 1st Division with your Brigade must capture all the bridges."

I reiterated that I considered the operation impossible and his superior commanders should not demand the impossible from him.

To this, he replied rather lightly: "The Red Devils and the Polish Paratroopers can do anything."

"Well," I said, "you must realise, General, that if my theories are right, your glider will come slap down into the middle of a German trap and you will be killed or captured."

"Well, give me your solution to the problem," he suggested.

I demurred, saying that as I was only a brigade commander, it was hardly my position to do so; but he urged me on, assuring me that our discussion would remain completely private.

"At least two divisions are needed," I said. "One for the Nijmegen area and another to hold the high ground and capture the bridges."

Browning smiled and shrugged his shoulders.

I think I was right and the later fighting at Nijmegen, during the Arnhem battle, gave some support to my theory. But that is anticipating events.

I never got the order in writing, because on September the 10th Operation "Comet" was cancelled and we went wearily back to our camps to await the next bright idea.

We did not have long to wait: only two days later, in fact, I was called to Urquhart's Headquarters for a conference. When I arrived, all the other brigade commanders were already there, some of whom I had not met before; also present were all the other independent unit and glider commanders.

Roy Urquhart stood before a large scale map, showing France, Holland, Belgium and most of Germany. I noticed that the flags and markers had been re-arranged and a new code name—"Market Garden"—had replaced "Comet".

"D-Day," said Urquhart, "is the 17th of September."

That meant we had five days only in which to prepare and launch the vital operation which we now know from General Montgomery's Memoirs was intended to bring the war to a victorious close in 1944. Plenty has been written about this battle, and the reasons for it, and many people have produced theories as to why it was a dismal, costly failure.

General Urquhart, after fourteen years' silence, gave his viewpoint as the Divisional Commander in his book published last year called *Arnhem*—yet this impressive and very honest account is in some ways incomplete: it concentrates on the battle fought on the north bank of the Neder Rhine, largely ignoring the fighting which took place on the south bank; and then for two days of the battle, Urquhart was cut off from his Headquarters and was not in control of the fighting.

The whole world knows how the Allied Airborne Army planned to capture vital bridges over the Dutch rivers, and how XXX Corps under General Sir Brian Horrocks was to have thrust through with a division of tanks up the one road, wrecking everything in its path in a surprise and desperate attempt to relieve the parachutists and force open the gate wide into Germany. We all know that this attempt failed—and at what an appalling cost!

Yet that was still to come. For the group of commanders who gathered at Urquhart's Headquarters that evening, it was just another projected operation that would probably not come off. I heard one of my British colleagues remark:

"I bet this one will be another abortive effort."

I sensed an air of: I've heard all this before among those gathered there. At the time, there was nothing to indicate how vital this was, and certainly no unusual pressure was put on to impress us of its importance.

Browning had already given his outline orders to Urquhart for the British and Poles to capture the bridges at Arnhem, build a bridgehead on the north bank of the Neder Rhine and assist XXX Corps to break out to the north. Our other task was to destroy all enemy flak in the area.

German strength and resistance were both reported to be negligible, consisting mainly of labour and training units and a few beaten-up tank regiments, which were re-forming.

Urquhart decided to drop his force in three groups, one each day for three days. The point that struck me immediately, as in the planning of operation "Comet", was that all the dropping zones were at least six miles away from the objectives. The 1st Parachute Brigade had to march six miles to the Arnhem bridges, thus making it clear to the Germans exactly where they were going.

The Polish Brigade was ordered to drop on the south bank of the Neder Rhine in the area of Elden, about one mile south of Arnhem. Our immediate task was to cross the bridges which, according to Urquhart's plan, would already be firmly in the hands of 1st Parachute Brigade, and then dig in on the eastern edge of Arnhem, facing the river Ijssel.

Urquhart said to me at the end: "If by any chance the 1st Brigade has not taken the Arnhem bridges, you will have to capture them on the way through."

To make matters more difficult, my Brigade Group was flying out on different days in completely separate parties. The glider lift was travelling on D-Day plus One and Two, with 1st Air Landing Brigade, and was supposed to join up with us on D-Day plus Three. My Second Line Ammunition—main reserve— would be with the gliders on the north bank of the river, while the main party were landing on the south and, in the event of heavy fighting, we would need that ammunition badly. I would there-fore have to issue strict economy orders.

"Market Garden" followed very closely the lines of "Comet" and most of the commanders made few, if any, notes about it.

At the end Urquhart asked: "Any questions?"

Not one brigadier or unit commander spoke.

I looked round, but most of them sat nonchalantly with legs crossed, looking rather bored and waiting for the conference to end. Questions were buzzing round my head, but I quickly sensed that if I started asking questions it would delay the end of the meeting; I would be unpopular with all of them and I did not think that it would be any use anyway. I was certainly not in a good mood, having been told that the plan was so limited that my battery of 75 mm. howitzers would not go by glider, but would travel with the sea lift.

Most of that night I spent working in my Headquarters, sorting out the details, and I arranged for the operational briefing to take place at 2 p.m. the following day.

13th September 1944 was not a very auspicious day. I am not a superstitious man, but I had so many doubts about the Arnhem operation that I could not help noticing bad omens to add to my worries.

The Operations room was in an old house on the outskirts of Stamford, heavily guarded, and only those with a special password were allowed to enter.

I divided the Brigade into three battalion combat groups, each with its complement of signals equipment, medical supplies, medium machine guns, explosives, mines, et cetera. These groups were to drop and fight together. To the First Battalion Group I gave the task of capturing the Arnhem bridge, if it was not already in the hands of 1st British Brigade, and crossing the river to the eastern outskirts of Arnhem. The Second Battalion Group was to give them covering fire from the south and west approaches and capture a pontoon bridge. Whilst the Third would be destroying anti-aircraft and searchlight units around the dropping zone and organising a ferry west of the main bridge to get men and equipment across.

I knew in the initial stages I would be without most of my heavy guns and ammunition reserves and we would not join up with them until we had crossed the Rhine. Urquhart had promised at the original conference to have sufficient river crossing equipment left on the banks for us to use, and also to send jeeps from the 1st Parachute Brigade to help clear the dropping zone.

I impressed on my commanders—and told them to impress it also on their men—that this operation would not be a picnic. In spite of British assurances and Intelligence reports to the contrary, I expected hard and bitter fighting. Anyone looking at the map could see how important the Arnhem area was to the Germans and those who thought the Germans did not recognise the fact were very shortsighted. Yet, I was told that Browning's Headquarters were still receiving reports from 21st Army Group that enemy units were few and of low quality. Dutch resistance continued to report German tank units in the Arnhem district, but these were totally discounted. This, I thought, was arrogant optimism completely unjustified.

I did not pass on all my disquiet to my commanders, however; I kept most of it to myself and prepared for the worst. They went back to their units and issued orders, giving out all the information, except the date and actual locality of the assault.

The following day I met Urquhart and had a serious discussion with him. "Do you realise, General," I asked, "that your defence perimeter is ten miles round, in a wooded and inhabited area? Your strength will be very thinly dispersed."

"I quite agree," he replied. "But there will be no heavy German resistance and it is a risk we can well afford to take."

He also repeated his assurance that he would make certain the Engineers' river-crossing stores for the ferry would be available and that British paratroopers would defend my dropping zone.

Urquhart added at the end that all signs pointed to the fact that this operation would not be cancelled and was very much on.

I drove back to Stamford with a heavy heart, much worried over Urquhart's optimism.

Five days is not very long to plan a battle and it is a very short time indeed to teach private soldiers a new plan in which, as paratroopers, they are required to know a lot more than normal soldiers and will have to act on their own initiative. Compared with 6th Airborne Division, who had been given three months in which to plan and prepare for D-Day, we were fighting the clock.

There is much more preparatory paper work to an airborne operation than to a normal type of battle. The whole brigade had to be divided into small compact groups of sixteen to eighteen men for each aircraft. Equipment containers had to be put into the bomb racks and the loads carefully worked out. Each man carried his own equipment and, in addition, many wore leg-kit-bags containing vital supplies, such as radios, medical gear, parts of mortars or machine guns. Also in the fuselage of the planes would be other bundles to be pushed out of the door, such as folding bicycles. Every man was loaded to the maximum, but no one was allowed to be overloaded, as this might cause casualties either from dropping too quickly or upsetting the parachute.

They all carried a personal weapon, pistol, sten gun, rifle or bren gun, plus ammunition; hand grenades; field dressings; personal kit; and spare ammunition. Over this went an overall, then the parachute and a Mae West—we looked quite a sight!

The heavy equipment was sent off by sea, with orders to follow XXX Corps into Arnhem as closely as possible, but it would not be available to us until after the battle.

An amusing incident happened concerning this column: my Quartermaster, Lieutenant-Colonel Rotter, an elderly man, kept pressing to be allowed to jump into Holland in spite of an attack of lumbago and I had not the heart to refuse, although I was certain he would seriously injure himself. Hearing that the officer in charge of the supply company had been killed and looking upon it as a golden opportunity to get rid of Rotter without hurting his feelings, I asked him to go over and sort out any problems, convinced that, by the time he returned, we would have flown. But he was back very quickly and in the end flew with us—his luck held and his legs remained unbroken, in spite of my pessimism!

The strictest security precautions were imposed on all my men, but it soon became obvious to anyone that the Brigade was preparing for an operation. The troops were confined to barracks and with wives and girl friends continually calling and being refused permission to see their menfolk, they were not slow in assessing the situation. With the Brigade split between seven different camps, security was extremely difficult. I was touched, but surprised, to hear from our Depot in Scotland that local kirks had offered up special prayers for our protection and success. A number of men had been on education courses at universities and technical schools when the operation was initiated; some, but not all, I had recalled, leaving the others to finish their studies. That did not satisfy them: they deserted their books and came to Stamford of their own accord, begging permission to join their comrades.

A former Deputy Brigade Commander, a dear friend, Colonel Kaminski, turned up demanding to fly with us. He had left the Brigade simply and solely because of his age and had been appointed Airborne Adviser to the Inspector General of Training. Another officer, Lieutenant Slesicki, a lawyer, abandoned a nice safe job and asked for his old job as a company commander. Both these men flew with us and Slesicki was the first Polish officer to be killed at Arnhem.

It was remarkable how the tremendous spirit of the Brigade rose as the day of action drew nearer. I knew most of my men by name, I was very fond of them, even the tough old offenders had turned out well. We had confidence in each other and my only doubt was what their initial reaction would be on landing in the middle of a fight without the gradual build-up which most ordinary troops receive. One can train in battle-simulated conditions; yet in spite of the element of danger, everyone knows it is only a game, and the first shots that kill often produce very different reactions. The toughest often turn out to be more afraid that the meak and mild. But we had done our best.

The kindness and affection which we received from our British friends was a great comfort to us all. We were, after all, a long way from our families and lacking that love and family spirit that most British and American soldiers still had. They could at least receive letters, but our loved ones were completely cut off, many languishing in Russian slave camps, and in our more sombre moments we often felt very, very lonely.

Luckier than most, I did have my brother and sister-in-law living in Edinburgh. She sent me a small image of Our Lady of Czestochowa with the message: *May Our Lady preserve you in all you do*. But I had no news at all of my wife and son in Warsaw.

Because of my preoccupation with plans and staff work, I often toiled late into the night, disregarding the personal life of my subordinates. My aide-de-camp, Captain Sieczkowski, was very much in love with his wife and naturally they wanted to see as much of each other as they could. Looking out from my office window into the main street of Stamford one evening, I noticed a young lady walking up and down the pavement, who kept glancing up at my window. Calling my aide, I asked who she was.

"It is my wife," he blushed.

I realised how selfish I was, dismissed him immediately and he gratefully hurried off. Next morning, he told me:

"My wife asked last night in which aircraft I would be flying. I told her that obviously I would be in the same plane as you and her reply was: 'Thank goodness—in that case you'll be safe: Old Sosab is always lucky.'"

Throughout the Polish Army, I had a reputation for good luck and often, after accidents and fatalities, I would hear soldiers comment: "That was because 'Old' was not here." "Old" and "Old Sosab" were nicknames they had given me through the years and were both terms of affection, although I was a bit doubtful about the constant reference to my age! In the Polish Army, as in the British, a nickname is a reassuring sign of popularity and of the confidence in which one is held by the troops.

The last few days were intensely active; we packed and assembled, we checked and repaired, we oiled and we greased, we went to the airfields and filled containers and other equipment. The men going by glider went off to airfields in southern England; I sent off liaison officers to Divisional Headquarters and I even had Polish War Correspondents attached to my Headquarters. At last, it seemed, we had done everything possible and on the 16th September we went to our beds in the knowledge that on the following morning the operation would start.

September 17th, 1944, was a Sunday, a perfect autumn day. The leaves of the trees were only just beginning to take on their golden tints, the grass under my feet was emerald green as always, dahlias and early chrysanthemums flowered in profusion. I had been to Mass and was walking slowly back to my quarters, my thoughts wandering and straying. I was looking forward to a farewell lunch with my landlady, Miss Mason, who had saved a fine bottle of Burgundy for the occasion. The forthcoming battle had almost receded into the back of my mind, but I kept thinking about Urquhart and hoped that he would be lucky. He had always been very friendly to me and had put up with all my outspoken criticisms with a good heart. I came out of my reverie, my face, eyes and ears drawn to the sky by the increasing roar of aircraft engines. I looked up and, silhouetted against the sun, only a few hundred feet up, was a vast air Armada in formation flying eastwards. Operation "Market Garden" had been launched.

Chapter X

ARNHEM

I<small>T WAS</small> impossible to distinguish the private from the general,
or the corporal from the captain. They sat awkwardly on
uncomfortable, canvas bucket seats along each side of the
plane's fuselage. They all looked the same. Like bulbous bellied
clowns, legs foreshortened by their bulk, and with round-topped,
brimless helmets and chin straps, they took on the appearance of
misshapen dwarfs, huddling together for protection.

They sat, grave-faced and motionless, as the aircraft engines
roared and subsided under the fingers of a young American pilot
manipulating the controls from his cabin. Only occasionally did
their eyes stray and then only to watch my reactions. Their
questing glances searched for a sign of nerves, of fear, confidence,
or worry. But I knew they were looking, and what they were
looking for. I *was* afraid, my nerve ends *were* jangling like fire
bells, I *was* worrying like hell and my confidence was badly shaken
by the lack of information about the operation. Yet I smiled
casually and confidently, half-yawning as if I was completely at
ease. Then their eyes left my face to exchange reassuring flickers
with nearby comrades.

"'Old' is all right—so why worry?"

Chalked on the nose of our Dakota was the number 110 and
marshalled in front were other identical planes. Behind were
more, parked at 45-degrees to the perimeter track on concrete
aprons, each crammed with men and equipment.

The twin engines gradually increased momentum and slowly
the propellers eased the machines along. Here and there along
the track edge, small groups of soldiers and aircraftsmen, waved
and mouthed unheard farewells. We would soon be airborne,
heading for Arnhem and whatever fate awaited us. Overloaded
bodies leaned to the angle of the plane and jerked as it slowed or
accelerated. The aircraft braked and stopped, engines ticking
over.

Men eased their backsides away from protruding metal points
and bars. They wriggled more firmly into parachute harnesses

and peered, with difficulty, out of the small windows, in efforts to see what was happening. After a period of endless time, the figure of the Jumpmaster appeared at the cabin door and with a careless shrug of his shoulders bellowed:

"Weather's too bad—operation's cancelled for twenty-four hours."

Men cursed loudly, repetitively, venomously. Others screwed up their faces near to tears with disappointment; some sighed resignedly. Try to imagine the effect of this cancellation, and for the second time running! Just before take-off on an operation, everyone is keyed up to a high pitch. Once in the sky, an air of fatal acceptance descends and all is well. But twice we had screwed up our courage and twice it had been smashed to bits. This was no fault on the part of senior officers; it was simply bad, lousy, unlucky weather. While men fought and died and suffered on Dutch soil, awaiting our coming with hope, we sat helpless on an English airfield, reluctant landlubbers.

My Quartermaster's staff, back in the camps, was nearly mad with frustration. Each day they collected the kit we left behind and carefully stored it away. They cancelled orders for vast quantities of food. Then in the evening, back we came with empty stomachs to be filled and with the need to lie down and sleep.

There was only one good thing to be said for this second delay, and that was that we would have longer to look at the new operational plans, which had only been issued early that morning.

But let us go back to D-Day—the 17th September—and follow the sequence of events leading up to our departure.

*　　*　　*　　*　　*

When General Urquhart and his Divisional Headquarters had departed I found, to my horror, that wireless communications with them from England were almost non-existent. Most of the news I received from official sources only confirmed what I had already seen in the newspapers—and it was not very heartening.

Attached to my Headquarters was a very pleasant British officer, Lieutenant-Colonel George Stevens, who had been appointed my Chief Liaison Officer. He was as worried as the rest of us over the lack of news and the bad communications. I had no radio contact with Division at Arnhem. General Browning had left with Corps from Moor Park, and even they did not have a long range transmitter. Somewhere in the Ascot area was the Base Headquarters of the 1st Allied Airborne Army under U.S. General Paul Brereton, but this was not much use to me, because Browning was commanding the troops on the ground and only from him could fresh information be obtained and alterations made in the plans.

On D-Day plus One we read in the newspapers that the Allied Airborne Army had landed in Holland. The 1st Airborne Division was fighting in the Arnhem area and some elements had reached the bridge. But they only held one end, the Germans still clung to the other and heavy fighting was going on.

Additional news brought by Stevens gave me a slightly fuller picture, but it was nothing like clear. One thing I knew for certain was that the element of surprise had been lost. Time was working in the Germans' favour. Any further jumps into Arnhem would be expected by the enemy and dealt with accordingly. On this day, the first batch of Polish gliders took off from Manston to land successfully with other paratroopers and gliders which formed the second divisional lift.

That evening, which I reckoned to be my last in England for some time, I sent off an official report to Polish Headquarters informing them we were on the point of leaving.

I had previously collected all my gear and stowed it in a cupboard in the office. At my billet, I left most of my personal possessions in my bedroom and told the landlady:

"Don't worry, Miss Mason, nothing will happen to me. Look—I'm not even packing properly."

She smiled and assured me that everything would be carefully looked after. I went to bed around 10 p.m. to get as much rest as possible.

We were due to take off at 10 a.m. and the troops had been ordered to be at the aircraft by nine-thirty. It was a dull foggy morning but we had learned by experience that the early morning weather was often like this, normally clearing very quickly. As I drove through the airfield with my aide, we became part of a vast military machine sorting and organising order out of chaos. Jeeps weaved in and out of parked planes, which loomed out of the mist. Groups of men with heavy containers lifted them up to the jaws of the bomb bays. In neat rows lay parachutes, helmets, haversacks and weapons. Y.M.C.A. vans served tea, chocolate and cigarettes without asking for money, and long-legged American airmen, bright scarves round their necks, grinned amiably, trying to understand the broken English of my troops.

Here and there engineers made last-minute adjustments to aircraft engines and sometimes the slipstream sent helmets and jumping smocks scooting over the field, with owners rushing madly after them. My driver pulled up at the Headquarters aircraft and my fellow passengers gathered round to hear the latest news.

"Will the weather clear, sir?"

"What do you think, sir, are our chances of taking off?"

Questions beat down on me.

I replied briefly: "I am still waiting for the met. report."

I busied myself with last minute adjustments of personal kit and then drove off again, stopping here and there to talk to my men.

An aircraft skipper ambled up while I was speaking with one group to tell us in a slow drawl:

"Jesus Christ, I hope we take off today. Do you'se guys realise that if I fly to Holland and back today, I will have finished my operational tour of duty and will be going Stateside."

He grinned hopefully and did a little tap dance of pure unsophisticated happiness. They were a grand bunch of airmen and we could not have asked for better crews or planes.

Another American Sergeant told us both his parents were pure Dutch.

"But Goddam it," he added, "I've never seen the country and today I shall only fly over it."

All the time we kept glancing at the sky and across the airfield trying to measure the visibility. Ten o'clock came and went. The hours slowly slipped by; midday, 1 p.m.—and still the mist clung to the earth. A weather reconnaissance plane took off and circled the field, but returned with no apparent result.

Finally at 3 p.m. the Station Commander greeted me:

"I sure am sorry, General, but it's no good today. Come back tomorrow and we'll try again at 10 a.m."

Luckily I had not ordered the lorries to return to camp and soon the staff organised the troops, getting them back to their billets. I went to Headquarters and was sitting in the office when Colonel Stevens reported:

"Your second glider lift took off this morning from Down Ampney and Tarrant Rushton—the weather was better down there—but I'm sorry to say I have heard an unconfirmed report that they were destroyed by the Germans during landing."

The news hit me hard and I was too dazed to reply immediately; but it flashed through my mind that perhaps my premonitions were coming true.

Yet in fact the picture was very different to the one described by Stevens.

Thirty-five Polish gliders had set off and thirty-four arrived over the landing zone, where they were met by a murderous anti-aircraft fire from all types of German guns. The pilots kept their planes dead on route and released the thick nylon tow ropes from the gliders' wings exactly over target. Later they let go these ropes, which fell from the sky like giant snakes writhing and coiling as they tumbled to the ground.

Gliders came down at all angles and from every direction. Some were on fire before they landed; jeeps with punctured petrol tanks flooded the wooden aircraft and red hot flak turned them into flaming infernos. Several gliders swooped into the trees, breaking off their wings, but the passengers and equipment remained unharmed.

From out of these engineless planes swarmed the Poles, who blew off the tails with explosive charges and hustled away with the guns and vehicles which had been stowed inside.

The Germans who had previously concentrated on the aircraft, now turned their artillery and machine guns on to the troops. They all had to run a gauntlet of fire to get off the exposed landing area; in some cases they had to fight their way against marauding enemy infantry.

As they formed up under the protection of a railway embankment, they asked:

"Where do we go?"

An officer told them:

"To the south to 1st Division. But we are surrounded by the enemy and must fight our way through."

A column of jeeps, trailers and anti-tank six-pounders prepared to go. Every man had his weapon at the ready and medium machine guns were mounted for action. The column drove as fast as it could and there were several false alarms, as civilians or British soldiers yelled that there were enemies up ahead.

But without making direct contact with the Germans, the column charged through the debris-littered streets, gazing in awe at the terrible destruction all around. They reported to Divisional Headquarters at the Hartenstein Hotel, where a staff officer ordered the remaining six-pounder guns into a position not far from the hotel.

Eight guns landed, but because of the devastating German fire, only three were ever unloaded from the gliders. One of these went into action against enemy armoured vehicles on the landing zone and was never seen again.

Early next morning, on the 20th September, I went to the office to see if any fresh news had come in. I had not been there long, when Stevens arrived bringing new orders.

Our landing zone had been changed: we were now to drop some four miles west of the original area near the village of Driel. We would then cross the Neder Rhine by means of a ferry near Heveadorp, held by 1st Airborne Division, and reinforce them at Oosterbeek.

This was quite a blow. We were due to take off in about three hours and there we were with a complete change of plan. To make matters worse, my force was divided between two air-fields. I ordered Major Thon in command of the troops at Spanhoe to come and see me and telephoned the two airfield commanders, telling them to delay take-off until 1 p.m. We had thought it difficult enough having only a few days to pre-pare for battle, and now we had to completely re-organise within a few hours.

I rapidly briefed Major Thon and then drove to the airfield. Gathering my men on the grass near an aircraft dispersal bay, I quickly had the new dropping zone marked on a map and pointed out fresh assembly points to my junior commanders and routes to the Heveadorp ferry.

The meteorological report was again unfavourable and the airfield lay swathed in a fine mist, which threatened to completely blanket us for ever. My officers and troops took the change of orders in their stride and still exuded confidence. At 2 p.m., as I have already described, we climbed into the planes and taxied to the end of the runways.

Then the take-off was cancelled.

However, it did give us twenty-four hours to review the situa-tion and I made several alterations in the detailed planning, which were passed on to the units. Colonel Stevens went off to try and get the latest front-line news. He never rested the whole of this period; backwards and forwards he went, seeking out information and worrying senior officers to make sure we had the best available Intelligence. He returned that night, looking very tired but, punctilious as ever, saluted and said:

"Sir, the situation is pretty confused. 1st Parachute Brigade is fighting in the western outskirts of Arnhem, one battalion has been cut off and is facing heavy odds at the bridge. The rest of 1st.

Airborne Division is battling in the Oosterbeek area under heavy pressure from the north and west. The Germans still hold the northern sectors of Nijmegen and the bridge over the River Waal is in the enemy's hands."

"And what about XXX Corps' progress up the road?" I asked.

"They appear to be bogged down and making little headway."

"What was the time of this report? Is it a fresh one, or hours old?"

"I cannot tell you, General; I only know it is the latest information I can get."

I realised just as well as he did that it could easily be hopelessly out of date and, by the time we jumped, the situation might be entirely different. There was no doubt that the operation was not going according to plan, in fact it had gone badly astray and we could well be dropping into Holland to reinforce defeat. I made up my mind immediately.

"I must speak to General Brereton at Allied Airborne Army Headquarters. It is now two days since I received any orders from Browning or Urquhart, and it is clear that 1st Airborne Division is in a dangerous position. Unless I can be assured by a senior officer at Army Headquarters of the exact situation around Arnhem, the Polish Parachute Brigade will not take off."

Stevens looked startled, but he knew very well that I meant every word and off he went, determined to get fresh information.

It was a dreadful decision to have to take, especially in view of the possible consequences, not only to the British troops at Arnhem, but also to the charges which would have been levelled in my direction, accusing me of every military crime. I would have been branded a coward; I would have been charged with refusing to obey lawful orders; I shudder to think of what might have happened.

Yet, looking back, I would take the same course again.

My reasons were, I think, sensible. Our job was to drop to the south of the Neder Rhine and cross the ferry to reinforce the British paratroopers. I had every reason to believe that I was dropping into battle on a set of orders hopelessly outdated and not designed for the present situation. Would I have been right to land my troops into the unknown, with every chance of being annihilated, without taking every possible precaution? I am sure the answer is: No, I would not have been justified.

I got very little sleep that night. I paced my office for hours and then paced the bedroom. When I lay down, my mind ran through nightmares of losing battles, of overwhelming forces of Germans, and of standing before a Court Martial answering charges that I had deliberately sacrificed my Parachute Brigade.

At about 7 a.m., 21st September, there was a knock at my door and Stevens came in. Looking at him closely, I noticed he appeared satisfied.

"The ferry at Heveadorp is in British hands, and the dropping zone hasn't been changed."

"Good!" I cried. "Then we can take-off today."

Shortly afterwards, I received a telephone call from the Chief of Staff Allied Airborne Army wishing the Brigade Good Luck. I then sent off a coded telegram to Polish Headquarters saying: *Weather permitting, we are off today.*

Take-off was set for noon. Saltby airfield was once again the scene of great activity, while the inevitable September mist clung to the ground, obscuring the vast hangars, control tower and the hundreds of aircraft ringing the field, waiting for the all-clear.

Continual waves of talk, questions and answers descended on me wherever I went. I was pleased with the men's spirit. In spite of the rough conditions and previous cancellations, they were as keen as ever and longing for battle.

At 11 a.m. the crews arrived and set about preparing the planes; they were mostly youthful, with majors and colonels young enough to be my sons. They treated my grey hair with respect and I suspect privately thought it a bit peculiar that such an old general should also be a parachutist.

Noon came and still the mist persisted. The station commander asked me in for coffee and with Stevens and Sieczkowski, my aide, we drove to airfield Headquarters. We had only taken a sip from the scalding cups, when the news arrived that the weather had cleared. With a hurried round of handshakes and cries of Good Luck we hustled out to the jeep and drove off to the waiting column of planes. An almost audible sigh of relief went round the aircraft when the news was heard. But not everyone was convinced; a sergeant near me grunted:

"It will be the same as yesterday and the day before—I won't believe it until we are in the air."

I struggled into my parachute and joined the line of men waiting to be inspected by the Stick Commander, Lieutenant Dyrda. He called us to attention.

"Left turn," he shouted, and we inspected the parachute and equipment of the man in front.

"About turn," he ordered—and we inspected the man to the right.

Then Dyrda looked us over. When he was satisfied, he said: "Stick emplane."

Like ungainly beasts of burden, we walked and staggered to the aircraft. Crew members helped us up the steps and we sank gratefully into the bucket seats; most of the talking stopped and we sat expectantly. Through the door I could see the pilots sitting on the grass, getting a final briefing from the operation commander. The group dispersed to their planes. One young captain informed us:

"We are flying in formation and the trip will take about two and a half hours. I'll give you plenty of warning before you reach the dropping zone. Good luck."

He entered the cabin and was gone. On him depended our safety until the time came to jump.

The fuselage trembled as the engines started and very soon we were part of a slow-moving convoy heading for the runway. Peering through the wide-open door and windows, we got brief glimpses as the Dakotas took off in line ahead formation, nose to tail, only seconds between them. At last it was our turn. The pilot pushed the throttles forward; the aircraft shot ahead, we bounced and bumped on the runway and then we were into the smoothness of the air. I looked at my watch. It was 2.15 p.m.: our great adventure had started.

We climbed steeply into dense low-lying rain clouds. It was nerve-racking, as we knew we were in tight formation, and it was agony hoping that we would not collide with other planes—only fifty feet off course would have been enough. Above the clouds we floated on whiteness and all around lay a majestic Armada of planes, so close that it seemed possible to reach out and touch the wingtips of the neighbouring aircraft. We floated motionless and, if it had not been for the roar of engines, we would have felt that time stood still.

After about half an hour a crew member came back to inform us that we were flying at nearly ten thousand feet and would stay at this height until we started the gradual descent to the target.

One of the paratroopers shouted:

"Wouldn't it be fun to jump from this height? I'd like it very much."

"You would drown in the North Sea—that's where we are," retorted another, pointing out of a small round window through a gap in the clouds to a choppy grey expanse of water.

Conversation was entirely restricted to shouted comments about time and distance; none of us felt like talking. I am sure I speak for all of us when I say that our hearts beat violently when we thought of what was in store. Our breath came in shuddering gulps and our insides were a tight mass of anticipation.

Yet I managed to sleep and relax until imperceptibly the nose of the plane pointed downwards and pressure in the ears told us that we were gradually descending. A crew member came from the cabin and, pointing downwards, shouted:

"We are over Belgium and coming down to operational height."

The air rushing in the open doorway became warmer, bringing some life and feeling back into our frozen limbs.

The layer of cloud was much thinner over the continent and soon we were flying beneath them, in full view of the soldiers and civilians who gazed up in open-mouthed astonishment at the hundreds of roaring tightly-formationed planes.

We stared in awe at the fleeting pictures which came to us through the small windows.

"Look there," shouted someone near me. "Look at the burning buildings."

"D'you see that crashed plane over there?" another cried out.

The roads and fields were pitted with deep bomb holes and scarred by artillery shells. The burnt-out hulks of lorries and tanks dotted streets and meadows. Here and there it was possible to see small groups waving wildly at us. At regular intervals there were smoking fires, forming a straight line, which we seemed to follow. I think it was a guide line into Arnhem, but the smoke spread a haze over the land, making it all seem unreal.

The American Jumpmaster came to the rear of the plane, taking up a position by the door, from where he could help us when the time came.

"Only twenty minutes to go," he shouted, pointing at his watch and holding up the fingers of both hands twice.

We all busied ourselves looking over the equipment, ensuring that all was in order. The Stick Commander came to give us a final check-over. We sat looking up at a point just above the door, where we knew a red and a green bulb would flash as a warning when it was time to jump.

"Five minutes to go," yelled the Jumpmaster.

Like one man, we lumbered to our feet and hooked our static lines to a cable running along the roof and locked them with securing pins. The plane started to weave about, and rise and fall, while we heard thuds like drum beats from outside. At first, none of us realised what it was and put it down to getting nearer the ground and hitting warm currents of air. It was not until I noticed several puff-balls of white smoke that I realised it was German flak. We were under fire! But it was all so remote and—in a way—unimportant compared with the battle we were about to face. It was a difficult time for the pilots: the Dakotas were unarmed, with thin petrol tanks and no defence at all from shells. In addition, they had orders to keep strict formation and not to take any evasive action. Those young American pilots kept perfect station in spite of the sight of flaming torches of hit planes plummeting to earth.

The red light came on.

"Action stations," screamed Dyrda.

We shuffled up the corrugated floor, bunching as close as possible. There were four long minutes still to go. An exploding anti-aircraft shell burst too near for comfort, bouncing the plane to one side. We lurched and recovered our balance.

The green bulb shone ghostlily above the door space and simultaneously the Jumpmaster shouted:

"GO!"

At the same moment the plane bucked as a crash under the belly indicated the first of the equipment containers had dropped from the bomb rack. The leading man pushed out a bundle of folding bicycles and in an instant flung himself into space. Number Two, Three, Four, and so on, each with a gentle push from the Jumpmaster.

Then it was my turn.

Following the man in front, I leaned forward, grasped both sides of the door and as the slipstream tried to push me back, I stepped with my left foot into nothingness. Hunching my shoulders and bending my legs, like an autumn ripe apple I fell. I was about to reap what I had sown in hard work and training. In a flash, I wondered: Had I planted well? Would I reap a good harvest?

I felt the tug of the parachute webbing on my shoulders—I was floating down. All round me, as far as the eye could see, other paratroopers were descending. The man nearest to me let out the string of his kit bag until it dangled thirty foot below, countering the oscillation of his body. Looking up, I saw with horror a Dakota, with flames pouring from both engines: yet I noticed too that the plane kept on a steady course and paratroopers still came in order out of the door. The rattle of machine guns grew louder as the thunder of the planes died away. Balls of cotton wool still appeared among the parachutes, but now they had a vicious crack of defiance.

I saw the green grass of Holland coming up to greet me, my feet touched and I sprawled sideways into the dampness of Europe. My right hand went automatically to the harness release box: I turned the metal disc, banging it smartly and the harness fell from my shoulders and groin. I rolled and the khaki canopy collapsed to the ground. Standing up, I unzipped my outer overalls and let them drop to my feet, while my eyes searched anxiously around. Shells were whistling down and mortars bursting with their characteristic explosive crack. Machine guns were ranging the whole area. I saw unorganised groups of men getting themselves out of their harnesses and others unpacking containers; but, further away, I noticed orderly files of troops marching firmly towards rendezvous points. I picked out the group of trees where my Headquarters had been ordered to assemble. My landing had been near a canal and, if I had drifted only a few more yards, I would have had a very wet welcome to Holland.

Nearby, I saw one soldier with his head in the grass and his backside sticking in the air.

"Don't stay there," I shouted. "You'll get a very painful wound; get off to your rendezvous."

Directing other soldiers who looked enquiringly at me to the assembly point, I made my own way there.

On the slope of a moist dyke I came upon the body of one of the first of my soldiers to be killed. He lay on the grass, stretched out as if on a cross. A bullet or a piece of shrapnel had neatly sliced off the top of his head, but his face was in repose without regret or hate. I wondered how many more of my men I would see like this before the battle was over, and whether their sacrifice would be worthwhile?

At the Brigade rendezvous, I found my aide-de-camp and the thought went through my head that his wife's trust in my luck had been justified; she would be very thankful. The Wireless Officer already had a transmitter working and was asking out-stations to report their strength and state of readiness to move.

Smoke put down by our mortars was drifting across the fields, obscuring our movements from the enemy, who was raking the

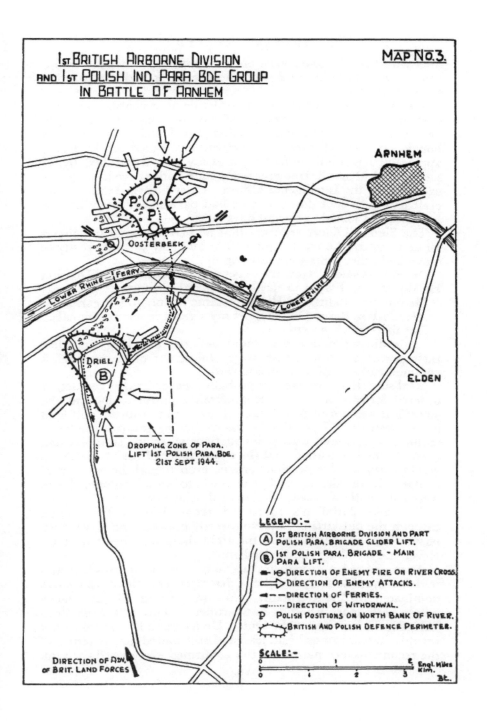

1st BRITISH AIRBORNE DIVISION AND 1st POLISH IND. PARA. BDE GROUP IN BATTLE OF ARNHEM

MAP No. 3.

ARNHEM

P
P (A) P

OOSTERBEEK

LOWER RHINE   FERRY

LOWER RHINE

DRIEL

(B)

ELDEN

DROPPING ZONE OF PARA.
LIFT 1ST POLISH PARA. BDE.
21ST SEPT 1944.

LEGEND:-

(A) 1ST BRITISH AIRBORNE DIVISION AND PART
POLISH PARA. BRIGADE GLIDER LIFT.

(B) 1ST POLISH PARA. BRIGADE - MAIN
PARA LIFT.

DIRECTION OF ENEMY FIRE ON RIVER CROSS.

DIRECTION OF ENEMY ATTACKS.

DIRECTION OF FERRIES.

DIRECTION OF WITHDRAWAL.

P   POLISH POSITIONS ON NORTH BANK OF RIVER.

BRITISH AND POLISH DEFENCE PERIMETER.

SCALE:-

0   1   2   3   Engl. Miles
0   1   2   3   Km.

Bt.

DIRECTION OF ADV.
OF BRIT. LAND FORCES

area with fire. In some spots on the Dropping Zones my troops were having to fight their way into the cover and comparative safety of the woods.

We sat on the verge of a road bordering an orchard, and I saw over my head the tempting sight of rosy red apples just asking to be eaten. I could not resist; reaching up, I picked one from its bough. It was delicious. Colonel Stevens joined me in a ripe apple and I was still munching it as my troops marched by. I soon found that all Headquarter's staff had arrived, with the exception of the Intelligence Officer. Later I learned that his air-craft had been shot down, but he had parachuted safely behind our lines and joined us several days later.

The Signals Officer reported that he had managed to contact all units except the 1st Battalion. The 2nd and 3rd were ready to move and other units were forming up.

"Good," I said. "Now try to get in touch with the 1st Division Headquarters. I want to speak to General Urquhart."

He returned to his set. His voice came plainly to our ears:

"Hallo Fox Baker Oboe report my signals report my signals." But there came no answer.

Little did we realise that radio batteries had long since lost their power and the British were almost cut off from wireless communication with the outside world.

Realising that we would probably never make contact, I ordered forward a strong reconnaissance patrol to look at the ferry; if it was not in Allied hands they were to capture and hold it. To save time, I got the battalions moving towards the ferry, saying I would send further instructions when the situation had been clarified. I trusted that the commander of the 1st Battalion would carry out his previous orders, even though he was out of contact. It was already dark, which was to our advantage. There were still civilians about, who greeted us as liberators.

The 2nd Battalion's route led them through Baarskamp, through the outskirts of Driel to directly opposite the Heveadorp ferry. The 3rd Battalion on the right flank was directed at De Nevel, a dyke along the Neder Rhine.

As we passed a crossroads, a young woman approached and told me that the ferry had been destroyed and the crossing was dominated by the Germans, who also covered all the nearby points with machine guns and artillery. This was Miss Cora Baltussen, a member of the Dutch Underground. I thanked her warmly; it was just as I had feared; I still waited for the return of the reconnaissance patrol but this confirmed every word she said.

Several times on the march to Driel, enemy shells and mortars got our range and, with unpleasant accuracy, sent us diving into the ditches and gutters.

Faced with a completely new situation, I had to make a fresh plan, so I moved with my staff into a deserted farmhouse. We blanketed the windows, set up some pressure lamps and were soon at work on the maps. I was deeply engrossed in the task, when the door was flung open; I looked up with angry words on my lips:

"What the hell . . ."

My outburst froze in mid-air, for an incredible figure staggered in. Dripping with water and spattered with mud stood a near-naked man, clad only in underpants and a camouflage net round his face. Suddenly I recognised Captain Zwolanski, whom I had sent as Liaison Officer to Urquhart.

"Oh!" I uttered rather pointlessly. "What are you doing here?"

"I have just swum the Rhine to bring you the latest news, sir."

"Yes," I said. "It looks as if you have. Well, tell me about it."

One of my staff threw a blanket over Zwolanski's shoulders, who had begun to shiver. He gratefully accepted a chair and started to talk.

"We saw you fly in and watched the drop, and immediately tried to contact you on our radio, but with no luck. General Urquhart was very worried about how he was going to get in touch with you, so I suggested I should swim across. He asked me to tell you that the ferry was taken by the Germans on the night 20th-21st, but tonight he will bring rafts to the river to carry the Brigade to the north bank. To help your crossing, he will carry out a sweep further along the river."

"How am I going to get my messages to General Urquhart?" I asked.

"I shall swim back with them, sir, the same way that I came," Zwolanski replied at once.

It was a very gallant offer, as the river was under close observation by the Germans.

I gave him my instructions:

"Tell the General that I will keep a close watch on the banks for the arrival of the rafts, and will start the crossing as soon as they are there. I shall come over with the first troops."

I shook Zwolanski's hand and watched his naked body disappear from the room.

Shortly after, I left the house and wandered down to the river to see that the patrols maintained a good look-out. It was about 10.30 p.m. The Germans were keeping up a regular pattern of night firing. Artillery shells came down on pre-arranged points and mortars thudded into the river bank. Machine guns on fixed lines fired warning to anyone foolish enough to approach.

I heard midnight strike from the bell of the church tower and all was still. Even the Germans seemed to have quietened down; there was no sign of activity further up the river and the banks were silent.

Meanwhile, on the north side, the British paratroopers with soldiers of my glider lifts were fighting an heroic battle against overwhelming odds. Urquhart, hard pressed, with his force split into several pockets had given up the unequal struggle for the Arnhem bridge and was consolidating the tattered force around Oosterbeek, trying to maintain a small bridgehead on the north bank and be ready for the expected reinforcements of my Brigade and following troops of XXX Corps. But he was unable to keep the ferry, and the British never got across with their makeshift rafts.

In a shell-pocked hole in the ground, two Polish soldiers sat, unshaven, red-eyed and haggard, writing with pencil stubs on pieces of wood. A passing English sergeant looking down as he went by, stopped, his eyebrows raised:

"What in God's name are you two doing?"

Glancing up from their work, one replied:

"We are trying to save the burial party trouble. When they find us dead here, they will also find two crosses with our names, rank, numbers, and even the correct date, because we change it every morning."

The Sergeant slapped his thigh with glee and laughed. It was not pessimism or fatalism; it was the kind of macabre joke that those soldiers in the Arnhem waste cracked and enjoyed.

But as I stood on the south bank, I heard the church clock strike 3 a.m. and I was worried. My thoughts went back to the September campaign, when I had been left with troops cut off without orders. It was obvious by then that, even if the rafts did appear, we could not possibly cross the river in the dark—and to do so in daylight would invite destruction.

Quickly I went back to Headquarters and called the Deputy Brigade Commander, Colonel Jachnik.

"You are to stay here with the 3rd Battalion group," I ordered. "If the rafts come, you will go over and report to Urquhart. I have decided it is too dangerous for the Brigade to remain here and am moving it to Driel, where we shall dig in and await an opportunity to cross."

Within half an hour the men were once again on the move. I went to the head of the column and led the Brigade into the Driel area. It was pitch black, just about one hour before dawn. With great luck, the approach march passed without incident. I directed the unit commanders to their sectors, telling them to get dug in quickly. I knew the area was overlooked by the Germans, and if we were caught in the open we would suffer heavy casualties.

The noise of our arrival woke the inhabitants, who were soon offering the men all possible help. We advised them to get into their cellars before the Germans started shelling, but they would not take heed of our words. They lent the troops spades and shovels to dig the trenches and, as the earth was very soft, our men soon reached quite a depth. We were in a rough circle round the village with my Headquarters near the main cross-road. The medical dressing station settled into the village school. As the first gleam of dawn came to the eastern sky, the 3rd Battalion led by Colonel Jachnik arrived. The Colonel reported that the rafts had failed to arrive and there had been no sign of British activity on the opposite bank.

As I thought, the ground occupied by the enemy on the northern side overlooked our trenches; with the light came the shells, and with the shells the victims. The first German shell killed Lieutenant Slesicki and wounded several civilians. I urged them to take cover in the cellars and to evacuate the village, but many refused to go.

I ordered that as many men as possible should get to sleep, so as to be rested for what I expected to be a night of activity. But at Brigade Headquarters there was not much rest for the staff. The civilians were helpful and gave us a good idea of where the German positions were and how they covered the area; I was told that the Heteren neighbourhood was not permanently occupied by the enemy, but they visited it most days with a strong patrol, which came across the river from Heelsum and Renkun.

To find out more, I ordered out a reconnaissance patrol of company strength under Captain Wardzala to look into the village of Elden and the bridges at Arnhem, and also, if possible, to bring back a prisoner. Another strong patrol I sent in the other direction to Elst, with orders to slip through the enemy without fighting and try to contact XXX Corps to tell General Horrocks our position.

In addition, I sent out a one-man assault patrol on a motor-cycle. This was a brave young officer, Lieutenant Detko, relying on his dash and audacity to get through to Nijmegen. He drove off with great élan, his exhaust roaring defiance as he disappeared into No-Man's-Land. He reached the centre of Elst without incident, but there he ran into a German company and a troop of tanks. They shot him up but, in spite of wounds, he somehow crashed through and went on to make contact with 43 Division and got the information to General Thomas.

Captain Wardzala's patrol returned some hours later with a prisoner and two British airmen who had been shot down. The bridges at Arnhem were blown and the approaches to the wreckage strongly held by the enemy in pillboxes and trenches. They had laid an ambush for a German patrol, but had been ambushed in return, only narrowly escaping. In the fight they had caught one very frightened German soldier.

The other patrol, which went to Heteren, confirmed what we had been told by Miss Baltussen. We also learned that some British troops were in the village, hidden by civilians, and we later sent out and brought them into our perimeter.

Meanwhile, the Germans had been concentrating heavy artillery and mortar fire onto our defence area. Every movement brought a reaction from the enemy and it soon taught my men fieldcraft and caution. I went round all the units to see how they had settled in. We were under fire from the north and the south-east. In the south, the Germans were harassing the landing zones, where my supply company were still collecting equipment from containers and hampers.

I went out with my aide to look at some nearby units. I was carrying my steel helmet in my hand, as the day was warm and the helmet not too comfortable. At a company headquarters, a sergeant spoke to me:

"Please, sir, put on your helmet. It is dangerous; you must not be wounded."

I realised how right he was and immediately put it on. Walking round the trenches, I heard one old soldier say to a less-experienced campaigner:

"Now you can stop worrying: 'Old' is here and he's a very lucky man—nothing will go wrong while he's around."

It was good to see that the men's morale was very high.

My battalions were spread over a fairly big area and as I did not have a lot of spare time, I took a lady's bicycle which I found leaning against the wall of my Headquarters and cycled off to visit the western sector. The troops seemed to find it highly amusing: the sight of their General riding a lady's bicycle in the middle of the battle. I did not mind, if it amused them, and it certainly was a quick way of getting about.

The company in the extreme western position protected the main road leading to Heteren and also guarded the river crossings. I was told that the defences were complete and anti-tank mines laid in and alongside the road. I stood with the Company Commander looking through field glasses at all the approaches. It was about midday and I was feeling hungry and wondering what sort of meal we would be getting at Brigade Headquarters.

I was just about to put down the glasses, when I noticed a troop of three tanks coming towards us from the west. They were in full view of the Germans and not a shot was fired against them; I naturally presumed them to be enemy tanks. The Company Commander shouted orders to his anti-tank gunners, but he added:

"They will amost certainly drive over our mines and be blown up."

He told them to hold their fire and we sat, fascinated, watching them approach destruction. Only then, as they got nearer, did I notice they were carrying British recognition marks. I shouted to the Company Commander to stop them running over the mines; a forward platoon officer stepped out and halted them, only just in time.

A troop of tanks from the Household Cavalry had charged forward from XXX Corps to join us. The young captain commanding them told me how he had avoided the enemy but, for me, the most important thing was that his wireless sets were in direct contact with XXX Corps Headquarters. I was able to send to General Horrocks a detailed position report of all my troops, and tell him that we were holding the south bank of the river, through which he would be able to assault and rescue 1st Airborne Division.

Directing the tank troop to an area near Brigade Headquarters I ordered my men to look after them. They were soon overcoming the language difficulties and chattering away like old comrades.

German pressure increased all around. Shortly after midday I received a wireless message that the unit collecting supplies from the dropping zone had been forced to retire; the officer in charge also warned that it looked as if a strong attack, including tanks, might be launched on the Brigade area.

Soon after other battalion commanders reported that the enemy
was preparing to assault. The artillery barrage and machine-gun
fire increased and soon my farmhouse headquarters was rocking
to the explosions. The rapid fire of German machine-guns got
louder and closer; then I heard the familiar tattoo of a Bren and
a tattered fusillade of rifle fire. Putting on my steel helmet, I went
out to have a look at the battle developing.

In a lush meadow just outside the farmhouse, chewing placidly,
was the new brigade mascot, a young white billy-goat which the
troops had befriended. It stayed quiet, unworried by shot and
shell, tethered to a long rope. It looked at me expectantly for a
titbit. Every time a soldier passed, the goat received a biscuit or
a cigarette. I patted it and it responded with a butting motion of
its head.

I made my way to the nearest trenches where I could see
troops firing. Jumping into one of the fox holes, I asked the
man:

"Show me your target."

He indicated a small copse several hundred yards away, where
I got a quick glimpse of field-grey uniforms.

"They are much too far away for your rifle," I told him.
"Don't waste your ammunition; you may need it badly later on.
Wait until they are within range and you are sure you can hit
them."

The soldier nodded and I gave him a reassuring smile.

Awaiting a pause in the mortar barrage, I hoisted myself out
of the moist trench and scuttled off to the Battalion Headquarters.
The commander was busy giving orders to his mortar platoon for
a concentration of fire on what appeared to be enemy forming-up
points. I approved his plan and was well pleased with his efficient
preparations.

From the reports that came in, there did not appear to be much
to worry about, apart from the tanks. I had already ordered the
anti-tank men to get far forward to deal with them, before they
got too close. But, as I was without my glider lift, the six-pounder
guns had never arrived and I had to rely on the Piat, which was
a very short-range weapon and not terribly effective against the
thick armour plating of these massive monsters.

Lieutenant Mikulski sent in a report from his company that the
Germans were driving Dutch civilians, including women and
children, in front of the infantry. I did not have time to check this,
because from the extreme south-west sector a commander informed me that enemy tanks, in spite of several hits with Piat

and plastic hand grenades, had broken through his protective screen.

I turned to the English tank captain standing in my Head-quarters:

"Some German tanks have got inside my defences. Can you help me, Captain?"

"Well, General," he hesitated, "my job is really only to recon-noitre and I am waiting for fresh orders from Corps Head-quarters."

I butted in: "But this is an emergency. You must fight if you are attacked—and if you don't help, we may be over-whelmed."

The young officer agreed immediately.

"Where do you want me to go?"

"Get a tank started and I will show you the way."

He left and soon I heard the roar of a tank engine and the grinding rattle of its tracks.

Throwing my map case at my aide, I shouted:

"Follow me!"

I rushed into the farmyard, picked up my bicycle from where it lay and, putting one foot on a pedal and swinging my other leg between the saddle and handlebars, I pushed off. I pedalled towards the tank and, waving my arms, which made the cycle wobble dangerously, I indicated that they should follow me. The tank roared and off I went, pedalling like hell in front of the clattering monster to avoid being run over. My aide chugged along behind, the map-board swinging madly from his shoulders. Amazed paratroopers looked at us from their trenches: it must have been quite a sight.

At one road intersection, a group of soldiers turned and waved, grinning and cheering. At another point, an officer shouted:

"Look out for snipers!"

Sure enough, we both soon heard the crack and whine of shots whistling near us.

The Company Commander, who had been warned we were on our way, stepped out and showed us on his map where the trouble was. The British officer joined us and we quickly decided the best site for the armoured vehicle. The tank trundled off and soon we heard the reassuring crack of a British tank gun bolstering our defences and the Germans withdrew.

We cycled back through Driel to Brigade Headquarters. The streets were strewn with broken glass from shattered windows and here and there a building burned and smoked as a result of shell-fire. Few civilians were about, except for an occasional stretcher party, taking injured women or children to a first-aid post. Yet these Dutch people were in good heart; they were convinced that liberation had come to stay and had no thought of defeat or re-occupation.

All day long the Germans snapped and ripped at our defences and my troopers fought back with a very newly acquired technique. They soon learned the tricks of battle and the sixth sense of knowing when to put their heads down and when to move about. Casualties were surprisingly low, which showed good discipline. The Germans made a tremendous effort to wipe us out. They realised very well that we were holding the south bank of the Neder Rhine, so that the Army could sweep through.

Little snippets of the battle were told to me later by officers and men alike.

Lieutenant Richard Tice, my young American, was killed that day by treachery. His platoon was holding a sector of the front and were awaiting an attack from a group of advancing German infantry. Tice told his men to hold their fire until the Huns were very close. At about two hundred yards distance, one or two voices were heard shouting:

"Don't shoot, don't shoot!"

Tice at once told his men: "Don't fire—I think they are Americans."

They kept their guns ready, but held their fire and waited. When the advancing group got within about one hundred yards, they suddenly dropped to the ground and started firing machine-guns and rifles point blank into our positions. It was a trap. Tice ordered the troops to retire singly to the shelter of some nearby buildings, whilst he and another man covered the withdrawal with Bren-gun fire. When Tice ran for cover, he was shot down by a machine-gun.

At the church, Padre Mietki was busy holding funeral rites. The steeple attracted a large amount of artillery fire, because it was thought to be used as an observation post. The enemy was right. Sergeant Halocha was up there, but as the fire became very intense, he was ordered down; within minutes, the spot where he had been sitting was hit three times in succession.

A Sergeant in the cemetery was sewing the bodies of comrades into blankets. Above and looking down at them from a cross hung a statue of Christ with an expression of infinite pity and compassion on His face. A shell burst through the chapel roof, knocking over the Sergeant; the cross fell with a crash on the stone floor, but through the dust of the explosion he saw the statue of Christ miraculously unscathed.

An officer on his rounds found a dead cow lying not far forward of the trenches in No-Man's-Land. His mind jumped to the obvious conclusion: That means fresh meat—it was an enormous and very dead cow within carrying distance. But when he asked for volunteers to go out and cut off some meat, nobody seemed very keen; it occurred to him that it was not very reasonable to ask men to risk their lives to fetch in a luxury. However, his mouth watered: the temptation was too great. He spoke to the Platoon Commander and asked from which part of the body came the best steaks; the Platoon Commander did not know, but he was inclined to think it came from the front and he agreed to help in the carving. They opened their service knives and ran out to the cow, cutting and hacking off an enormous lump of bloody meat and hustled it back to safety. There were, needless to say, plenty of volunteers to cook and eat it!

At the Forward Dressing Station in the school, my surgeons worked wonders in the most primitive surroundings. Throughout the night, they toiled at life-saving operations, using oil lamps, often with the room rocking over their heads to the drumming of mortar bombs all around. Back at Headquarters I found wounded lying in the corridors waiting to be treated; I gave an encouraging word to each of them and was amazed by their cheerfulness.

A Royal Air Force Sergeant had turned up during the day; he had been a rear gunner in a Stirling bomber which had been shot down. He acquired a rifle and joined in the fighting.

After the usual lunch of tinned meat and vegetables, and tea made from a block of milk, tea and sugar, I went up to the farm-house loft to get some sleep, leaving strict orders that I was to be awakened should anything unusual occur.

I had hardly had the proverbial forty winks, when I was brought back to wakefulness by the arrival of two British officers, Colonel Mackenzie, Urquhart's Chief of Staff, and Lieutenant-Colonel Myers, Chief Engineer, who had bravely rowed across the river in a rubber dinghy. I had not seen Mackenzie since Scotland, when he had conveyed to Browning my disapproval of a projected operation.

He told me they were on their way to XXX Corps to tell General Horrocks exactly how critical the situation was north of the Rhine.

"General," he ended, "every man you can get across the river to help 1st Division will be invaluable. Even five or ten might make a difference."

I agreed wholeheartedly with him and said I had made every effort, but without boats, rafts or bridges, how could I get any men across? Mackenzie knew very well I had no boats. Colonel Myers then made an offer.

"I think we can help. There are some small three-man rubber dinghies, which can be pulled backwards and forwards across the river on hawsers."

Delighted to hear this, I told my Chief Engineer to discuss the plan with Myers and later I heard that by this method, using only four boats, the maximum number of men we could hope to get across during the hours of darkness was two hundred, and this would depend on the operation being unopposed. I sent orders to the 3rd Battalion Commander to get his troops ready and the 8th Parachute Company was detailed to cross first. The start was scheduled for 9 p.m. and the engineers prepared the launching areas about a mile and a half north of Driel, just opposite Ooster-beek church.

At dusk I was handed a report which informed me of a column of troops advancing on my south-west perimeter. There was some exchange of fire, but it was soon realised that the column was British and shortly afterwards I welcomed Colonel George Taylor of the Duke of Cornwall's Light Infantry from 43rd Division, which had come up the route taken by the tank troop much earlier in the day. I had been wondering why troops had not immediately followed up the tanks and I was delighted to see the British infantry. Taylor told me that his Brigade should be arriving in the Valburg area—five miles south—by late night or early morning.

Included amongst his vehicles were two DUKWs—amphibious vehicles—to help the river crossings. My Chief Engineer thought these heavy craft would be useless, as they would be unable to cross the ditches and banks leading to the water, but in spite of his advice they were driven down to the Rhine, where they bogged down, useless for the whole operation.

As 9 p.m. approached, all was quiet at the river crossing points and except for a muffled thud and odd grunt, there was little to show what was being prepared. The Germans seemed to suspect nothing. The assaulting company had two two-men dinghies and two one-man dinghies: only six men could cross at a time, a slow and laborious process. Hardly had the first boat crossed, when into the black sky shot a German parachute flare. A faint red spark fizzed and then the magnesium caught, spreading a brilliant white, blinding light down on the river. Two other boats were half-way across. Enemy Spandaus commenced spraying the river, stirring up small waves, making the water boil with hot steel. Mortars started ranging on our bank, falling in the middle of the troops gathered for embarkation.

One of the first men across to make contact with the British was Lieutenant Smaczny, commanding the 8th Company. Let him tell his story:

A British guide met me on the north bank and said he would take us to the Headquarters of the Airlanding Brigade located in Oosterbeek. Other guides were left to bring on the rest of my men as they arrived. The guide told me he knew the way perfectly and we followed as he set off in the darkness. The route led us along littered streets flanked with wrecked houses; the noise of fighting was very close and all around, but apart from flashes and odd flares, we could see nothing in the pitch black. As we passed up the middle of a street, we suddenly heard, loud and clear, a German voice say:

"Feldwebel—hier sind die Tommies!"

An answering shout came from the other side of the street. We realised we were walking between two groups of Germans.

"Fall down flat," I screamed.

Not a moment too soon; machine-gun and rifle fire burst out from both sides, only just above our heads.

"We can't stay here," I shouted to the guide. "When I fire a burst from my sten, dash off with the others and I'll cover you."

Blindly, I fired a sten magazine into the top windows on the left and quickly inserting a new magazine, sprayed the right-hand buildings. The Englishman jumped to his feet and, closely followed by my men, ran down the street, but unfortunately he was killed by a burst of bullets. I then threw a hand-grenade into the nearest door and, as it exploded, I made off as fast as my trembling legs would carry me. At the end of the street, we were welcomed by red-bereted British soldiers.

During that night we only managed to get fifty men across. By 3 a.m. only one rubber dinghy was left undamaged and as dawn neared and I saw more clearly the state of affairs, I gave orders for the crossing to stop. We had done all we could to go to the aid of our hard-pressed British comrades. The 8th Company suffered very heavy casualties in the attempt.

Those who crossed, joined up with the Poles who had landed by glider, and were formed into a fighting group.

1st Airborne Division was still giving a good account of itself. German tanks often drove through their positions and enemy infantry sometimes penetrated amongst them, but somehow they never managed to overwhelm those brave young men. That day, in roughly dug positions, mangled and shattered by shells, not far from the Hartenstein Hotel in Oosterbeek, on the verge of the ever-decreasing perimeter, the remaining six-pounder anti-tank guns of the Polish Battery fired until the barrels of the weapons were hot in an effort to keep the enemy at arm's length. They knocked out two tanks and damaged and frightened off many others.

Inside the Hartenstein Hotel, one of the few wireless sets still working was manned by a group of my signallers, who were continually praised by General Urquhart for their determination in keeping communications going.

I later heard of the deeds of some of my men north of the Rhine. One story sticks in my mind: an officer was walking round the trenches, cheering the men with a word or two and giving out the scant information that he had. Nearing one trench, he heard a groan and, going up to it, saw a sergeant lying at the bottom.

"What's the matter with you?" the officer asked.

"Oh, nothing, sir."

Thinking the Sergeant was losing his nerve, the officer delivered a short lecture on keeping his head and controlling himself.

Some time later, as he returned, he went to see if the man was better.

The sergeant indicated a bloody bandage wrapped round a twisted leg.

"What's that?" queried the officer. Replied the Sergeant: "I was hit in the leg, but I dressed it myself."

"But when I asked you before, you said it was all right."

"Yes, sir, but there was a lot of shelling and I did not want you or anyone else to be exposed—so I dressed the leg myself."

He adamantly refused to go to hospital.

The battle also had its lighter moments as, for instance, when a Corporal walked up proudly to his Company Commander and produced from inside his grubby battle dress blouse a bunch of ripe blue grapes which he had discovered in a deserted and broken greenhouse!

The morning of 23rd September came grey, dank and foggy, and with it the enemy shelling and mortaring increased. I learned

from the Duke of Cornwall's Light Infantry that their Brigade
had run into enemy resistance near Elst and was held up. They
were ordered to reconnoitre to the south to try and make the
Brigade's task easier.

At 9 a.m. a liaison officer arrived from Airborne Corps with
orders to report back to Browning the exact situation on my
front. I had sent plenty of information already, but he apparently
wanted to check it.

He said that the Brigade was to make another attempt to cross
the river that night and forecast that the leading Brigade of 43rd
Division would break through to the south bank during the day.
It did cross my mind as to why we had been chosen again for the
crossing, particularly as I knew the infantry had plenty of boats
and troops experienced in river assaults, but I remained silent. I
agreed to try once more on two conditions.

"I shall need more boats—there's only one left from last night's
efforts—and I shall also need full supplies of ammunition and food
for my men."

These the officer promised.

"We can get as many boats as you need from 43rd Division."

He also assured me of long-range artillery support.

I pointed out to him that this plan made no provision for carrying across to 1st Division the vitally needed supplies.

"What they need more than anything is rations and bullets,"
I stressed and he agreed to look into it.

Before departing, he gave me the first official news I had received of my 1st Battalion, which had been dropped in the Grave
area after weather had delayed their arrival.

I sent my Chief of Staff to 43rd Division and he later returned
with details of the number of boats allocated and the rather
surprising news that we would have to supply the crews as well.
It seemed to me that engineers with experience would have been
better to man the boats; however, I had no choice.

We busied ourselves devising a new plan, allocating men and
materials to the boats. The whole Brigade was to cross, and I was
personally most excited and keen to get my men into the battle:
we all felt the tension and how crucial this night was for all
of us.

That afternoon we watched a heroic attempt by the Air Force
to drop much-needed supplies to the remnants of 1st Division.
Fighters preceded the transport planes, with the object of shooting
up and silencing the German anti-aircraft guns; but as soon as the
Hun gunners saw the Spitfires peeling off to the attack, they

ceased fire and went under cover. The fighters emptied their cannons at every likely target; the noise was horrific and dust drifted over the whole area, choking the men and obscuring the view. Then came the fresh thunder of heavier engines and we saw a massed formation of Royal Air Force Stirling bombers approaching with bomb doors open, ready to drop their vital loads to the paratroopers. The German flak guns opened up immediately and at short range on the aircraft. The giant planes ignored the shells, seeming almost to brush them aside. Multi-coloured bunches of large flowers appeared in the sky, as the supply parachutes blossomed out, carrying down the containers and pan-niers. Hardly had they vanished over the trees, when a formation of United States Air Force Dakotas appeared: The Germans guns switched targets and poured ruby-coloured tracer shells into the defenceless planes. One staggered, as it was hit by a barrage of projectiles; it levelled out and we could see the figure of a crew man still pushing out baskets and bundles. Another plane, hit in the rudder, circled out of control and still supplies came tumbling out. Smoke poured from both engines, then they flamed and suddenly the plane lifted its nose and dropped helplessly to earth; there was an enormous flash and a violent explosion. The crew must have perished with their aircraft. The brutal fact was that precious few of these supplies ever reached the hands of the British, as the Germans were occupying the dropping zones and no one had told the Royal Air Force to switch targets.

It was terrible to sit so impotently on the wrong side of the river, while our British comrades and some of my troops fought and died north of the river, so near and yet so far away. We could not help ourselves; we remained poised and ready, awaiting the arrival of the boats and hoping that the forthcoming night's attempt would not be too late. But time was running out.

I was so busy that I had completely forgotten the significance of September 23rd. During the afternoon, my aide-de-camp came to ask if I would go with him to another room, where he wished to show me something; he refused to say what it was and, con-siderably puzzled, I followed. I cannot remember what I expected, but was amazed to find all the staff gathered round an iced cake commemorating the Brigade Anniversary. I was deeply touched and surprised that they had remembered in the midst of battle.

The promised supplies for us were late in arriving, but it did not really matter, as the boats were also late, and it was not until after midnight that we were ready, although the supplies for 1st Division never reached us. Nothing went smoothly: we had been promised boats of a certain size, but those delivered were completely different, so at the last moment we had to change all the loading plans to ensure that self-supporting groups of men went over, and not unprepared bits and pieces of units.

I was also worried because we had to cross in the same area as on the previous night and I feared that the enemy would have laid on fixed lines of fire and mortar-shelling programmes. The initial stages were difficult, as the leading troops had to carry the heavy boats several hundred yards to the water from where the British Engineers had left them. They moved as silently as possible through the darkness; exploding shells and flares briefly lit the countryside. The men slipped and staggered under the weight of the boats and, as they approached the river, a factory not far off burst into flames, lighting up the whole area. I never found out if they were German or Allied shells that started the conflagration, but the subsequent blaze made it very difficult for us.

Those carrying the first boats were met with a withering hail of fire from machine-gunners as they launched their burdens into the fast running water. Only one boat was launched and it floated empty and abandoned downstream, because all the crew and passengers had been killed or wounded. Other boats sank into the mud with insufficient men to move them. It would have been madness to stay in what was virtually a death trap and those following were ordered to retire and try from another launching point. The approaches to the river were obstructed by dykes and ditches which criss-crossed the surrounding ground and men soon lost themselves and wandered aimlessly in circles, until directed to the new positions.

I set up my forward Headquarters behind one of the dykes in order to keep a close watch on battle developments. The new crossing point was even nearer to this spot and I viewed the groups of men forming up, while silently congratulating the officers and non-commissioned officers for the way they tackled the job. Behind the wall of the dyke it was comparatively safe: out in the open the troops were at the mercy of the machine guns and the continual blast of mortar bombs and deadly flying shell fragments.

I heard an officer cry out:

"Lift boat!"

Several teams trudged off into a slippery meadow sloping down to the water. For a moment we saw them silhouetted against the factory blaze on top of a bank, and then they vanished into the river; the momentum of enemy fire increased to a tremendous peak, when the whole world seemed to be exploding around us, and at Headquarters we watched and waited. Hour by hour, all through the night, we received messages of boats getting across and of boats being sunk; every time I went out to have a look round, files of stretcher-bearers trudged past bringing back the wounded and others marched forward, ready and eager to take their place.

Suddenly, and without warning, there was an enormous explosion which seemed to enter my head and expand it. I felt my feet knocked from under me; then for a second or two, I lay deafened and still. Then I was on my feet again.

"Is everyone all right?"

An air burst had exploded immediately above us and it was remarkable how little damage was done: the only person to be wounded was the Chief Engineer, who had been sitting next to me.

Just then a messenger came running up.

"Sir," he panted, "the embarkation point is under heavy fire; there are many casualties and the situation is very grim. The Embarkation Officer would like your orders."

Grabbing my helmet, I ran off, shouting back over my shoulder:
"I'll sort it out."

Then I heard the voice of my old friend, Colonel Kaminski, cry out:

"You can't do it alone; I'm coming."

The two of us ran down to the bank: it was quite true. An inferno of shells, bombs and bullets were dropping right on the spot; there was a hell of a noise, continual flashes, the reek of cordite and cries of anguish from the wounded men. It was impossible to get order out of it and, in fact, not desirable as dawn was not far off. Troops still stood bravely at the embarkation points, helping men on and wounded bodies off, but I told the officer in charge:

"Stop everything. It will soon be dawn. Get those remaining back to safety."

In an orderly manner they retired and I followed them wearily back. When the final count was handed to me, I learned that over two hundred Polish soldiers had got across to join in the fighting around Arnhem. These men moved into position with the 1st Division and came under command of Brigadier Shan Hacket who put them at the crossroads of the *Utrechtse Weg-Station Weg* at Oosterbeek.

The battle moved backwards and forwards a yard at a time. Trenches were occupied for a short while by the Poles and then by the Germans. Many fox-holes were within a few yards of each other. The buildings overlooking the crossroads were hotly contested and a lot of very hard house-to-house fighting took place with the inevitable casualties. Captain Gazurek, the Battalion Commander, and a Company Commander, Lieutenant Pudelko, were killed.

All the open spaces were continually swept by the fire of both sides; unburied human and animal bodies lay swollen and revolting in these areas. In all the house-cellars women and children crouched under the roaring waves of battle, grateful for the odd pieces of chocolate and food which the troops handed to them with words of good cheer and hope.

The anti-tank guns continued firing at giant tanks which kept appearing all round the perimeter. They did not stop firing until the last gun was put out of action on the 25th.

I went back to the Dressing Station, well satisfied with the night's work and proud of my brave men, but when I saw the long lines of wounded awaiting treatment, I was very sad. The cost in life and limb of that crossing had been very heavy.

Inside the wrecked building, by the light of candles and paraffin lamps, the surgeons toiled and sweated. Their operation overalls were smothered in blood and the whole place reeked of human flesh. They had replaced the white operating caps with steel helmets and the sweat from their brows dripped from the chin straps and orderlies wiped this away continually. On one side of the battered room on a stretcher table lay a ghost of a man, blood pumping into him from a plasma tube slung from the wall. Others lay moaning or patiently waiting for attention and those able to walk moved among them offering sips of water and cigarettes.

The Chief Surgeon, Dr. Milian, was pale and wan. Glancing up and seeing me, he finished sewing up a wounded abdomen and came to talk.

"You must get some sleep, Doctor," I ordered.

"How can we," he replied. "As long as we have benzedrine we will all keep going."

It was such a spirit that imbued us all at Arnhem, and many men were saved by this gallant band of medicos who would have died had there been any less sufficient to the occasion.

This was 24th September 1944, the eighth day of the Arnhem battle. North and south of the Neder Rhine the unequal fight continued, a fight which I felt certain could still be won if the heavy units of XXX Corps managed to break through. After a final check up on the situation and a cup of tea, I fell into bed hoping to get at least three hours' sleep. But it was not to be: within an hour I was awakened by the aide-de-camp.

"A British General has arrived in an armoured car and wants to see you."

I had just struggled to my feet when General Horrocks entered and introduced himself. I was pleased to see him; he was the first high-ranking officer to visit me during the battle and we all took a very good view of his coming into the front line. He shook hands warmly and said that he had called in to tell me that my 1st Battalion was on the way up and should be joining us within a few hours. He also asked for full details of the situation on my front.

As briefly as I could, I described the battle and gave him my appreciation: the remnants of 1st Airborne Division with part of my Brigade were north of the Rhine, holding isolated pockets; they did not even have a permanent path to the river, although there was a corridor which was continually being interrupted by the enemy. I showed Horrocks where we had crossed and one other spot where I thought a crossing was feasible, but told him that, with increasing German opposition, if he wanted to get any more units over, he should set about it immediately. Thanking me, he then asked me to attend a conference at 43rd Division Headquarters afterwards. He drove off smiling and waving at my troops.

Colonel Stevens, who had managed to scrounge a jeep from somewhere, drove me back to Valburg, where the Headquarters of 43rd Division was hidden in some orchards. Compared to my riverside abode, this was absolute luxury. Caravans and lorries stood about, carefully camouflaged; there were big marquees for staff officers and messes and smaller tents for living accommodation. Officers and troops were shaved and well dressed, and although one could not but help making comparisons, I was not jealous; as an Airborne Commander, I expected to rough it much more, and live and eat in the same conditions as my soldiers.

I went to see Major-General George Thomas, the Divisional Commander. What a difference there was between the two of us! He was clean and smart, in a well-creased service dress and red-banded peaked cap, and he gave out an air of well-being and satisfaction. In contrast, I wore a camouflaged airborne smock, with belt and pistol; from my helmet dangled a net and multi-coloured strips of hessian, my battle dress trousers were stained and

wet and my boots caked with dirt. I had shaved, but I was generally dishevelled.

Horrocks arrived in a flurry of vehicles and quickly moved into
the briefing tent, where he ordered two river assaults for that
night. One was to be carried out at the sunken Heveadorp Ferry
by the 1st Battalion Dorsets, together with one of my battalions,
taking with us as many supplies and medium machine guns as we
could carry. The rest of my Brigade was to attempt another
attack in the same place as we had already tried for two consecu-
tive nights, but this was to be a secondary operation.

General Thomas started giving his more detailed orders and,
turning to me, said:

"Your 1st Battalion will go with the Dorsets."

"Excuse me, General," I retorted, "but *one* of my Battalions
selected by *me* will go there."

Thomas flushed red and, if it had not been for some soothing
words from Horrocks, there might have been a real row. Thomas
was most displeased and he very soon showed that he was not
going to forget it.

The conference ended and I was walking towards the jeep with
Colonel Stevens when Thomas came up to us. He ignored my
presence, although he was well aware that I spoke English,
and addressed himself only to Stevens. He gave some further
instructions to my British Liaison Officer and then walked off
without offering to shake hands or making any sign in my
direction.

Stevens and I drove off to Nijmegen, where Corps Headquarters
was located. It was interesting to drive along this route; a lot of
hard battles had been fought and the countryside was considerably
devastated. The high ground overlooking the town was held by
the United States 82nd Airborne Division and from the sound
of the shell-fire, quite a battle was still raging. It crossed my
mind that if Operation "Comet" had been carried out, the
position which my Brigade was supposed to have occupied near
Nijmegen, without the friendly forces on that high ground, would
not have been very pleasant.

We were greeted in a most friendly fashion by Corps staff
officers, who bombarded us with questions about the battle,
which we did our best to answer. It was a pleasure to sit down at
a well-appointed luncheon table, with mess waiters to attend on
us. The food was served on china plates and a good cook had
worked wonders with Army rations supplemented with what
appeared to be locally purchased titbits. How much better than

the meagre lunch I would have had out of a mess tin at the front line!

Browning was also at this meal and, towards the end, he caught my eye and asked if I would go to his caravan before leaving again for Brigade.

Browning, immaculate as ever, came to the point as soon as I entered.

"My main task now, Sosabowski, is to keep open the road from Nijmegen to Eindhoven. The Germans are continually cutting it and I also want to bring up all our seaborne vehicles as near to the front as possible."

I agreed that there was still quite a job ahead and asked him what he thought of the chances of successfully assaulting the Neder Rhine. I emphasised that the longer the attack was delayed, the stronger would become German resistance; even more so when the enemy learned that the main Allied forces were approaching the south bank. Browning's reply positively amazed me:

"The river crossing may not succeed as there is no adequate equipment."

Thunderstruck, I asked: "Why, in heaven's name, not?"

"Because it is impossible to get the equipment up to the river."

"But ambulances are getting through regularly to Driel; they have evacuated some of my wounded and, if they can do it, so can the bridging lorries."

Browning repeated what he had said, adding that the Germans had cut the road and nobody knew when it would be clear again. He hoped it would be soon.

I felt it was incredible and, speaking my mind freely, I told him so.

"Every hour, every minute that 1st Airborne Division is left on the other bank, means more killed and wounded. We are so near to them—we must make a final effort."

I fear that my forthrightness hurt Browning's feelings, for he quickly indicated the end of our conversation.

I drove off rapidly with very mixed feelings from the Corps area and went straight back to Brigade Headquarters.

Written orders, confirming the morning's conference, arrived from 43rd Division at about 5 p.m. fixing the time for the assault at 9 p.m. Early in the evening, I welcomed Major Thon, the Commander of my 1st Battalion, who had just arrived with his unit after being missing since the operation commenced. He explained how they had taken off at the correct time on the 21st from Spanhoe Airfield, but then the planes had returned to base owing to bad weather on instructions radioed from Headquarters. He was powerless to do otherwise, because as long as paratroopers are airborne, they come under the orders of the Air Force. He was very upset when he realised that the bulk of the planes had gone on to complete their mission in Holland. They finally took off on 23rd September and dropped near Grave in the area occupied by the 82nd United States Airborne Division. This battalion was a very welcome addition indeed and I ordered them to prepare to follow the Dorsets in the main assault.

Just before 9 p.m. my 2nd Battalion was poised at our crossing point, ready to go. Stevens arrived at my Headquarters with a message from General Thomas delaying the operation, owing to the non-arrival of boats for the main crossing.

"When do they expect to get the boats?" I asked.

"They haven't the faintest idea; they may never get them at all."

There was a pause and then, taking a deep breath, Stevens went on.

"Are you willing, sir, to give up the boats held by you and hand them over to the Dorsets, so that the main assault can be put in?"

At this, the following questions immediately came to the fore-front of my mind: Where is the biggest effort? where are most of the supplies? The answer to both was: With the Dorsets. Even so, I was reluctant to let the boats go, as with the previous night's success in getting the 3rd Battalion across, I was confident that I could get the rest of the Brigade over. Yet, in view of the much bigger effort to be made further along the river, I turned to my Chief Engineer and told him to transfer the boats to the Dorsets' crossing point.

However, owing to this unforeseen delay, the Dorsets did not start before midnight, by which time it was pretty obvious to the Germans where the assault would take place and, when it was launched, they were met with murderous machine-gun fire, which raked the men and riddled the boats. Wounded soldiers were swept screaming downstream and unmanned craft drifted, circled and sank. The Dorsets took a horrible beating that night. The worst of it was that not a single pound of supplies, equipment or ammunition ever reached its destination—to bolster the weakening resistance in the ever-decreasing perimeter around Oosterbeek.

That morning, 25th September, saw us stuck in exactly the

same spot as on the previous days; no progress at all had been made. Yet, at this time, a route was wide open, the Oosterhoud–Wolferen–Valburg road, along which ambulances and other vehicles were passing quite safely. This had been known to Corps Headquarters for almost three days; along this route had come the Household Cavalry tank troop; followed after some delay by the Duke of Cornwall's Light Infantry; and still later the remainder of an infantry brigade had come up it. To my mind it was fantastic that the main units of XXX Corps had not made a really determined effort to get along the fourteen miles of this road separating them from the Neder Rhine. The troops seemed to be marking time when speed was most essential.

The situation with my Brigade at this time was as follows: on the north bank, under direct command of General Urquhart, were my men who had flown in by glider with jeeps and anti-tank guns; plus, of course, most of the 3rd Parachute Battalion with the parachute elements of the anti-tank and signal companies, which had got over on the previous nights. Under my command on the south bank I had the 1st and 2nd Battalions, engineers, medical units and the remainder of the administrative units.

During the day I received from 43rd Division a plan for the evacuation of the remnants of 1st Division back across the river. It was to be a night withdrawal and speed and silence were vital. My Brigade was detailed to help guide the men when they reached the southern bank and direct them to Nijmegen; after that, I was to move my troops back to the same area. Any equipment that could not be carried was to be destroyed on the spot; it was obvious we would be withdrawing in full daylight and in my detailed orders to Unit Commanders I said they should travel in small groups and rendezvous further south at Valburg.

As dusk fell that evening, my men plodded out in the rain through the mud into the fields and took up positions to act as guides to any soldiers who were lucky enough to escape from the enemy. The overwhelming German forces kept up a continual barrage from weapons of all shapes and sizes; the boom and rattle of their explosions formed a background to which we were completely accustomed.

I had done all I could and decided to get some sleep. The ground floor of the farmhouse was a very busy and overcrowded place and I crept into a niche by the fireplace to avoid being trodden on. I was awakened by a tremendous crash and I opened my eyes, which were at once filled with dust. There was chaos all around.

I heard Colonel Kaminski crying: "General, General, are you all right?"

"Yes—what the hell has happened?" I yelled in reply.

Someone lit a candle and by its dim guttering flame we could see a jagged hole in one wall, through which a shell had blasted. In another room, we could hear the groans and cries of wounded men. My mind went back to the Headquarters I had occupied in the aircraft factory in Warsaw during the siege—my luck had not deserted me! But my luck had not spread to our billy-goat mascot; a flying shell fragment killed him where he stood, tethered by his rope.

On the north bank, the British and Polish survivors prepared for the evacuation. The Polish group was ordered to act as a rearguard and cover the approaches to the river, while the British troops crossed. With faces blackened, boots covered in sacking, and all pieces of metal bound to deaden any sound, they prepared to guide men through the rain and slush to the swiftly flowing water.

Meanwhile, a burial party hastily interred the dead. Over one small mound of muddy earth was erected a ragged cross made from a bough and a twisted number plate wrenched from a wrecked jeep. It read:

Lieutenant K
Polish Paratroopers
24-9-1944

Others were buried where they lay in crumbling fox-holes and shell-pits.

The long files of men began the slow and dreary march to the river about 9.30 p.m. The drenching rain drummed down, masking the sound of squelching boots and the groans and cries of the wounded. Every now and then, the Germans let fly blindly with a barrage of mortar bombs, which landed indiscriminately along the crowded river approaches. Occasionally, a searchlight beam probed the darkness, illuminating the meandering columns of soldiers, who froze like statues as the light struck them.

The rearguard was told that, when the last survivor had passed through their lines, they would be informed. But the order for them to move never arrived. At 3 a.m. the officer in charge took the decision on his own shoulders and they joined on the end of a straggling line of exhausted and wounded troops. They stood, quietly patient; those who were unable to stand any longer sat or lay dozing in the mud. Stuck in the middle of an open meadow, they were suddenly illuminated by several parachute flares, shortly followed by a salvo of bombs. One burst landed across a line of men; several of them, already wounded, were killed or more severely injured. Their comrades gathered them up, sending them forward for priority in the boats.

As they neared the river, it was possible to hear the muffled roar of motor-boat exhausts, interspersed with the crash of shells and the staccato *brrrrrrp* of Schmeisser machine guns.

At 4 a.m. some Poles reached the banks and found that only one boat was left operating, although there was still something like five hundred men north of the Rhine; they were unlikely to be able to cross by boat. Suddenly, the implications of the situation struck the men and panic broke out, as about a hundred British troops rushed into the shallows, fighting to get aboard the lone craft. "Get back!" shouted an officer. "Behave like Englishmen!"

The struggling stopped and they returned to shore.

All semblance of order disappeared. It was everyone for himself. Men, singly and in groups, Poles and British, wandered along the bank looking for good places from which to swim the swirling waters. Many threw off their clothes, dived in and fighting the strong current, swam to the Allied side; others, many of them non-swimmers, turned back to join groups in hiding to await a suitable opportunity to escape; others again were captured by German patrols.

Many of the soldiers who swam across the Neder Rhine recalled afterwards passing through a battered broken house, where a Dutch civilian stood, handing out bottled fruit, taken from a precious hoard, to the exhausted troops.

In spite of instructions that they should proceed to Nijmegen directly, most of the Poles came instead to rejoin the Brigade. This was a most touching display of loyalty.

When the flow of men across the river ceased, I gave the order for the Brigade to evacuate Driel, and in small groups, well spaced out, they started plodding along the lanes leading to Nijmegen.

The Battle of Arnhem was over.

*   *   *   *   *

One thousand seven hundred Polish troops parachuted or glided into Holland; 1,310 marched out. Our less fortunate British comrades moved off to well-deserved rest and evacuation to England.

We marched, with all our heavy equipment, the fourteen miles to Nijmegen. Whilst in the town, I took the first opportunity of visiting Urquhart, who was resting there. He was in a low state, both physically and mentally, but he was pleased to see me; although we refrained from discussing the battle, his whole attitude was one of deep and bitter disappointment.

I had to report to Browning's Headquarters to collect fresh instructions. I was kept waiting in an office, where I went to sleep in an armchair; perhaps the delay was due to the preoccupation by everyone in preparing new plans.

We were allocated new positions in defence of an airfield not far from Grave on the banks of the River Maas. The sector was fairly quiet, although 712 German Division in the s'Hertogenbosch area constituted a grave threat to the lines of communication to Nijmegen.

I had also been told by a senior staff officer at Browning's Headquarters that I was under command of 157 Brigade of 52nd Lowland Division. To me this was a clear breach of regulations, as it meant that I, a Major-General, was taking orders from a Brigadier. Such orders are not given in any army and I could not tolerate it. As soon as my men were settled in their new positions, I despatched a message to Browning.

May I be released from under command of O.C. 157 Brigade. My reasons are as follows:
    1. The organisation of my unit;
    2. My seniority of rank.

To this Browning replied:

1. 1st Polish Para. Bde. was put under command 157 Inf. Bde. for the following reasons:

    (a) *Polish Para. Bde. had severe casualties and was inevitably disorganised owing to series of dispersed drops and action in which it had taken part.*

    (b) *157 Bde. H.Q. was established in an important area but badly needed a reserve immediately available in emergency to strengthen the few troops already there.*

2. The situation has now changed for the better. 1st Polish Para. Bde. will therefore revert to directly under command of British Airborne Corps with effect 08.00 hrs. 29th Sep.

3. 1st Polish Para. Bde. will maintain present dispositions and tasks, working in very close liaison with 157 Inf. Bde.

I was very surprised that such orders were ever given, as from my point of view, Browning appeared to have deliberately slighted me, and then objected when I complained. He knew—or should have known—my nature very well, and he must have realized that I would react strongly to being ordered around by a Brigadier. Equally, he knew very well that my Brigade had never been exactly disorganized; we had been dispersed and split up, we had suffered casualties, but I had remained in full control at all times.

As soon as circumstances permitted, I produced a full written report on the battle and I also enclosed a statement of our present situation.

The Polish Liaison Officer from 21st Army Group Headquarters called on me in the course of his duties and I made it clear to him that the Polish Parachute Brigade was not to be integrated into any British unit and our independence was to be maintained. I also asked that he should do his best to prevent our being used as ordinary infantry of the line, not only because of our specialist role, but because we had little chance of getting more volunteers and I still had in mind the possibility that we might be able to fight in Poland.

For several days, we stayed in the muddy, damp dug-outs which made up the line along the River Maas. We were mainly occupied with patrolling at night, which kept us in contact with the enemy and enabled us to capture a prisoner or two. Many wild rumours of German parachutists started at this time and this caused a fire fight one night between my supply column and a British unit, during which two Poles were killed and several wounded.

On the 28th of September one company took over guard duties on the Waal bridge at Nijmegen and other canal bridges. This was mainly a precaution against enemy frogmen, who had drifted down with the current without being seen and had succeeded in blowing up the railway bridge.

I also lent General Gavin, Commander of 82nd U.S. Airborne Division, a couple of patrols, because his men had been unable to capture any Germans. We were both delighted when the first patrol out brought back a sergeant-major as a prisoner.

On October the 7th, we set off by lorry for Brussels, from where we hoped to fly to England, but only a few were taken by air; the rest of us were switched to Ostend and embarked for Britain on four landing craft. On arrival at Tilbury on the 12th of October, the inevitable Customs Officer came aboard, asking if we had anything to declare.

"Yes," I replied. "We have a large quantity of Eau de Cologne—or Rhine Water."

He roared with laughter and went on his way.

One of the very first things I was shown on my return was my obituary notice, which appeared in the *Glasgow Herald,* on the strength of which my brother in Edinburgh had received several telegrams of condolence.

It was a triumph of German propaganda. My jeep had gone by glider and, shortly after landing, the driver was wounded and captured. The Germans who looted the vehicle must have been delighted to find a bottle of whisky which I had stored away and, unfortunately for my relatives and friends, they also found a case labelled with my name. With this very circumstantial evidence, Goebbels' propaganda machine broadcast three times that I had been killed in action!

CHAPTER XI

PERSONAL REFLECTIONS

THERE were eight thousand casualties as a result of the Battle of Arnhem. Montgomery has said "In years to come it will be a great thing for a man to be able to say 'I fought at Arnhem'." Those who came back alive will certainly agree; the dead cannot speak for themselves.

It is no part of this book to disillusion the parents, wives and children of those who died. They all believe that their loved ones died because it was necessary for the cause. As in all British battles involving huge casualties, the commanders get fame and the soldiers' deeds are entered in the glorious annals of history.

Yet I would like to analyse the battle and give my views on some of the reasons why the battle failed to gain all its objectives. Any criticism I make is certainly not directed at the brave soldiers. Wrong decisions by commanders do not affect the personal heroism of individuals; in fact, they often serve to increase it.

The nine days around Arnhem have something in common with the two months' siege of Warsaw. Both battles were fought with tremendous bravery because those involved believed help was at hand, though in each case it never came.

The first question which comes to mind about Arnhem is: *If all had gone well, would the plan have worked?* The only possible answer is that, had it succeeded, the war in Europe would have ended in 1944 and the wastage of human lives and the vast expense would certainly have been considerably reduced. The sacrifice at Arnhem would, in that case, have been well worthwhile.

It is now common knowledge that Eisenhower and Montgomery were at variance over the way to bring the war to a swift conclusion. Montgomery favoured one swift single thrust into the Ruhr and then on to Berlin. Eisenhower, backed by General Omar Bradley, preferred to combine with Montgomery's plan another attack by the American Armies through the Saar; as a result, he did not give priority to Arnhem until it was too late.

I think that it has never yet been taken into account, consciously or unconsciously, that national pride played a large part in this decision. If the British plan had resulted in the Germans suing for peace, think of the cries of: Who won the war? The same would have happened if the Americans had succeeded. There were similar cases in Italy, particularly over Rome.

From a political point of view, it was preferable for the coup de grâce to be given by both Allies together.

The facts, as given by Eisenhower and Montgomery, show that, while the agony of Arnhem was in progress, these two commanders were arguing about priorities and only on 22nd September did Ike finally agree to give full support to 21st Army Group; but, of course, this was too late to affect the immediate operation.

It was on the 3rd of September that Montgomery and Browning first conceived the idea of an airborne assault to capture the bridges over the Rhine and Lower Rhine. Browning flew to Montgomery's Field Headquarters on that day and again on the 10th.

At this stage, in view of the plans being made and Eisenhower's refusals, the question arises: *Should Montgomery have continued?*

All battles contain an element of risk, but it is the commanders' responsibility to reduce this risk to the minimum. It is a sign of a good commander if he takes into consideration the unexpected possibilities.

The object of Operation "Market Garden" was to end the war in 1944. Montgomery was well justified in taking the risk, although he had not been given the support of equipment and planes for which he had asked.

Monty's estimation of what he needed to win this battle was as follows:

1. *The 1st Allied Airborne Army, consisting of 82nd, 101st U.S. Airborne Divisions, 1st British Airborne Division and the Polish Independent Parachute Brigade.*
2. *A daily air supply of 1,000 tons.*
3. *The covering of the right flank by 1st U.S. Army.*
4. *Sufficient transport aircraft for the paratroopers.*

Of these four main requirements, Montgomery only received the first in full—the Allied Airborne Army; all his other requests were modified or never fulfilled. The maximum daily air supply ever received was five hundred tons, or exactly half of the requirement. The right flank was never covered by 1st U.S. Army during the operation. The operation was launched and continued with insufficient aircraft, because many of the American planes were still being used to supply 12th U.S. Army Group.

It is a common military maxim that where the main effort is directed, there also should be the maximum concentration of troops and supplies.

I preferred Montgomery's plan for a single thrust, by-passing the Siegfried Line and going straight through the Ruhr into the wide north German plain, where the tanks could have been used to the best advantage. The Saar thrust would have had to blast its way through the Siegfried Line, pillbox by pillbox, a slow and costly business; the only reason I can think of for the Supreme Commander's dilatoriness is that he was waiting to find out the weakest of the two plans.

As a general reflection on the number of plans produced and the imagination with which they were thought up, I can only say that we were lucky that the ones prior to "Market Garden" were never launched. Operation "Comet", for instance, which was designed to capture the Nijmegen Bridge, in my considered opinion, did not have the slightest chance of success.

When Montgomery gave the go-ahead for "Market Garden" he was well aware of the difficulties facing him. Between the Guards' Armoured Division on the Albert–Escaut Canal and Arnhem were six water obstacles: three rivers and three canals. Over sixty long miles separated 2nd Army's spearhead from Arnhem. Only one narrow ribbon of a road led straight across the polder lands and tanks were forced to remain on it; any that ventured into the fields would certainly have bogged down. To my mind, 2nd Army should at least have reached the Wilhelmina Canal, about twenty-five miles nearer to Arnhem and been ready with strong forces to push ahead.

But one of the biggest blunders of all was the complete and utter failure of the Allied Intelligence system to correctly assess the number of German units, and their type and capabilities. I had personally protested to Urquhart at early briefings that the enemy were not only being under-estimated in size, but also in their reactions. It was a bit of a joke amongst airborne officers that Browning was a little apt to chuck in a bit of enemy opposition as and where it suited his purposes. He was also inclined to be a bit over-confident—"The Red Devils with the Polish Para-troopers can do anything"—and tended to brush aside, in a very arbitrary manner, any difficulties placed in his way. In fact the Wehrmacht was waiting in force and not with low-grade troops, but with top-line paratroopers and panzers. The German High Command had certainly not failed to realise the importance of Arnhem as a gateway into Germany.

It is as well to point out here that Airborne troops, to my knowledge, were never at any time used as much as sixty miles ahead of the main forces. I have always maintained that paratroopers, lightly equipped as they are, must be relieved as quickly as possible by stronger infantry and tanks.

The Airborne Army should never have been dropped so far ahead. It was extraordinary optimism to ever dream that they could have been relieved in thirty-six hours as was planned.

These were mistakes in higher strategy; and now we come to tactical details.

The main weapon of airborne forces is the element of surprise. Troops dropping from planes or travelling in gliders can land in the heart of enemy positions before the enemy are aware of what is happening. The lightly-equipped paratroopers, who are trained for immediate instinctive offensive action, can take full advantage of the resulting chaos amongst the defenders. In Normandy, gliders of 6th Airborne Division successfully crash-landed on top of bridges and even in the middle of a coastal battery. Yet in the plans for Arnhem, the dropping zones were, in some cases, as much as six miles from the objectives. The troops had to fight their way towards targets which thus became perfectly obvious to even the most stupid of German commanders. What would be the point in dropping thousands of paratroopers in that area, except to capture the Rhine bridges?

The technical experts, who advised Urquhart that the soggy ground around the bridges was unsuited to gliders, were talking through their hats. American and British gliders at that time were capable of landing in the most restricted places, being highly manœuvrable, and there are many cases where glider pilots deliberately drove their planes into woods, smashing the wings against tree trunks, in order to stop their planes. Urquhart, advised by his Divisional Staff, did ask Royal Air Force Transport Command to drop men and gliders both sides of the bridges. The Air Force refused to do this, because they said German flak was too heavy; they even refused to put in a small Coup-de-Main Party.

Nobody appears to have stepped forward and pointed out the vital importance of capturing the bridges, which were well worth the possible loss of a few transport aircraft. Did the Airborne commanders ever bring pressure to bear on the Air Force? There was a strong feeling in the Airborne that the Air Force were not co-operating to the fullest extent.

One should not place too much blame on Urquhart's shoulders. He was brought into Airborne without any previous experience; he described himself as "very much a landlubber". He was appointed to command of the Division after the War Office had removed one of their most experienced parachutist generals, Eric Down. This was a strange policy on the part of the War Office, and it is hard to see why a non-Airborne general was appointed, when there were experienced Airborne officers available, such as Brigadier Gerald Lathbury, who had commanded a battalion in North Africa and a brigade in Sicily, and Brigadier "Shan" Hackett.

In my view, Urquhart's appointment was not a happy one. His Brigade Commanders did not take it too well and he, like most soldiers outside the Airborne Corps d'Élite, must have felt a little out of his element. The decision to put him in command showed an unjustified lack of confidence in the other Brigade Commanders.

Like many other World War II Generals, Urquhart started off with a pre-conceived error. He was of the opinion that once paratroopers had landed, they could be used as ordinary infantry. But this was completely wrong. Why waste specialist troops, trained at great expense, in jobs that can be done by the infantry? Armoured and infantry engagements are two entirely different types of battle; the difference between ordinary infantry and paratroopers is as wide. Airborne forces are lightly equipped and cannot be expected, unless enormously reinforced and supported, to carry out normal infantry tasks.

In his Memoirs Montgomery rather grandly takes on himself full blame and responsibility for the failure of Arnhem, but although, as Army Group Commander, he was ultimately responsible, he is, in my opinion, being much too generous. Mistakes were made at Army, Corps and Divisional levels.

Shortage of aircraft was a vital factor. The plan was to fly in 1st Airborne Division and the Polish Brigade in three separate lifts at twenty-four-hour intervals. Even with the lack of aircraft, there was no reason why there had to be such a long delay between each drop. The planes could have flown back to England, re-fuelled, loaded and returned to Holland within twelve hours. All operational lifts would thus have been completed in thirty-six hours and all the men would have been on the ground before the bad weather set in on the 19th of September.

There was, also, no reason whatever why the men could not

have dropped at night. This might easily have resulted in fewer casualties in the initial stages. In fact, "Comet", the cancelled operation, had included a night drop in the plans. 6th Airborne Division had jumped in pitch darkness into Normandy on the 5th of June. The delay between the lifts allowed the Germans to fight each group separately.

All the errors, however, were not on the Airborne side. I believe, in spite of the planning mistakes, the battle could have still been won if the Land Forces had shown more determination and drive.

Montgomery's orders to General Horrocks read: *The thrust northwards to secure the river crossings will be rapid and violent and without regard to what is happening on the flanks.* Responsibility for the flanks was allocated to VIII and XII Corps. Did the Corps do their best to push on? XII Corps on the left flank delayed its start twenty-four hours to the 18th!

It took XXX Corps four days to cross the Waal at Nijmegen, by which time they should have covered all sixty miles into Arnhem. Throughout the whole of this period, one cannot sense any great urgency amongst the commanders or the troops of Horrocks' Corps.

On the night of 20th September, the Guards' Armoured Division and 43rd Division were in Nijmegen, only nine miles short of Arnhem, and the bridge was still intact. On the 21st my Brigade dropped on the southern bank of the river. We held a wide stretch of the approaches and were firmly in possession of the ground, but no great effort was made to reach us. Not until lunchtime on the 22nd did the tank troop of the Household Cavalry come into my positions at Driel. They were followed in the evening, along exactly the same route, by the Duke of Cornwall's Light Infantry, who found the road free of the enemy. There was some fighting in the area of Elst, but the road via Oosterhout–Valburg–Driel, right up to the Neder Rhine, was wide open. Yet, in spite of this, and with even ambulances travelling along it, no large bodies of troops were moved up for a river assault. General Thomas of 43rd Division had hung around Nijmegen for some time and, when he did move, it looked a bit half-hearted.

Horrocks came up to the front line to see me on September 24th. I am convinced he still thought that a river crossing was both possible and desirable. That night, the 24th-25th, Thomas launched the Dorsets across the Rhine but, I think, in the wrong place. The attempt was a failure and resulted in awful casualties.

The Corps Commander, Horrocks, then planned a major assault for the following night. Browning, however, was against it; he thought that it could not succeed. He passed on this opinion to General Dempsey who transmitted it to Monty. Montgomery decided immediately to call the whole thing off and the plan, Operation "Berlin", was made to evacuate the 1st Airborne Division.

Browning was wrong. In every action comes a crisis. At that moment, the battle can be swayed one way or the other, dependent on the luck or superior planning of either side. Victory or defeat lie along a very thin razor edge. It is incredible to me that Browning, Chief of British Airborne, despite the shortage of river-crossing equipment did not use all his powers to encourage and persuade Horrocks, Dempsey and Montgomery to have a final go. We were so near victory at that time; at long last, troops and heavy equipment were up to the Neder Rhine; it only needed one final effort by the units south of the river, and I am sure they would have streamed across to the relief of 1st Airborne.

I have often wondered, if Montgomery had been with Brian Horrocks at Nijmegen on the 25th September, whether he would not have endorsed Horrocks' plan to carry out a major assault; and then, perhaps, the Battle of Arnhem would have been turned into a victory instead of a defeat.

Chapter XII

LAST POST

LITTLE did I know, when I brought my Brigade back to England from Europe, that our battles were over. I was still convinced that the Polish Parachute Brigade would be reinforced, re-equipped, and flown to Poland to help in the liberation of our country. But, unknown to us simple soldiers, political forces were already at work which prevented this plan ever being carried out.

To go back a little to the period just after the battle, I heard on October 2nd that we were to move back to England. This news was conveyed to me in a letter from General Browning.

I had previously learned that my Government had decided to confer on him one of Poland's highest military awards the Star of the Order *Polonia Restituta* and I immediately despatched the following message: *May I on behalf of officers and other ranks under my command, as well as myself, express our best congratulations.*

Browning replied in the following terms:

Dear General,

Thank you for your communication with regard to the award by your Government to me of the Star of the Order Polonia Restituta. *I can assure you that I genuinely consider that it is indeed an honour to have this order conferred on me, and I thank you for the congratulations of yourself and your officers and men.*

However, I am going to be absolutely candid, and I say to you that the award of a Polish decoration, at the present time, to me is unfortunate. As you must be most fully aware, my relationship with you and your Brigade has not been of the happiest during the last few weeks; it has been very different, in fact, from the days when your brigade was in Scotland and I and my headquarters did our best to obtain a sufficiency of training equipment for you, against the policy of the War Office at that time.

When I say that the award is unfortunate I would hasten to repeat that I do most genuinely consider it an honour.

I fear, however, that the award of this decoration must make you and your brigade feel equally awkward, owing to our relationship lately.

For your own personal information, I have received word that your brigade will be withdrawn to the United Kingdom for reconstitution.
Yours sincerely,
Frederick Browning.

I did not understand his reference to the recent deterioration in our relationship and I replied to Browning's letter immediately:

Sir,
Will you please allow me to reply on the part of your letter where you wrote that your relationship with me and the Brigade Group was not of the happiest during the last weeks.
If I should dare to confirm this opinion of yours, I would like to express my greatest regret for the part I had in this state of affairs.
I would like, however, to assure you, sir, that without any regard to the personal relationship, I always was and am trying—according to my best possibilities and with the greatest soldierlike loyalty:

To execute all orders you, as my operational superior, have and will give me.
To tell you always and openly all my doubts—if I should have any—in regard to the way of executing tasks which you have given me. I shall also always report to you if the troops under my command are sufficiently prepared to fulfil the tasks, because I consider it to be my duty, whereas the final decision belongs to you.

I take also this opportunity to mention that I always considered it an honour and pleasure to get under your command, as I am sure to receive just and equal recognition for the troops under my command and that the delay in being placed under your command was personally much regretted as well by myself as by my troops.
May I also be allowed to state, that although the motion for your award was put forward at the end of last year, the time passed since then has changed nothing but only increased the merits of your work for this Brigade Group.
Please accept, sir, once more, my apologies if at any time my opinion was expressed in such a way or with words you did not like.
Yours sincerely,
Sosabowski.

On our way back to England I was most amused to see a British newspaper carrying a picture of myself with the caption: *Polish Commander-in-Chief dismissed.* It was a mistake, the picture should have been of General Sosnkowski, whom the Russians hated.

Considerable pressure had been brought to bear on the British Government to get him removed and the Polish President, Mr. Raczkiewicz, was persuaded by the Prime Minister, Mr. Mikolajczyk, to sign the dismissal order. It was a sad blow to us, as he had been a great supporter of the Parachute Brigade.

I did not dream then that three months later I would follow him.

Back in camp in Lincolnshire, we settled in and cleared up the inevitable mess which any unit finds itself in after a battle; then the men went on leave. Before departing, they were issued with operational Parachute badges and warned to behave themselves. I told them not to be bombastic or boastful, but to maintain good discipline and be modest in their behaviour.

"Let other people praise you—not you yourselves," I told them.

I assured them of my trust, but said that on their return I would ask those who had misbehaved to step forward from the ranks on parade and confess to any misdemeanours. This I did, and several men came forward; however, I ordered them to step back into the ranks and did not punish them, satisfied by their confidence in me.

In spite of the original agreement between the Polish Commander-in-Chief and the British that after one operation my Brigade should revert to the direct control of the Polish Headquarters, I received orders from Headquarters British Airborne Corps placing me under command of 1st British Airborne Division. All instructions which followed indicated that the Brigade was fast losing its independence and was well on the way to being integrated into the 1st Division. Urquhart also sent me a letter confirming that I had been placed under his command and saying he wanted to discuss training problems with me. I replied on 4th November saying I would be delighted to see him but, regarding the question of command, I was awaiting instructions from Polish General Headquarters. I also sent a similar signal to Browning.

General Kopanski, Chief of the Polish General Staff, to whom I had sent a report, acted immediately, and on the 22nd November he told me that the British authorities had agreed that the independence of my Brigade was to be retained and we would not become part of the Division. To me and to my troops it was terribly important that we should remain independent. We were an outward and positive sign to the Polish nation that we were still fighting for them.

On December 1st, I heard that Browning had written to General Sir Ronald Weeks, Deputy Chief of the Imperial General Staff, suggesting that I should be removed from my command. The main reason he gave was that I was too difficult to collaborate with. This suggestion and a copy of his letter were sent to General Kopanski, who was acting for the Commander-in-Chief, and were shown to me.

Why Browning decided to take action at this time, I am unable to understand. He was in the process of giving up his job as Airborne Chief and handing over to General Richard Gale; he would have had no further dealings with me anyway. However, with such a suggestion coming from the War Office, it was impossible for the Polish Government to refuse. I was sacked and appointed Inspector of Disposal Units. Yet I never looked upon my dismissal as a defeat; I considered it a moral victory, as I left the Brigade at the height of its success. President Raczkiewicz wrote to me on 9th December 1944:

Dear General,
It is from necessity that I must remove you from the command of the 1st Polish Independent Parachute Brigade. I would like to underline the merits of your service in this post and your proven character on the battlefield.
I would like also to mention especially the fact that it was your energy and resolve which built up the Parachute Brigade.
With cordial respect,
W. Raczkiewicz.

It was only left for me to pack my bags and go.

Looking back after all these years, I realise how wide the gulf was separating Browning and myself. He seemed to have the notion, not uncommon in the British Army, that most foreigners are fools and must be treated accordingly. In such circumstances, it is not surprising that small differences grew out of all proportion; but what I do not understand is why on occasions he should have taken personal offence.

Urquhart also never quite understood the Polish point of view. In his book *Arnhem* he wrote of me: *He was, of course, a political leader as well, a role which led him into queer paths. There were times when I could not be certain whether he was debating a point from the military angle or merely trying to put over the Polish political cause. He fell out badly with General Browning on two or three occasions, and even at the end their relations were not of the best.*

I am not a politician, I never have been and never will be; but I love my country above all things and my first allegiance was always to Poland, as was that of my compatriots. Perhaps Urquhart realised this, for he dedicated his book *To all ranks who served in the 1st Airborne Division in September 1944 and their Comrades in Arms of the 1st Polish Parachute Brigade Group.*

My dismissal was badly received by the Brigade and on Christmas Eve I was informed that two of my units, one at Wansford and another at Peterborough, had gone on hunger strike in protest. This was a serious breach of military discipline and I immediately arranged to visit all units. At each camp, I addressed a parade speaking to them as a father to his wayward sons:

"Boys, what do you expect to achieve by this action? Do you think that under pressure from you the President of Poland will change his mind? Of course he won't. Be sensible and go at once to the dining-room, where I will eat a meal with you."

They dismissed and I went and sat with them, eating the same food, sharing their jokes. This was certainly against military discipline and custom, but I did not want anyone to suffer because of loyalty to me.

An official formal handing-over parade to my successor was arranged for Boxing Day. I knew that this would be an emotional occasion—and possibly inflammable, needing careful handling.

There is a tradition in the Polish Army that the retiring commander appears before the assembled ranks and kisses the flag. I did not kiss the flag; I only said Goodbye. I only left my men physically; we were never spiritually parted.

If I had my time all over again, I would not change it; I would live every moment the same way and I have few regrets.

Poland still stirs restlessly under the yoke of oppression and, if I do have regrets, the greatest is that I was never able to take my troops back to Poland to give my countrymen the freedom for which they long. There are thousands of young men still waiting the chance to fight for liberty, under that same motto engraved on the steel blade of my sabre:

For Honour and Glory